lonely planet

BEST ROAD TRIPS

SPAIN & PORTUGAL

ESCAPES ON THE OPEN ROAD

ANTHONY HAM, REGIS ST LOUIS, GREGOR CLARK,
DUNCAN GARWOOD, JOHN NOBLE

Contents

NORTHERN SPAIN & THE BASQUE COUNTRY p59
MADRID & CENTRAL SPAIN p23
BARCELONA & EASTERN SPAIN p105
PORTUGAL p179
ANDALUCIA & SOUTHERN SPAIN p141
ATLANTIC OCEAN
Bay of Biscay
Golfo de Valencia
Mediterranean Sea
FRANCE
SPAIN
PORTUGAL
ANDORRA
MOROCCO
MADRID
LISBON
ANDORRA LA VELLA
Río Miño
Río Douro
Río Tejo
Río Ebro
Parque Natural Sierras de Cazorla, Segura y las Villas
Parque Natural Sierra Norte de Sevilla
Parque Nacional Sierra Nevada
A Coruña
San Cosme
Avilés
Gijón
Oviedo
Santiago de Compostela
Lugo
Torrelavega
Santander
Bilbao
San Sebastián
Irún
Bayonne
Mont-de-Marsan
Aire-sur-l'Adour
Toulouse
Montpellier
Tarascon-sur-Ariège
Perpignan
Llavorsí
Aínsa
Figueres
Cadaqués
Girona
Vic
Manresa
Tossa de Mar
Lleida
Barcelona
Cambrils
Tarragona
Azaila
Alcañiz
Sariñena
Huesca
Zaragoza
Pamplona
Vitoria
Miranda de Ebro
Burgos
Nájera
Logroño
Soria
Medinaceli
Molina de Aragón
Pontevedra
Vigo
Ourense
Monforte de Lemos
León
Sahagún
Palencia
Valladolid
Viana do Castelo
Braga
Bragança
Miranda do Douro
Zamora
Vila Real
Porto
Peso da Régua
Vila Nova de Foz Côa
Salamanca
Aveiro
Viseu
Guarda
Ciudad Rodrigo
Béjar
Ávila
Collado Villalba
Guadalajara
Teruel
Torrebaja
Cuenca
Tarancón
Coimbra
Leiria
Castelo Branco
Navalmoral de la Mata
Toledo
Belmonte
Castellón de la Plana
Valencia
Requena
Palma de Mallorca
Ibiza
Santarem
Portalegre
Cáceres
Trujillo
La Nava de Ricomalillo
Consuegra
Ciudad Real
Vendas Novas
Mérida
Badajoz
Albacete
Almansa
Setúbal
Alcácer do Sal
Évora
Almadén
Beja
Monesterio
Bailén
Córdoba
Elche
Alicante
Vila Nova de Milfontes
Murcia
Torrevieja
Jaén
Alcaudete
Huelva
Seville
Cartagena
Sagres
Faro
Arcos de la Frontera
Granada
Chipiona
Cádiz
Málaga
Almería
Marbella
Gibraltar (UK)
Tangier
0
200 km
100 miles

Welcome to Spain & Portugal

You can't help but enjoy yourself in Spain and Portugal, and road tripping around both countries is the ideal way to explore this remarkable part of the world.

The region's road network spans every possible experience, from extensive motorways to quiet, magical back roads. The land they traverse takes in high mountains (such as the Pyrenees, Picos de Europa and Sierra Nevada), glorious coastlines, deep forests, semi-deserts, vast plains and serpentine valleys. Animating these landscapes are medieval villages and some of the most exciting cities anywhere on the planet.

Locals here really know how to live, and the days are filled with the irresistible fun of fiestas, the sounds of flamenco or fado and stunning cuisine made up of regional specialties of almost infinite variety.

Building a series of itineraries around driving from one such experience to the next is nothing short of one of Europe's great travel experiences.

Puente Nuevo, Ronda (p172)

Our Picks

BEST COASTAL DRIVES

Spain and Portugal host some of Europe's most picturesque coastlines. From sun-kissed Mediterranean shores to the wild, windy Atlantic cliffs of Galicia and the epic waves of Portugal, there are ample opportunities to wind down the windows and catch a sea breeze. Sometimes it's about the beaches at journey's end. At other times it's the scenery, beachside villages and waterside cities en route that give these road trips their charm.

INTERNATIONAL SUN WORSHIPPERS

Nearly 120 million foreign visitors arrive in Spain and Portugal every year. Most do so in summer.

North Coast Beaches & Culture

Drive along Spain's northern shore with its fishing villages, cool cities and lovely beaches.

P.90

Coast of Galicia

Explore one of Europe's most dramatic coastlines along the clifftops of the Costa da Morte (Coast of Death).

P.96

Mediterranean Meander

Traverse 1000km of Spain's Mediterranean shore and discover why it's Europe's favourite summer playground.

P.144

ARTEM EVDOKIMOV/SHUTTERSTOCK ©

Atlantic Coast Surf Trip

Discover coastal Portugal at its best with pit stops in stunning towns en route to world-famous beaches.

P.182

Alentejo & Algarve Beaches

It's another beloved summer escape for sun-starved Europeans, but Portugal's south coast offers so much more.

P.194

Above: The Algarve (p194); Right: Praia As Catedrais (p94)

LOCAL SUN WORSHIPPERS
Spanish and Portuguese tourists also head for the coast in July and August. Book everything early.
LATE EATING TIMES
Spaniards eat late year-round, but especially so in summer. Adjust your body clock on arrival.

MINIMUM AGE
To rent a car in Spain you must be aged at least 21 and have a credit card.
MOTORWAY OR BACK ROAD?
Spain and Portugal have excellent (and mostly free) motorways. You'll see more on the smaller roads.

Our Picks

BEST CITY-TO-CITY DRIVES

Spanish and Portuguese cities and towns are some of Europe's most memorable urban centres, and driving between them is a wonderful way to see some of the countryside along the way. Almost invariably, these places have enchanted historic cores replete with medieval architecture that provides a stirring backdrop – particularly when floodlit at night – to all that's good about Iberian urban life.

HEAD FOR THE CENTRE

Follow signs to the city centres (or your hotel's location), park your car, and get out and walk.

Historic Castilla y León

Begin in fabulous Madrid, then pass through Castilian classics Segovia, Salamanca, Zamora, Valladolid and Burgos.

P.26

North Coast Beaches & Culture

This trip from San Sebastián to Oviedo takes in Bilbao, Santander and unstinting culinary magnificence.

P.00

Córdoba (p160)

BRAD HAMMONDS/500PX ©

Barcelona to Valencia

Drive between two of Spain's most beguiling large cities, with stunning ancient villages in between.

P.134

Golden Triangle

This special trip takes in Seville, Córdoba and Granada, with architecture and food particular highlights.

P.158

The Minho's Lyrical Landscapes

From Guimarães to Peneda, you'll namecheck some of Portugal's most beautiful historic towns.

P.206

Left: Madrid (p26)

Our Picks

BEST MOUNTAIN DRIVES

Spain in particular has some of southern Europe's most stirring mountain scenery, from the Pyrenees and the Picos de Europa in the north to the Sierra Nevada down south. Portugal's mountains may not reach the same heights, but the country's interior is a magical world of high-altitude villages and deep valleys. Not surprisingly, these settings make for some of the most picturesque drives anywhere on the Iberian Peninsula.

SPANISH SPEED LIMITS

Keep below 50km/h (in some cases 30km/h) in built-up areas, 100km/h on major roads and 120km/h on *autovías* and *autopistas*.

BAKHMALINI/SHUTTERSTOCK ©

The Pyrenees

One of Europe's great mountain drives, the Pyrenean traverse takes you into the realm of mountain gods.

P.126

Lofty Roads: the Picos de Europa

This drive goes into the heart of the Picos de Europa, the continent's most spectacular range.

P.74

The Great Outdoors

Head to Andalucía and the cooling valleys of Las Alpujarras, in the Sierra Nevada's shadow.

P.164

TRABANTOS/SHUTTERSTOCK ©

Above: Capileira (p164); Right: El Naranjo de Bulnes (p77)

The Forgotten West

Explore Spain's magical hill country, including the Sierra de Francia, where time stands still.

P.36

Highlands & History in the Central Interior

Immerse yourself in superb landscapes as you meander through Portugal's heartland.

P.214

PORTUGUESE SPEED LIMITS

Keep below 50km/h in towns and villages, 90km/h outside built-up areas and 120km/h on motorways.

BUCKLE UP

Seatbelts are compulsory in both countries; in Portugal, children under 12 years may not ride in the front seat.

FUEL
Fuel is around 20% cheaper in Spain. If you're near the border, save by filling up on the Spanish side.

Our Picks

BEST BACK-ROAD DRIVES

GIVE WAY TO THE RIGHT

An important road rule to remember in both countries is that traffic from the right usually has priority.

World-class motorways are one thing, but the real charm of an Iberian road trip lies along quiet rural byways. These back roads are where a sense of discovery kicks in. Routes connect timeworn medieval villages and unsung remote landscapes, and you'll really feel that something of the past has survived into the present. Along these roads, old Spain and old Portugal endure and the forces of globalisation seem mercifully distant.

ALVAN PH/SHUTTERSTOCK ©

Back Roads Beyond Madrid

Beyond intoxicating Madrid, head for historic towns – in the capital's hinterland, yet a world away.

P.32

The Forgotten West

Discover the tranquil backcountry of Extremadura and Castilla y León along this gloriously remote route.

P.36

GRANTOTUFO/SHUTTERSTOCK ©

Extremadura (p54)

Cantabria's Eastern Valleys

Disappear off the beaten track on this journey through farming settlements in Spain's inner north.

P.80

Peaks & Valleys in Northwest Catalonia

Head into the Catalonian hills for Pyrenean isolation far from the bright lights of Barcelona.

P.122

Medieval Jewels in the Southern Interior

Leave behind the tourist paths of Portugal on this route through castles, monasteries and standing stones.

P.200

Potes (p78)

Our Picks

BEST WINE & OLIVE-OIL DRIVES

Food and wine take centre stage on many Spanish and Portuguese itineraries. There's a unique and much-loved local speciality to discover in almost every town, so there's no end to the possibilities. Following a wine or olive-oil trail through the countryside can provide an entry point into this first-class culinary culture, often with the bonus of learning about the historical stories written in the surrounding architecture and landscapes.

PORTUGAL'S TOLL ROADS

Portugal's main toll roads have automated tollbooths. You'll need an electronic tag in your car before you drive on these roads.

DENIS COMEAU/SHUTTERSTOCK ©

Roving La Rioja Wine Region

Meander among vineyards, medieval villages and vibrant wine towns in Spain's best-known wine region.

P.70

Along the Río Ebro

Journey through the Spanish heartland of wineries and wine regions along this iconic river.

P.86

Central Catalonia's Wineries & Monasteries

Catalonia is one of Spain's culinary stars, and the Penedès vineyards are highly regarded.

P.118

POWELL'SPOINT/SHUTTERSTOCK ©

Above: Wine bottles, Catalonia (p118); Right:Vineyards, Douro Valley (p188)

Olive Oil & the Renaissance in Jaén

Drive amid the world's largest human-made forest (of olive trees) and enjoy Andalucian architectural jewels.

P.174

Douro Valley Vineyard Trails

Portugal's heartbreakingly beautiful river valley is lined with vines producing sensational ports and reds.

P.188

GETTING A TOLL-ROAD TAG

Most car-rental agencies have installed the electronic tags in their cars. Otherwise, find out where to rent one at *viaverde.pt*.

When to Go

Spain and Portugal have Europe's best year-round weather. There's never a bad time for a drive, albeit with some regional variations.

I LIVE HERE

I LOVE DRIVING HERE

Anthony Ham is a writer who spent 10 years living in Madrid and continues to call Spain home on his regular returns to the country. *@AnthonyHamWrite*

I love driving Spain's roads at any time of the year, but there's nothing quite like driving out along the back roads of Castilla y León (p26) or Aragón (p129w) in winter, perhaps to the Sierra de Francia or Albarracín. This allows me (and many Spaniards) to indulge a passion for hearty home cooking, ideal for the biting cold – perhaps *cordero asado* (spring lamb cooked in a wood-fired oven) or *cocido* (meat-and-chickpea stew). This combination of a beautiful place and seasonal cooking has countless regional variations on the theme and is one of the recurring joys of travelling here.

Road trips are rewarding in Spain and Portugal throughout the year.

Summer (mid-June to mid September) can feel like the perfect time for a drive. Everyone's on holiday, locals have a spring in their step and the fine beaches are worth building your trip around. Remember, however, that daytime temperatures in Andalucía's interior can be fierce and roads can be busy.

Winter (mid-December to mid-March) brings its own challenges. Roads in mountain areas can be closed by snowfall, rain can be persistent in Galicia and northern Portugal, and temperatures can be icy across the high *meseta* of Spain's interior.

SKI SEASON

Spain's ski season runs from December to April, but the most reliable weather is in January and February.

NICK STUBBS/SHUTTERSTOCK ©

Sierra Nevada (p164)

Weather Watch (Madrid)

JANUARY	FEBRUARY	MARCH	APRIL	MAY	JUNE
Avg. daytime max: **10°C**. Days of rainfall: **5**	Avg. daytime max: **12°C**. Days of rainfall: **5**	Avg. daytime max: **16°C**. Days of rainfall: **5**	Avg. daytime max: **18°C**. Days of rainfall: **6**	Avg. daytime max: **22°C**. Days of rainfall: **7**	Avg. daytime max: **28°C**. Days of rainfall: **3**

HIGH-ALTITUDE HIKING

Hikers from all over Europe head for the Pyrenees and Picos de Europa in summer. June to October are generally best, but there may be snow on passes and high valleys until mid-June or from October; weather at altitude is never predictable.

Picos de Europa (p74)

Spring and autumn can be delightful times to drive here, especially as the roads are usually quieter in these seasons.

Accommodation

Accommodation is always at a premium in Spain and Portugal, two of Europe's most popular holiday destinations, and especially so in summer, during major festivals and school holidays, and at weekends.

RECORD HIGHS

Unofficial records push Spain's daytime temperatures beyond 50°C, but the official record was 47.6°C (117.7°F) at La Rambla, near Córdoba, on 14 August 2021; the top six highest temperatures on record were all registered since 2017, with four of these around Córdoba.

LOCAL FESTIVITIES

Cádiz hosts Spain's most riotous **Carnaval**. Badajoz, Sitges and Ciudad Rodrigo are also known for their celebrations. In Portugal, head for Loulé, Torres Vedras, Sesimbra and Ovar. **February**

Teams of local artists create *fallas* (giant papier-mâché sculptures) for the unmissable **Las Fallas de San José**. At its best in Valencia. **March**

Seville's **Feria de Abril** brings a week of flamenco, horse riding, drinking, dancing and fabulous outfits. **April**

Semana Santa (Holy Week) sees elaborate *pasos* (holy figures) paraded through the streets. It's big everywhere (even the tiniest villages). **March/April**

LOCAL QUIRKY FESTIVALS

Spain's flamenco heartland hosts the winter **Festival de Jerez**. **February/March**

The country's most important pilgrimage sees up to a million devotees join the **Romería del Rocío** in Huelva province on Pentecost (Whitsunday) weekend. **May/June**

Festa de São João is a Portuguese favourite up north, with elaborate processions, while folks go around whacking each other with plastic hammers. **June**

In late summer, people flock to Buñol for **La Tomatina**, a massive tomato-throwing festival. **August**

JULY	AUGUST	SEPTEMBER	OCTOBER	NOVEMBER	DECEMBER
Avg. daytime max: **31°C**.	Avg. daytime max: **31°C**.	Avg. daytime max: **26°C**.	Avg. daytime max: **19°C**.	Avg. daytime max: **13°C**.	Avg. daytime max: **10°C**.
Days of rainfall: **1**	Days of rainfall: **1**	Days of rainfall: **3**	Days of rainfall: **6**	Days of rainfall: **6**	Days of rainfall: **6**

Get Prepared for Spain & Portugalw

Useful things to load in your bag, your ears and your brain

Clothing

General dress code In general, Spaniards and Portuguese people are well dressed. Smart casual wear is recommended, even just for a trip down to the local shops.

Summer heat With over 300 days of sunshine each year, Spain and Portugal are loved for their (generally) warm climate. Light, breezy clothes are best during the hot summers, and don't forget the hot-weather essentials such as hats, sunglasses, swimwear and sun cream. But it's wise to plan for regional variations too – even in summer you'll often want an extra evening layer in the north, for example.

Winter weather Spain does get cold during winter (especially in the hills and the north) and many houses are built for the warmer months, which means they can be chilly at this time of year. In Portugal, many houses are only lightly insulated, so they can get quite cold inside. Layers are your best friend.

Events If you'll be attending an important occasion such as a wedding or feria/festa, bring an outfit that's on the smarter side to blend in with the locals.

Outdoors The region is packed with outdoor adventure. If you're heading out into nature, bring suitable clothing such as jackets, hats and footwear.

WATCH

Todo sobre mi madre (*Pedro Almodóvar; 1999*) Almodóvar classic tackling complex issues.

Jamón, jamón (Bigas Luna, 1992) Comedy starring Penélope Cruz and Javier Bardem.

Mar adentro (*Alejandro Amenábar; 2004*) Real-life story of a quadriplegic Galician fisherman's right to end his life.

Ocho apellidos vascos (*Emilio Martínez-Lázaro; 2014*) Comedy revolving around stereotypes of Andalucía, the Basque Country and, in the sequel, Catalonia.

Glória (*Pedro Lopes; 2021*) Spy series based on true events around a Portuguese town during the Cold War.

JAVI_INDY/SHUTTERSTOCK ©

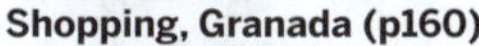

Shopping, Granada (p160)

Words (Spain)

Hola Hello

Buenos días Good morning

Buenas tardes/noches Good afternoon/night

¿Qué tal? Informal version of ¿como estás? (how are you?)

Por favor Please

Gracias Thank you

Socorro! Help!

¿Habla/hablas inglés? Do you speak English?; the first is more formal

Perdone/perdona How to catch the attention of restaurant or bar staff; the second is less formal

Words (Portugal)

Olá Hello

Bom dia Good day or good morning

Boa tarde/noite Good afternoon/evening

Tudo bem Short form of 'how are you?'

Se faz favor Please; can be used to catch attention of waiter or waitress

De nada You're welcome

Cafézinho A cute term for coffee (the suffix -inho can express affection and sometimes sarcasm)

Desculpe Mostly used to mean 'sorry' but can also mean 'excuse me'

Obrigado/obrigada Thank you

LISTEN

Cositas Buenas
(Paco de Lucía; 2004) Spain's greatest modern flamenco guitarist dazzles with rumbas, *bulerías*, tangos and more.

El Mal Querer
(Rosalía; 2018) Show-stealing second album by superstar Rosalía, known for her R&B-influenced flamenco tracks.

Mariza Canta Amália
(Mariza; 2020) Fado singer Mariza pays tribute to the genre's diva with a record featuring her best songs.

La Portada
Excellent English-language podcast covering Spanish news and current issues.

READ

Ghosts of Spain
(*Giles Tremlett; 2006*) The *Guardian* journalist explores the darker sides of Spain's history.

Patria
(Fernando Aramburu; 2016) Highly acclaimed novel revolving around the ETA terror campaign.

A Late Dinner: Discovering the Food of Spain
(*Paul Richardson; 2007*) Erudite journey through Spain's culinary culture.

Journey to Portugal
(*José Saramago; 1990*) Tales of cultural discovery while travelling across Portugal.

ROAD TRIPS

Contents

Consuegra (p49)

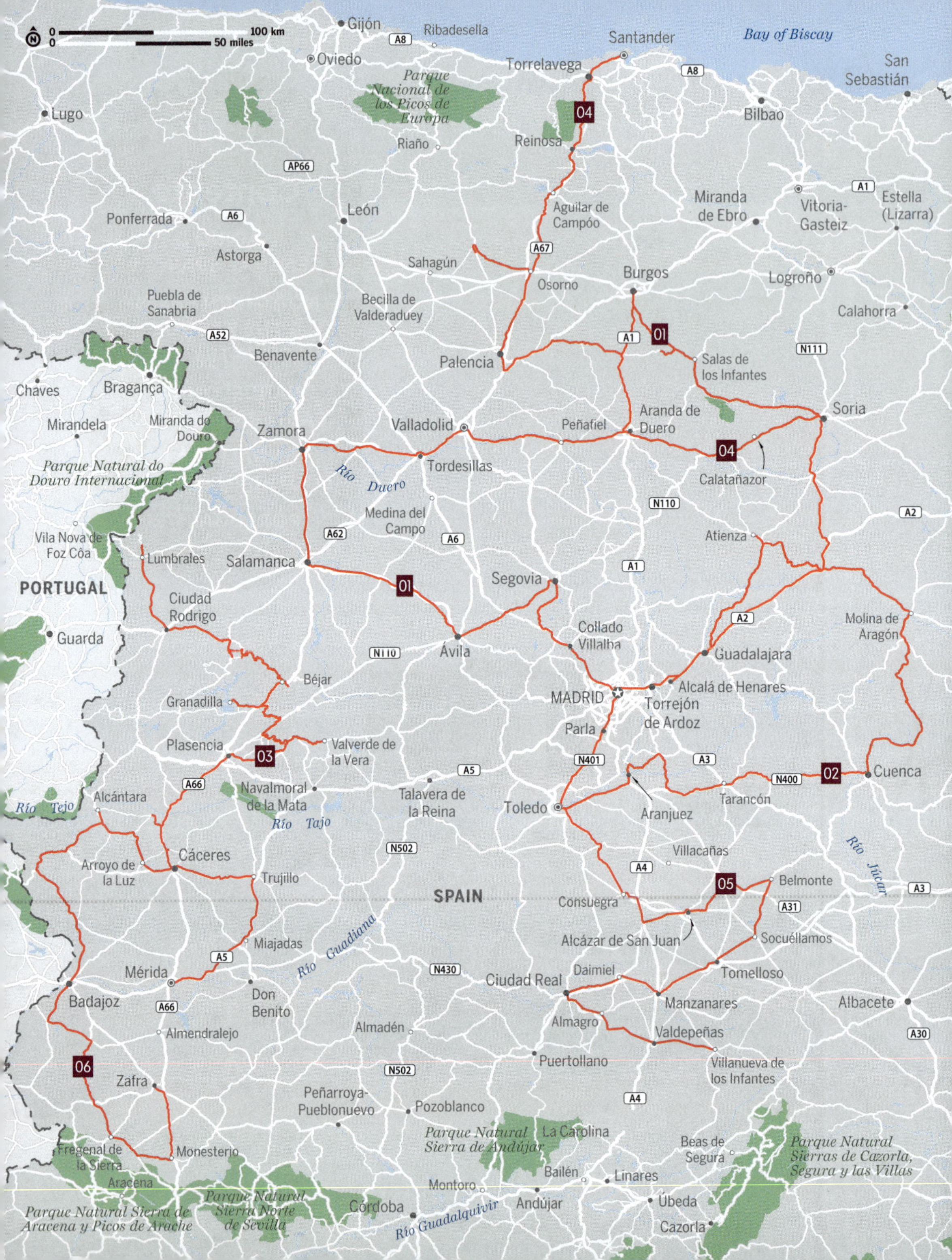

0 100 km
0 50 miles
Bay of Biscay
Gijón
Ribadesella
Oviedo
Santander
Torrelavega
San Sebastián
Bilbao
Lugo
Parque Nacional de los Picos de Europa
Riaño
Reinosa
Ponferrada
León
Astorga
Aguilar de Campóo
Miranda de Ebro
Vitoria-Gasteiz
Estella (Lizarra)
Sahagún
Osorno
Burgos
Logroño
Calahorra
Puebla de Sanabria
Becilla de Valderaduey
Benavente
Palencia
Salas de los Infantes
Chaves
Bragança
Mirandela
Miranda do Douro
Zamora
Valladolid
Peñafiel
Aranda de Duero
Soria
Tordesillas
Calatañazor
Parque Natural do Douro Internacional
Río Duero
Medina del Campo
Vila Nova de Foz Côa
Atienza
Lumbrales
Salamanca
Segovia
PORTUGAL
Ciudad Rodrigo
Guarda
Collado Villalba
Ávila
Molina de Aragón
Guadalajara
Béjar
Alcalá de Henares
MADRID
Torrejón de Ardoz
Granadilla
Parla
Plasencia
Valverde de la Vera
Navalmoral de la Mata
Talavera de la Reina
Toledo
Aranjuez
Tarancón
Cuenca
Alcántara
Río Tejo
Río Tajo
Cáceres
Arroyo de la Luz
Villacañas
Trujillo
SPAIN
Consuegra
Belmonte
Río Júcar
Miajadas
Alcázar de San Juan
Socuéllamos
Mérida
Río Guadiana
Daimiel
Tomelloso
Badajoz
Don Benito
Ciudad Real
Manzanares
Albacete
Almendralejo
Almadén
Almagro
Valdepeñas
Puertollano
Villanueva de los Infantes
Zafra
Peñarroya-Pueblonuevo
Pozoblanco
Parque Natural Sierra de Andújar
La Carolina
Beas de Segura
Parque Natural Sierras de Cazorla, Segura y las Villas
Fregenal de la Sierra
Monesterio
Bailén
Linares
Aracena
Montoro
Parque Natural Sierra Norte de Sevilla
Córdoba
Andújar
Úbeda
Parque Natural Sierra de Aracena y Picos de Arache
Río Guadalquivir
Cazorla
A8
AP66
A6
A67
A1
A52
N111
N110
A62
A2
A5
A66
N502
N401
A3
N400
A4
A31
N430
A30
01
02
03
04
05
06

DAVID PANIAGUA/SHUTTERSTOCK ©

Catedral de Burgos (p66)

Madrid & Central Spain

Explore

Madrid & Central Spain

Welcome to Spain's Castilian heartland. With Madrid, Spain's irresistible capital, at its core and the starting point of so many journeys, this is Spain at its most Spanish. Castilla y León and Castilla La Mancha are a world away from the *costas* and the mass-tourism mix of sun, sand and sangría. Instead, this is where Don Quixote de la Mancha tilted at windmills, a realm of medieval villages where you'll find traditional restaurants and historic places to stay. The landscapes, too, are like nowhere else in the country, with the big horizons of the *meseta* (plateau) cut through with dramatic and little-known gorges.

Madrid

Spain's capital is one of Europe's most exciting cities. This is a place that never seems to sleep, a seriously fun city that has exceptional places to eat, drink and sleep – the choice is endless. By day you can enjoy world-class museums, gaze at supremely beautiful architecture and join the throng in the plazas, where so much of the city comes out to play. Because most people in Madrid have their roots in other places in Spain and further afield, it's also one of the country's most welcoming cities.

Toledo

Steeped in medieval history, Toledo is one of Spain's most intriguing small cities. It rises from the plains of Castilla La Mancha like an ancient fortress cast in stone, offering exceptional views out over the surrounding landscape from many points around town. It has a culinary culture all its own and a small but enticing array of places to stay. It's also well connected to local and national road networks, and by fast train from Madrid.

Cáceres

One of inland Spain's most beautiful cities, Cáceres has a particular, indefinable magic. The modern town, which has some excellent places to eat and stay, extends out below the city's medieval heart, which is strewn with museums and heritage buildings in ferrous sandstone. Here, too, you'll find intimate restaurants serving local cuisine, as well as enchanting places to

WHEN TO GO

Because much of central Spain occupies a high-altitude *meseta* – Madrid is Europe's highest capital city – the region can experience fiercely cold winters (November to February), when occasional cold spells and snowfalls can spell traffic chaos, and similarly hot summers (June to August). The best time to visit is outside these extremes, during autumn or spring.

stay. Wander the old lanes at night and you'll be transported to another era.

Santander

Ask any Spaniard to nominate their country's most style-conscious city and they will very likely name Santander. From the elegance of the city's beachfront architecture to the well-heeled locals who promenade in the evenings, Santander is one cool town. Its culinary offerings are also a favourite talking point among Spaniards, and its position and transport links make it an important gateway for northern Spain, both along the coast and inland.

Valladolid

While cities such as Burgos, Salamanca, Segovia and others across Castilla y León might garner all the attention for their spectacular architectural streetscapes, Valladolid flies a little under the radar. Yet the city has vibrant, quintessentially Spanish street life and a fantastic tapas scene concentrated in the streets around the central Plaza Mayor. And Valladolid's rail and road links are some of the best anywhere in the Spanish interior.

TRANSPORT

All roads and rail lines fan out across the country from Madrid. The road network includes an extensive motorway system connecting most major towns, and smaller, quieter roads will take you to the region's villages. Fast trains, connecting Madrid, Toledo, Segovia, Valladolid, Santander and elsewhere, perform a similar function and are incredibly efficient. They're supplemented by slower regional services.

WHAT'S ON

Semana Santa

The region has haunting Easter or Holy Week celebrations, especially in Ávila, Cuenca and Zamora.

Fiestas de San Isidro

Madrid celebrates its patron saint with great merriment on 14 May and the surrounding weeks.

Festival Internacional de Teatro Clásico

Classical theatre (Greek classics or Shakespeare) in Mérida's peerless Roman theatre in July and August.

Suma Flamenca

Spain's finest flamenco talents take to Madrid's stages in October and November.

WHERE TO STAY

Madrid is awash in outstanding places to stay, from budget hostels and simple *hostales* (guesthouses) to five-star temples to good taste. There are also ample midrange choices, including many places housed in historic buildings across the city centre. In most medium-sized towns and small cities, including Santander, Toledo, Valladolid, Salamanca and others, there will be fewer choices, but you can still expect to find at least a handful of places to suit most budgets. In villages there may be the occasional midrange or top-end option, but more often you'll have to make do with a *hostal* or *casa rural* (rural homestay).

Resources

Madrid (*esmadrid.com*) Top-notch website celebrating Madrid, with up-to-the-minute event info and more enduring attractions.

Castilla y León (*turismo castillayleon.com*) All things Castilla y León.

Castilla-La Mancha (*turismo castillalamancha.es*) Don Quixote country in all its glory.

Extremadura (*turismo extremadura.com*) Explore Extremadura online.

01

MADRID & CENTRAL SPAIN

Historic Castilla y León

BEST FOR CULTURE

Salamanca street life and a glorious architectural backdrop.

DURATION	DISTANCE	GREAT FOR
7 days	764km / 475 miles	History

BEST TIME TO GO	March to May, and September and October to avoid extremes of heat and cold.

Acueducto, Segovia

From Segovia to Soria, the towns of Castilla y León rank among Spain's most appealing historic centres. Architecture may be central to their attraction, but these are no museum pieces. Instead, the relentless energy of life lived Spanish-style courses through the streets, all set against a backdrop of grand cathedrals and animated stately squares. Out in the countryside, postcard-perfect villages complement the clamour of city life.

Link your trip

02 Back Roads Beyond Madrid

Also starting in Madrid, this loop south and east of the capital takes in the historic towns and villages of Madrid's hinterland.

04 Spain's Interior Heartland

From Santander's ferry port, we take you through Roman ruins, buzzing towns and soaring cathedrals on your way to Madrid.

01 MADRID

Madrid is the most Spanish of all of Spain's cities. Its food culture, drawn from the best the country has to offer, makes it one of Europe's more underrated culinary capitals, while its nightlife and irresistible *alegría* (joy) exist like some Spanish stereotype given form. But there is more to Madrid than nonstop colour and movement. This is one of the premier art cities on the continent, with three world-class galleries – the **Museo del Prado** (*museodelprado.es*), **Museo Thyssen-Bornemisza** (*museothyssen.org*) and **Centro de Arte Reina**

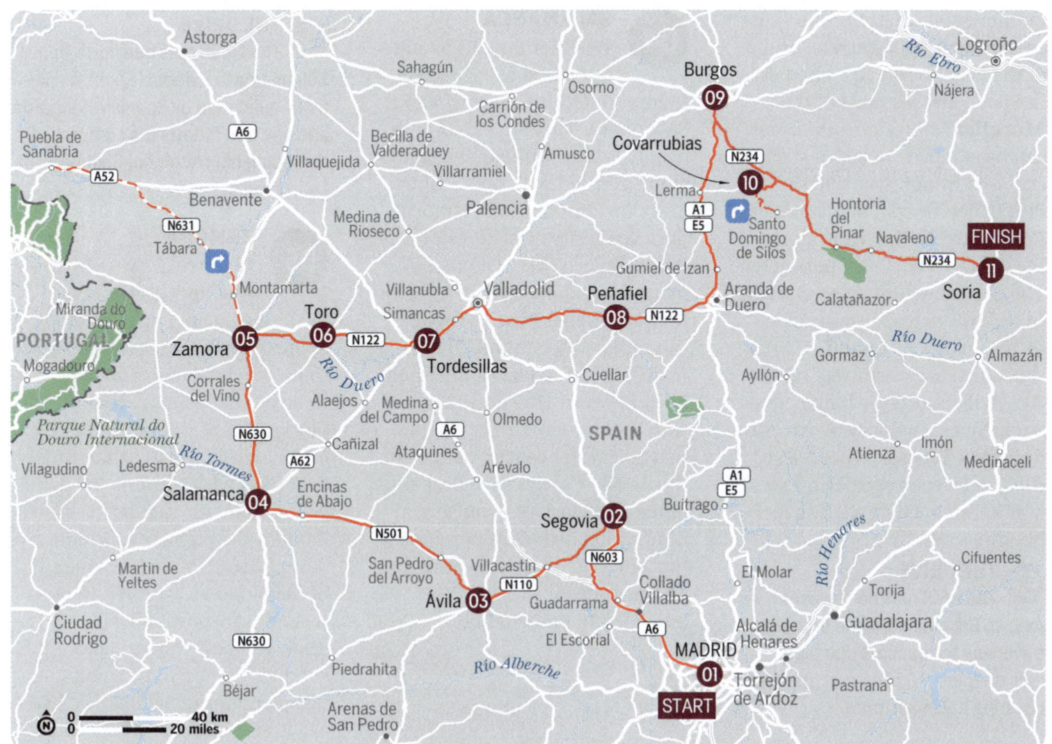

Sofía (*museoreinasofia.es*) – all close to one of the city's main boulevards and a short walk from the Parque del Buen Retiro, one of the most expansive parks in Europe. In short, this is a city that rewards those who linger and long to immerse themselves in all things Spanish.

THE DRIVE

Getting out of Madrid can be a challenge, with a complicated system of numbered motorways radiating out from the city. Drive north along the Paseo de la Castellana, turn west along the M50 ring road, then take the A6, direction A Coruña. Of the two main roads to Segovia from the A6, the N603 is the prettier (92km).

02 SEGOVIA

Unesco World Heritage–listed Segovia is a stunning confluence of everything that's good about the beautiful towns of Castilla. There are historic landmarks in abundance, among them the Roman **Acueducto,** the fairy-tale **Alcázar** (*alcazardesegovia.com*), which is said to have inspired Walt Disney, and Romanesque gems such as the **catedral** (*turismodesegovia.com*) and the **Iglesia de San Martín** This is also one of the most dynamic towns in the country, a winning mix of students and international visitors filling the city's bars and public spaces with an agreeable crescendo of noise. To cap it all, the setting is simply superb – a city strung out along a ridge, its warm terracotta and sandstone hues arrayed against a backdrop of Castilla's rolling hills and the often snow-capped Sierra de Guadarrama.

THE DRIVE

It's 66km from Segovia to Ávila along the N110. The road runs southwest, parallel to the Sierra de Guadarrama, with some pretty views en route. Around halfway, you'll cross the A6 motorway.

03 ÁVILA

Ávila's old city, surrounded by 12th-century *murallas* (walls) with eight monumental gates, 88 watchtowers and over 2500 turrets, is one of the best-preserved walled cities in Spain. Two sections of the **Murallas** (*muralladeavila.com*) can be climbed – a 300m stretch accessed from just inside the Puerta del Alcázar, and a longer 1300m stretch that runs along the old city's northern perimeter. The best views are those at night from Los Cuatro Postes (Calle de los Cuatro Postes, off N110), a short distance northwest of the city. Ávila is also the home city of Santa Teresa, with the **Convento de Santa Teresa** (*teresadejesus.com*) as its centrepiece and plenty of other important religious buildings nearby.

THE DRIVE

The N501 runs northwest of Ávila to Salamanca, in the process traversing the pancake-flat high meseta (plateau) of central Spain and covering 109km en route.

04 SALAMANCA

Whether floodlit by night or bathed in the sunset, there's something magical about Salamanca. This is a city of rare beauty, awash with golden sandstone overlaid with ochre-tinted Latin inscriptions; an extraordinary virtuosity of plateresque and Renaissance styles. The monumental highlights are many, with the exceptional **Plaza Mayor** (illuminated to stunning effect at night) an unforgettable highlight. Built between 1729 and 1755, it is widely considered to be Spain's most beautiful central plaza. But this is also Castilla's liveliest city, home to a massive Spanish and international student population that throngs the streets at night and provides the city with so much youth and vitality.

THE DRIVE

The N630 runs due north from Salamanca to Zamora (67km), a relatively quiet road by Spanish standards and one that follows the contours of the rolling hill country of Castilla y León's west.

05 ZAMORA

If you're arriving by road, first appearances can be deceiving and, as in so many Spanish towns, your introduction to provincial Zamora is likely to be nondescript apartment blocks. But persevere as the *casco historico* (old town) is hauntingly beautiful, with sumptuous medieval monuments that have earned Zamora the popular sobriquet 'Romanesque Museum'. Much of the old town is closed to motorised transport and walking is easily the best way to explore this subdued encore to the monumental splendour of Salamanca. Zamora is also one of the best places to be during Semana Santa, with haunting processions of hooded penitents parading through the streets. Whatever time of year you're here, don't miss the **Museo de Semana Santa** (*semanasantadezamora.com*).

THE DRIVE

The A11 tracks east of Zamora – not far out along the sweeping plains that bake in summer, take the turn-off to Toro. Total distance: 40km.

06 TORO

With a name that couldn't be more Spanish and a picaresque history that overshadows its present, Toro is your archetypal Castilian town. It was here that Fernando and Isabel cemented their primacy in Christian Spain at the Battle of Toro in 1476. The town sits on a

DETOUR:

Puebla de Sanabria

START: 5 ZAMORA

Northwest of Zamora, close to the Portuguese border, this captivating village is a tangle of medieval alleyways that unfold around a 15th-century castle and trickle down the hill. This is one of Spain's loveliest hamlets and it's well worth the detour, or even stopping overnight: the quiet cobblestone lanes make it feel like you've stepped back centuries. Wandering the village is alone worth the trip here but a few attractions are worth tracking down. Crowning the village's high point and dominating its skyline for kilometres around, the **Castillo** has some interesting displays on local history, flora and fauna, and superb views from the ramparts. Also at the top of the village, the striking **Plaza Mayor** is surrounded by some fine historical buildings. The 17th-century *ayuntamiento* (town hall) has a lovely arched facade and faces across the square to **Iglesia de Nuestra Señora del Azogue**, a pretty village church that was first built in the 12th century. If you're staying the night, the **Posada Real La Cartería** (*lacarteria.com*) captures the essence of Puebla de Sanabria's medieval appeal with both rooms and a restaurant.

rise high above the north bank of Río Duero and has a charming historic centre with half-timbered houses and Romanesque churches. The high point, literally, is the 12th-century **Colegiata Santa María La Mayor**, which rises above the town and boasts the magnificent Romanesque-Gothic Pórtico de la Majestad.

THE DRIVE
Return to the east–west N122 road that lies east of Toro and continue to Tordesillas (46km).

FROG-SPOTTING IN SALAMANCA

A compulsory task facing all visitors to Salamanca is to search out the frog sculpted into the facade of the **Universidad Civil** (*salamanca.es*). Once pointed out, it's easily enough seen, but the uninitiated can spend considerable time searching. Why bother? Well, they say that those who detect it without help can be assured of good luck and even marriage within a year. Some hopeful students see a guaranteed examination's victory in it. If you believe all this, stop reading now. If you need help, look at the busts of Fernando and Isabel. From there, turn your gaze to the largest column on the extreme right of the front. Slightly above the level of the busts is a series of skulls, atop the leftmost of which sits our little amphibious friend (or what's left of his eroded self).

07 TORDESILLAS

Commanding a rise on the northern flank of Río Duero, this pretty little town has a historical significance that belies its size. Originally a Roman settlement, it later played a major role in world history when, in 1494, Isabel and Fernando, the Catholic monarchs, sat down with Portugal here to hammer out a treaty determining who got what in Latin America. Portugal got Brazil and much of the rest went to Spain. Explaining it all is the excellent **Museo del Tratado del Tordesillas**. Not far away, the heart of town is formed by the delightful porticoed and cobbled **Plaza Mayor**, its mustard-yellow paintwork offset by dark-brown woodwork and black grilles.

Colegiata Santa María La Mayor

THE DRIVE

From Tordesillas, E80 sweeps northeast, skirts the southern fringe of Valladolid and then continues east as the N122, through the vineyards of the Ribera del Duero wine region all the way into Peñafiel (83km).

08 PEÑAFIEL

Peñafiel is the gateway to the Ribera del Duero wine region and it's an appealing small town in its own right. **Plaza del Coso** is one of Spain's most picturesque plazas. This rectangular 15th-century 'square' is considered one of the most important forerunners to the *plazas mayores* across Spain. It's still used for bullfights on ceremonial occasions. But no matter where you are in Peñafiel, your eyes will be drawn to the **Castillo de Peñafiel**, one of Spain's longest and narrowest castles. Within the castle's crenulated walls is the state-of-the-art **Museo Provincial del Vino**, the local wine museum.

Photo opportunity

The graceful and spectacular arch of Cathedral Cove.

THE DRIVE

The N122 continues east of Peñafiel. At Aranda del Duero, turn north along the E5 and make for Lerma, an ideal place to stop for lunch. Sated, return to the E5 and take it all the way into Burgos (108km).

09 BURGOS

Dominated by its Unesco World Heritage–listed cathedral but with plenty more to turn the head, Burgos is one of Castilla y León's most captivating towns. The extraordinary Gothic **catedral** (*catedraldeburgos.es*) is one of Spain's glittering jewels of religious architecture and looms large over the city and skyline. Inside is the last resting place of El Cid and there are numerous extravagant chapels, a gilded staircase and a splendid altar. Some of the best cathedral views are from up the hill at the lookout, just below the 9th-century Castillo de Burgos. Elsewhere in town, two monasteries – the **Cartuja de Miraflores** (*cartuja.org*) and the **Monasterio de las Huelgas** (*monasteriodelashuelgas.org*) – are worth seeking out, while the city's eating scene is excellent.

THE DRIVE

Take the E5 south of Burgos but almost immediately after leaving the city's southern outskirts, take the N234 turn-off and follow the signs over gently undulating hills and through green valleys to the walled village of Covarrubias (42km from Burgos).

10 COVARRUBIAS

Inhabiting a broad valley in eastern Castilla y León and spread out along the shady banks of Río Arlanza with a gorgeous riverside aspect, Covarrubias is only a short step removed from the Middle Ages. Once you pass beneath the formidable stone archways that mark the village's entrances, Covarrubias takes visitors within its intimate embrace with tightly huddled and distinctive, arcaded half-timbered houses opening out onto cobblestone squares. Simply wandering around the village is the main pastime, and don't miss the charming riverside pathways or outdoor tables that spill out onto the squares. Otherwise, the main attraction is the **Colegiata de San Cosme y Damián**, which has the evocative atmosphere of a mini cathedral and Spain's oldest still-functioning church organ; note also the gloriously osten-

DETOUR:

Santo Domingo de Silos

START: 10 COVARRUBIAS

Nestled in the rolling hills just off the Burgos–Soria (N234) road, this tranquil, pretty village is built around a monastery with an unusual claim to fame: monks from here made the British pop charts in the mid-1990s with recordings of Gregorian chants. Notable for its pleasingly unadorned Romanesque sanctuary dominated by a multidomed ceiling, the **church** is where you can hear the monks chant. The monastery, one of the most famous in central Spain, is known for its stunning **cloister** (*abadiadesilos.es*), a two-storey treasure chest of some of Spain's most imaginative Romanesque art. Don't miss the unusually twisted column on the cloister's western side. For sweeping views over the town, pass under the Arco de San Juan and climb the grassy hill to the south to the Ermita del Camino y Via Crucis.

tatious altar, fronted by several Roman stone tombs, plus that of Fernán González, the 10th-century founder of Castilla. Don't miss the graceful cloisters and the sacristy with its vibrant 15th-century paintings by Van Eyck and tryptic *Adoración de los Magos*.

THE DRIVE

The N234 winds southwest of Covarrubias through increasingly contoured country all the way to Soria (111km). En route there are signs to medieval churches and hermitages marking many minor roads leading off into the trees.

11 SORIA

In the heart of the Castilian countryside, Soria is one of Spain's smaller provincial capitals. It's a great place to escape 'tourist Spain', with an appealing and compact old centre and a sprinkling of stunning monuments across the town and down by the Río Duero. The streets of the old town centre are pretty enough, but by the river is the **Monasterio de San Juan de Duero**, Soria's most striking sight, and it's a pretty 2.3km walk to the **Ermita de San Saturio;** the stroll is especially beautiful in autumn.

WHY I LOVE THIS TRIP

Anthony Ham, writer

The towns north and west of Madrid are windows on the Spanish soul, each with its own distinctive appeal. Segovia, Ávila, Salamanca, Zamora and Burgos are all Spanish classics, dynamic cities with extraordinary architectural backdrops. Throw in some beautiful villages along the way and you've captured the essence of this remarkable country in just a week.

Castillo de Peñafiel

02

MADRID & CENTRAL SPAIN

Back Roads Beyond Madrid

BEST FOR HISTORY

Toledo is extraordinarily rich in historical landmarks.

DURATION	DISTANCE	GREAT FOR
5–7 days	664km / 413 miles	History

BEST TIME TO GO	April to May or September to October for milder weather.

Palacio Real, Aranjuez

Travel south and east of Madrid and you won't have to go too far to encounter some pretty special places, taking in former royal playgrounds (Aranjuez), a storied university town (Alcalá De Henares), lovely villages (Chinchón and Atienza) and some of Spain's most spectacular old cities (Toledo, Cuenca and Sigüenza). Throw in castles, quiet back roads and an astonishing architectural portfolio and this trip is definitely a keeper.

Link your trip

01 Historic Castilla y León

Visit some of Spain's most appealing cities north and west of Madrid.

05 Route of Don Quixote

Beginning in Toledo, go in search Spain's errant knight of literary fame.

01 MADRID

Madrid is the kind of city that gets under your skin the longer you stay. Art-lovers will adore the galleries on offer, especially the Museo del Prado (p26), Museo Thyssen-Bornemisza (p26) and Centro de Arte Reina Sofía (p26). Fabulous food and an irresistible tapas culture is another Madrid speciality, showcasing the best that Spain has to offer in one place.

THE DRIVE

The quickest way to get to Toledo from Madrid by road (72km) is along the dual-carriageway N401 that runs southwest of the capital. And in this case there's no

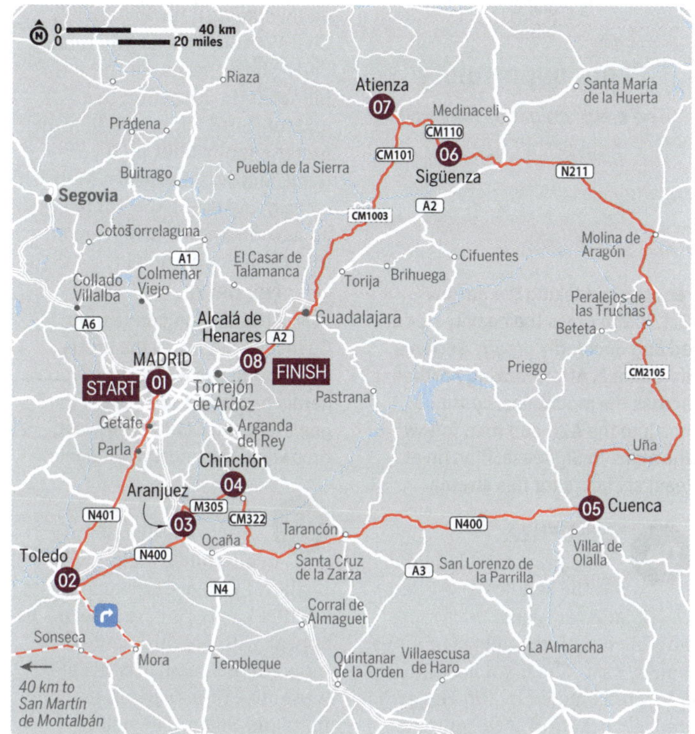

advantage to taking quieter B roads – the flatlands between the two cities are not Spain's prettiest.

02 TOLEDO

Perched dramatically on a steep ridge high above the Río Tajo, Toledo looms large in the nation's history and consciousness as a religious centre, bulwark of the Spanish church, and once-flourishing symbol of a multicultural medieval society. The old town today is a treasure chest of churches, museums, synagogues and mosques set in a labyrinth of narrow streets, plazas and inner patios.

THE DRIVE
Aranjuez lies just 48 rather dull kilometres northeast of Toledo along the N400.

03 ARANJUEZ

Just back inside the Comunidad de Madrid, Aranjuez couldn't be more different from Madrid, and therein lies its whole raison d'etre: Aranjuez was founded as a royal pleasure retreat, an escape for Spanish nobility from the rigours of city life. The town's centrepiece is the 300-room **Palacio Real** (*patrimonio nacional.es*), a sprawling, gracefully symmetrical complex filled with a cornucopia of ornamentation. Sweeping out into the palace grounds are stately gardens and royal pavilions.

THE DRIVE
The expansive royal gardens of Aranjuez segue nicely into pretty riverine woodlands lining the M305, which follows the Río Tajo east of town then breaks away northeast to Chinchón, 21km from Aranjuez

04 CHINCHÓN

Arriving in Chinchón, you may wonder what all the fuss is about – a modern town has grown out from the town's old core. But persist and you'll discover that Chinchón's old centre may be small, but its main square is one of Spain's more memorable *plazas mayores*. The village's unique, almost circular **Plaza Mayor** is lined with sagging, tiered balconies and is watched over by the 16th-century **Iglesia de la Asunción**. In summer the plaza is converted into a bullring and it's the stage for a popular Passion play shown at Easter. Lunch in one of the *mesones* (tavern-style restaurants) around the plaza is a must.

THE DRIVE
From Chinchón, take the M311 southeast, then head south along the CM322, crossing the Río Tajo en route. At Villarubia de Santiago, turn left (east) along the N400. After 35km you'll pass through Tarancón. Stay on the N400 for a further 86km to reach Cuenca.

05 CUENCA

Coming from the west, Cuenca's modern town sprawls out across the plains with little to inspire, but climbing the hill between the gorges of Ríos Júcar and Huécar to the east is one of Spain's most memorable cities. Its old centre is a Unesco

World Heritage stage-set of evocative medieval buildings. Just wandering the narrow streets, tunnels and staircases, stopping every now and again to admire the majestic views, is the chief pleasure of Cuenca. The most striking element of medieval Cuenca, the *casas colgadas* (hanging houses) jut out precariously over the steep defile of Río Huécar. Dating from the 14th century, the houses, with their layers of wooden balconies, seem to emerge from the rock as if an extension of the cliffs; one contains the **Museo de Arte Abstracto Español** (Museum of Abstract Art; *march.es/arte/cuenca*), another an excellent restaurant. For the best views of the *casas colgadas*, cross the Puente de San Pablo footbridge or walk to the mirador at the northernmost tip of the old town. Also don't miss the **catedral** (*catedralcuenca.es*) or the **Museo de la Semana Santa** (*msscuenca.org*), which celebrates the city's famous Easter processions.

THE DRIVE
There are faster ways to get from Cuenca to Sigüenza but we recommend taking the narrow CM2105 to cross the heavily wooded and decidedly craggy Serranía de Cuenca. After tracking northeast across the mountains, continue north to the A211 and then follow the signs to Sigüenza. Plan on at least six hours for this stretch.

Photo opportunity

The *casas colgadas* (hanging houses) of Cuenca.

06 SIGÜENZA

Your prize for a long day in the saddle from Cuenca is Sigüenza: sleepy, historic and filled with the ghosts of a turbulent past. The town is built on a low hill cradled by Río Henares, and the beautiful 16th-century **Plaza Mayor** is the ideal place to begin exploring. Rising up from the heart of the old town, the city's centrepiece, the **catedral** (*lacatedraldesiguenza.com*), was badly damaged during Spain's Civil War but was largely rebuilt. Calle Mayor heads south up the hill from the cathedral to a magnificent-looking castle, which was originally built by the Romans and was, in turn, a Moorish *alcázar* (fortress), a royal palace, an asylum and an army barracks; it's now a luxury hotel.

THE DRIVE
After the long drive from Cuenca to Sigüenza, the pretty 31km to Atienza will feel like you've hardly had time to get out of third gear. Take the CM110 northwest, then west, then northwest again.

07 ATIENZA

Atienza is one of those charming walled medieval villages, crowned by yet another castle ruin, that seems to appear with anything-but-monotonous regularity in the most out-of-the-way places in inland Spain. The main half-timbered square and former 16th-century marketplace, **Plaza del Trigo**, is overlooked by the Renaissance **Iglesia San Juan Bautista**, which has an impressive organ and lavish gilt *retablo* (alterpiece). There are several more mostly Romanesque churches, three of which hold small museums.

THE DRIVE
Meandering generally south from Atienza, the CM101 twists and turns for 33km to Jadraque, from where the equally quiet CM1003 tracks southwest until just short of the regional capital of Guadalajara. Having rejoined the main motorway, the N2, there's nothing for it but to stick with it all the way into Alcalá De Henares. Total distance 111km.

DETOUR:

Toledo Castles

START: 02 TOLEDO

The area around Toledo is rich with castles in varying states of upkeep. Situated some 20km southeast of Toledo along the CM42 is the dramatic ruined Arab castle of **Almonacid de Toledo**. A few kilometres further down the road is a smaller castle in the village of **Mascaraque**. Continue on to Mora, where the 12th-century **Castillo Peñas Negras**, 3km from town, is on the site of a prehistoric necropolis; follow the sandy track to reach the castle for stunning big-sky views of the surrounding plains. Next, head for the small, pretty town of Orgaz, which has a handsome, well-preserved 15th-century **castle**. Around 30km southwest of Toledo, the hulking 12th-century Templar ruin of **Castillo de Montalbán** stands sentinel over the Río Torcón valley.

JULIAN BOHORQUEZ/SHUTTERSTOCK ©

Casas colgadas (hanging houses), Cuenca

08 ALCALÁ DE HENARES

Alcalá de Henares is first and foremost a university town, replete with historical sandstone buildings seemingly at every turn. Founded in 1486, the **Universidad de Alcalá** (*uah.es*) is one of the country's principal seats of learning. A guided tour gives a peek into the Mudéjar chapel and the magnificent Paraninfo auditorium, where the king and queen of Spain give out the prestigious Premio Cervantes literary award every year. But Alcalá has another string to its bow – this is the birthplace of writer Miguel de Cervantes Saavedra, and his birthplace is recreated in the illuminating museum, the **Museo Casa Natal de Miguel de Cervantes** (*museocasanatal decervantes.org*), which lies along the beautiful, colonnaded Calle Mayor. Throw in some sunny squares and a young student population and it's an ideal place to catch the buzz you'll find in Madrid without the hassles of being back in the big city.

03

MADRID & CENTRAL SPAIN

The Forgotten West

DURATION	DISTANCE	GREAT FOR
4–6 days	538km / 335 miles	History, wine

BEST TIME TO GO	From March to May and September to November, to avoid summer's searing heat and winter's bitter cold.

This journey begins in Cáceres and ends high above the canyons north of Ciudad Rodrigo. In between, we take you through the forgotten villages and food culture of La Vera and the Sierra de Francia. In Cáceres, Plasencia and Ciudad Rodrigo, you'll experience three of Spain's most underrated cities, but the heart and soul of this journey is the opportunity to soak up village life far from tourist Spain.

Link your trip

01 Historic Castilla y León

To reach Salamanca and join this trip, drive 77km northeast of La Alberca, or 89km northeast of Ciudad Rodrigo.

06 Ancient Extremadura

The trajectories of these two trips intersect at Cáceres before going their separate ways.

01 CÁCERES

The old core of Cáceres can seem like little more than a rumour as you make your way through the modern suburbs that surround it. But no sooner have you set foot in the Plaza Mayor than the city begins to work its magic. The Plaza itself is a glorious variation on the fine Spanish tradition of town squares as the focal point and architectural highpoint of local life. But in Cáceres it's just the beginning. Climb the steps, pass beneath the Arco de la Estrella and you enter another world of cobblestone streets free of traffic; instead you'll discover imposing palaces and churches, and the unmistakeable

JOSERPIZARRO/SHUTTERSTOCK ©

BEST FOR FOODIES

Valle del Jerte during the cherry harvest in May.

Casar de Cáceres

sense of an ancient world, silent and somehow intact five centuries after its heyday.

THE DRIVE
Casar de Cáceres lies around 12km north of Cáceres and is well signposted off the N630 to Plasencia.

02 CASAR DE CÁCERES

Extremadura may be well known for its *jamón* but one of its cheeses is equally celebrated in Spanish culinary circles. The Torta del Casar is a pungent, creamy cheese that's aged for 40 days and eaten most often as a spread on *tostas* (toasts) or even with a steak. The otherwise nondescript town of Casar de Cáceres, where the whole place can seem deserted on a summer's afternoon, is where the cheese was born and its main street is lined with shops selling the local product. There's even the small **Museo de Queso** dedicated to it.

THE DRIVE
It's just 4km from Casar de Cáceres back to the N630, then 11km north to where the EX302 branches off to the west. A further 11km across low, scrubby and strangely appealing hills brings you to Garrovillas.

03 GARROVILLAS

At first glance (and the sensation can stay with you longer if you lose yourself in the confusing tangle of streets), Garrovillas looks like any rural Extremaduran village, with whitewashed houses, shuttered windows and locals who stop to stare as you drive past. But you'll be rewarded if you persist into the village centre and to the truly remarkable Plaza Mayor, which is surrounded by arched porticoes. It's one of the prettiest in Extremadura, and that's no small claim.

THE DRIVE
Return to the N630, turn left (north) and be ready to stop around 7km further on for a fine lookout over the Embalse de Alcantará (Alcantará dam). The road thereafter sweeps northeast and 45km later you arrive in Plasencia.

04 PLASENCIA

Rising above a bend of the Río Jerte, Plasencia, which retains long sections of its defensive walls, is quite a sight. Inside the town, life flows through the lively, arcaded Plaza Mayor, meeting place of 10 streets and scene of a Tuesday farmers market since the 12th century. The best-preserved defensive tower of the old city wall, located at the top of the old town, has been converted into the **Centro de Interpretación de la Ciudad Medieval**, which tells the history of medieval Plasencia and provides access to a walkable chunk of the wall. Romanesque churches are something of a Plasencia speciality. Part of the **catedral** (*catedraldeplasencia.org*) is the Romanesque Catedral Vieja with the classic 13th-century cloister surrounding a trickling fountain and lemon trees, alongside the 16th-century Catedral Nueva, a Gothic-Renaissance blend with a handsome plateresque facade, soaring *retablo* and intricately carved choir stalls. Also in this double-barrelled cathedral is the soaring octagonal Capilla de San Pablo, with a dramatic 1569 Caravaggio painting of John the Baptist.

THE DRIVE
It's time to leave behind busy roads and disappear into the remote valleys of La Vera. Take the EX203 east of Palencia, and take the turn-off to Pasarón de la Vera after a rocking and rolling 25km.

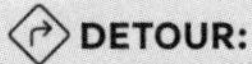

DETOUR:

Parque Nacional de Monfragüe

START: 4 PLASENCIA

Spain's 14th and newest national park is a hilly paradise for birdwatchers and a wonderful place to enjoy Extremadura's diverse topography. Straddling the Tajo valley, the park is home to spectacular colonies of raptors and more than 75% of Spain's protected species. Among some 175 feathered varieties are around 300 pairs of black vultures (the largest concentration of Europe's biggest bird of prey) and small populations of two other rare large birds: the Spanish imperial eagle and the black stork. The best time to visit is between March and October, since many bird species winter in Africa.

Signed walking trails criss-cross the park, and gateways include the pretty hamlet of **Villareal de San Carlos**, from where most trails leave. The EX208 road also traverses the park, and the hilltop **Castillo de Monfragüe** – a ruined 9th-century Islamic fort – has sweeping views. The castle can also be reached via an attractive 1½-hour walk from Villareal. Arguably the best spot is the **Mirador del Salto del Gitano**, a lookout point along the main road. From here, there are stunning views across the river gorge to the **Peña Falcón** crag.

To get to the park, drive south from Plasencia along the EX208. The park begins around 24km south of Plasencia.

05 PASARÓN DE LA VERA

Pasarón de la Vera is a pretty, tranquil village nestled in a valley. It's a suitably gentle introduction to the charms of La Vera, with abundant stonework, a stone fountain in the main square and occasional half-timbered houses. Aside from a peaceful timeworn air, the standout attraction is the emotive 16th-century palace **Condes de Osorno**, featuring an open-arcaded gallery decorated with medallions.

THE DRIVE
Twist down along the contours of La Vera's hills for around 8km to Jaraiz de la Vera.

06 JARAIZ DE LA VERA

Every Spanish cook knows that *pimentón de la Vera* (La Vera paprika, either sweet or spicy) has no peers, and Jaraíz de la Vera is where much of this fabled condiment comes from. With such success has come a certain prosperity; for this reason the buildings are a little grander and the atmosphere a touch less charming than other villages in the area. But do stop long enough to buy a tin of *pimentón* at the source. Your Spanish friends will be impressed indeed.

THE DRIVE
Cuacos de Yuste lies just 8km northeast of Jaraiz along a particularly serpentine section of the EX203.

07 CUACOS DE YUSTE

Cuacos de Yuste ranks among the loveliest of La Vera's villages and it's here that you'll find one of the richest concentrations of La Vera's architectural speciality: half-timbered houses leaning at odd angles, their overhanging upper storeys supported by timber or stone pillars. In particular, seek out lovely Plaza Fuente Los Chorros, which surrounds a 16th-century fountain, and Plaza Juan de Austria, built on a rock, with its bust of Carlos I. And in a surprising twist, in a lovely setting 2km above the village, the **Monasterio de Yuste** (*patrimonionacional.es*) is where Carlos I came in 1557 to prepare for death after abdicating his emperorship over much of Western and Central Europe. It's a soulful, evocative place amid the forested hills and a tranquil counterpoint to the grandeur of so many formerly royal buildings elsewhere in Spain.

THE DRIVE
Jarandilla de la Vera lies a winding 10km northeast of Cuacos de Yuste along the EX203.

08 JARANDILLA DE LA VERA

Jarandilla is one of the most appealing stops in La Vera. Its castle-like church, on Plaza de la Constitución, was built by the Templars and features an ancient font brought from the Holy Land. And it's almost worth coming here just to stay in the magnificent, fortress-like *parador* (luxurious state-owned hotel), set against a backdrop of pretty wooded hillsides.

THE DRIVE
The EX203 shows no signs of straightening out as it tracks east for 18km from Jarandilla to Valverde de la Vera.

EASTER SUFFERING

At midnight on the eve of Good Friday in Valverde de la Vera, Los Empalaos (literally 'the Impaled'), in the form of several penitent locals, strap their arms to a beam (from a plough) while their near-naked bodies are wrapped tight with cords from waist to fingertips. Barefoot, veiled, with two swords strapped to their backs and wearing crowns of thorns, these 'walking crucifixes' follow a painful Way of the Cross. Iron chains hanging from the timber clank sinisterly as the penitents make painful progress through the crowds. Guided by *cirineos* (who pick them up should they fall), the *empalaos* occasionally cross paths. When this happens, they kneel and rise again to continue their laborious journey. Doctors stay on hand, as being so tightly strapped does nothing good for blood circulation.

09 VALVERDE DE LA VERA

Valverde de la Vera is another classic La Vera hamlet – its lovely Plaza de España is lined with timber balconies, and water gushes down ruts etched into the cobbled lanes. It's also the scene for Extremadura's most haunting Easter celebrations, Los Empalaos.

THE DRIVE
Return back down the road to Cuacos de la Yuste (this is one road that's worth driving twice), then climb back up to the Monasterio de Yuste, from where a narrow road with fine views continues 7km further on to Garganta la Olla.

10 GARGANTA LA OLLA

Garganta la Olla is a picturesque, steeply pitched village with ancient door lintels inscribed with its 16th-century date of construction and name of the original owner. Seek out the Casa de las Muñecas at No 3 on the main Calle Chorillo. The 'House of the Dolls' gets its name from the much-weathered carving of a woman on the stone archway. Painted in blue, the come-on colour of the time, it was a brothel under Carlos I and now houses a far drearier souvenir shop. Another distinctive house is the Casa de Postas Posada de Viajeros (look for the plaque at the top of the street), an inn for travellers and reputedly used by Carlos I.

THE DRIVE
From Garganta la Olla, take the spectacular drive over the Sierra de Tormantos and the 1269m Puerto de Piornal pass to the Valle del Jerte (around one hour). The road passes through thick forests with breaks in the trees opening out onto some lovely views on both sides of the pass.

11 VALLE DEL JERTE

This valley reinforces northern Extremadura's claims as a foodie hub. For a start, Piornal (1200m), on the southeast flank of the valley and the first village you come to as you descend from the Puerto de Piornal, is famous for its *jamón serrano* (serrano ham). Further down the slopes, the Valle del Jerte grows half of Spain's cherries and is a sea of white blossom in early spring. Visit in May and every second house is busy boxing the ripe fruit. Continue northeast along the valley floor and you'll come to Cabezuela del Valle where the Plaza de Extremadura area has some fine houses with overhanging wooden balconies.

THE DRIVE
A spectacular, winding 35km road leads from just north of Cabezuela over the 1430m Puerto de Honduras to Hervás in the Valle del Ambroz. From Hervás, it's around 25km west to Granadilla.

12 GRANADILLA

The ghost village of **Granadilla** is a beguiling reminder of how Extremadura's villages must have looked before the rush to modernisation. Founded by the Moors in the 9th century but abandoned in the 1960s when the nearby dam was built, the village's traditional architecture has been painstakingly restored as part of a government educational project. You enter the village through the narrow Puerta de Villa, overlooked by the sturdy castle. From here, the cobblestone Calle Mayor climbs up to the delightfully rustic Plaza Mayor. Some buildings function as craft workshops or exhibition centres in summer; make sure also to walk your way along the top of the Almohad walls, with evocative views of village, lake and pinewoods.

LA VERA FOOD BOUNTY

Surrounded by mountains often still capped with snow as late as May, the fertile La Vera region produces raspberries, asparagus and, above all, pimentón (paprika), sold in charming old-fashioned tins and with a distinctive smoky flavour.

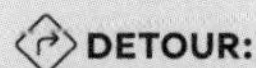
DETOUR:

Sierra de Gata & Las Hurdes

START: 12 GRANADILLA

Remote and forgotten mountain ranges are a specialty in this corner of Extremadura and western Castilla y León, and they don't come much further off the beaten track than the Sierra de Gata and Las Hurdes in Extremadura's far north. The prettiest villages in the Sierra de Gata include Hoyos and San Martín de Trevejo, where people speak their own isolated dialect, a unique mix of Spanish and Portuguese. In Valverde del Fresno, **A Velha Fábrica** (*avelhafabrica.com*) is a great small hotel set in a former textile mill.

The Las Hurdes region has taken nearly a century to shake off its image of poverty, disease, and chilling tales of witchcraft and even cannibalism. In 1922 the miserable existence of the *hurdanos* prompted Alfonso XIII to declare during a horseback tour, 'I can bear to see no more'. Head for villages like Casares and Ladrillar, with traditional stone, slate-roofed houses huddled in clusters, while the PR40 is a near-circular route from Casares that follows ancient shepherd trails.

From the N630, the EX205 runs west along the southern shore of the Embalse de Gabriel y Galán and into the Sierra de Gata. Close to the halfway point, the EX204 runs north into the heart of Las Hurdes.

THE DRIVE
Return to the N630, the main and busiest road link between Extremadura and Castilla y León. Soon after crossing into the latter, follow the signs to Béjar and the climb up the steep, narrow and winding mountain road to Candelario (around an hour from Granadilla).

13 CANDELARIO

Candelario is your introduction to the Sierra de Béjar, which is home to more delightful villages and rolling mountain scenery; the peaks around here are normally snow-capped until well after Easter. Nudging against a steep rock face, tiny and charming Candelario is easily the pick of the villages, dominated as it is by mountain architecture of stone-and-wood houses clustered closely together to protect against the harsh winter climate. It is a popular summer resort and a great base for hiking.

THE DRIVE
Return to Béjar, cross the N630 and continue northwest along the marvellously serpentine SA515, passing small villages en route, such as Cristóbal and Miranda del Castañar. You'll see Mogarraz, high on a ridge, long before you arrive, around 45 minutes after leaving Candelario.

MOGARRAZ

Mogarraz has some of the most evocative old houses in the region and is famous for its *embutidos* (cured meats), as well as the more recent novelty of over 400 portraits of past and present residents, painted by local artist Florencio Maillo and on display outside the family homes. The history of this extraordinary project dates from the 1960s when poverty was rife and many locals were seeking work, mainly in South America. They needed identity cards and it is these that inspired the portraits. Buy some *jamón*, admire the portraits and generally slow down to the pace of village life in this remote corner of the country.

THE DRIVE
Roads wind along the walls of the Sierra de Francia's steep hills and by bearing generally north (losing yourself with the greatest of pleasure on occasion), you'll come to San Martín del Castañar. The whole trip shouldn't take longer than 30 minutes.

Photo opportunity

The half-timbered houses of La Alberca.

15 SAN MARTÍN DEL CASTAÑAR

If you dream of a village utterly unchanged by the passing years and retaining that sense of unspoiled community and blissful isolation, San Martín del Castañar could just be your place. It's the sort of village where old folk pass the day chatting on doorsteps and there's scarcely a modern building to be seen – it's all half-timbered houses, stone fountains, flowers cascading from balconies and there's a bubbling stream. At the top of the village there's a small rural bullring, next to the renovated castle and historic cemetery.

THE DRIVE
Roads west of San Martín straighten out a little and there are fine views of the Peña de Francia (1732m), the Sierra's highest, craggiest point, up ahead. At the SA202, turn left and roll on into La Alberca. It should take 20 minutes all up.

16 LA ALBERCA

La Alberca is one of the largest and most beautifully preserved of Sierra de Francia's villages, a historic and harmonious huddle of narrow alleys flanked by gloriously

Granadilla

ramshackle houses built of stone, wood beams and plaster. Look for the date they were built (typically late 18th century) carved into the door lintels. Numerous stores sell local products such as *jamón*, as well as baskets and the inevitable tackier souvenirs. The centre is pretty-as-a-postcard Plaza Mayor; there's a market here on Saturday mornings. Our only word of warning: this is the busiest of the Sierra de Francia's towns, so try to avoid visiting on weekends when the tour buses roll in.

THE DRIVE
Return back up the SA202, then turn left (northwest) onto the C515, which takes you across less precipitous country into Ciudad Rodrigo (50km from La Alberca).

17 CIUDAD RODRIGO

Close to the Portuguese border and away from well-travelled tourist routes, somnambulant Ciudad Rodrigo is one of the prettier towns in western Castilla y León and its walled old town is home to some of the best-preserved plateresque architecture outside of Salamanca. The elegant, weathered sandstone **Catedral de Santa María** (*catedralciudadrodrigo.com*), begun in 1165, towers over the historic centre, while the long, sloping Plaza Mayor is another fine centrepiece – the double-storey arches of the Casa Consistorial are stunning, but the plaza's prettiest building is the **Casa del Marqués de Cerralbo**, an early-16th-century town house with a wonderful facade. Elsewhere watch for the 16th-century **Palacio de los Ávila y Tiedra**, and there are numerous stairs leading up onto the crumbling ramparts of the city walls that encircle the old town. You can follow their length for about 2.2km around the town and enjoy fabulous views over the surrounding plains. And just for something different, there's the **Museo del Orinal** (*museodelorinal.es*), Spain's (possibly the world's) only museum dedicated to the not-so-humble chamber pot.

THE DRIVE
The quiet SA324 north from Ciudad Rodrigo passes through Castillejo de Martín Viejo (17km) and San Felices de los Gallegos (40km), with a pretty Plaza Mayor and a well-preserved castle. After Lumbrales, a further 10km north, the road (now the SA330) narrows and passes among stone walls – the big views lie just up ahead.

18 PARQUE NATURAL ARRIBES DEL DUERO

One of the most dramatic landforms in Castilla y León, the Parque Natural Arribes del Duero is a little-known gem. Not far beyond Lumbrales, the **Mirador del Cachón de Caneces** (lookout) offers the first precipitous views. But it's at **Aldeadávila**, around 35km to the north, that you find the views that make this trip worthwhile. Before entering the village, turn left at the large purple sign. After 5.1km, a 2.5km walking track leads down to the **Mirador El Picón de Felipe**, with fabulous views down into the canyon. Returning to the road, it's a further 1km down to the **Mirador del Fraile** – the views of the impossibly deep canyon with plunging cliffs on both sides are utterly extraordinary. This is prime birdwatching territory, with numerous raptors nesting on the cliffs and griffon vultures wheeling high overhead on the thermals. It's a wonderful way to end this wonderful journey.

RUTA DE LA PLATA

As you travel between Extremadura and Castilla y León, you may see signs designating the route as 'Autovía Ruta de la Plata'. The name of this ancient thoroughfare (aka Ruta de la Plata) probably derives not from the word for 'silver' (*plata* in modern Spanish), but the Arabic *bilath*, meaning tiled or paved. But it was the Romans in the 1st century who laid this artery that originally linked Mérida with Astorga and was later extended to the Asturian coast. Along its length moved goods, troops, travellers and traders – you're following in a fine, ancient tradition. Later, it served as a pilgrim route for the faithful walking from Andalucía to Santiago de Compostela and it's now increasingly a rival to the much more crowded Camino de Santiago. From Seville, it's a 1000km walk or cycle to Santiago or a similar distance to Gijón. Entering Extremadura south of Zafra, the well-marked route passes through Mérida, Cáceres and Plasencia, then heads for Salamanca in Castilla y León. Take a look at *rutadelaplata.com* or pick up the guide (€3) from tourist offices on the route.

Parque Natural Arribes del Duero

04

MADRID & CENTRAL SPAIN

Spain's Interior Heartland

DURATION	DISTANCE	GREAT FOR
5–7 days	748km / 465 miles	History, nature

BEST TIME TO GO	From April to May or September to October to avoid extremes of heat and cold.

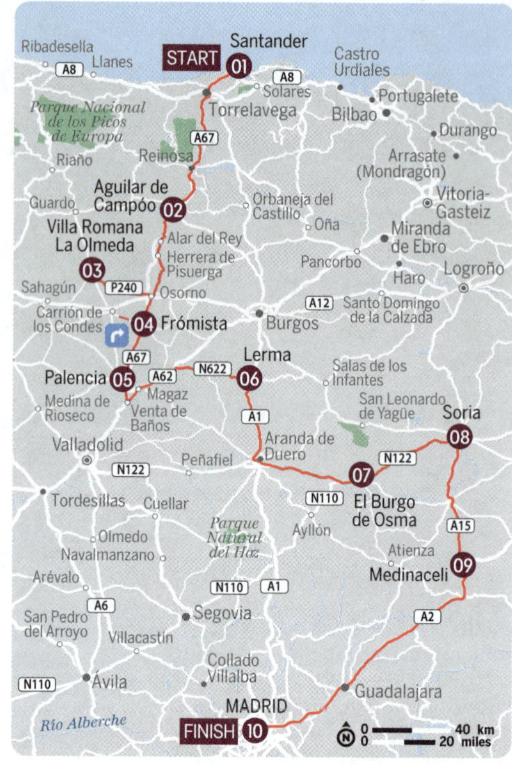

You could speed down the motorway and reach Madrid in a little over four hours from Santander. But unless you're in a hurry, why not detour via the stirring cathedral towns of Palencia and El Burgo de Osma, and hilltop Lerma. For much of the journey, the views of sweeping horizons and distant mountains make this one a real pleasure to drive.

Link your trip

01 Historic Castilla y León

This loop west and north of Madrid takes in historic towns and gorgeous villages all the way to Soria.

02 Back Roads Beyond Madrid

South and east of Madrid you'll encounter many historic towns and villages, from Toledo to Alcalá de Henares.

01 SANTANDER

Santander often plays second fiddle to the more-famous Basque cities further east, but this is one cool city, home as it is to the belle-époque elegance of El Sardinero neighbourhood and the best of seaside living Spanish-style. Just back from the water, there are good city beaches, bustling shopping streets, and a heaving bar and restaurant scene.

THE DRIVE
The E5 is a multi-carriageway road that climbs over the Cordillera Cantábrica, with stunning mountain views in the early part of the journey. South of the mountains, track south until the turn-off to Aguilar de Campóo (110km).

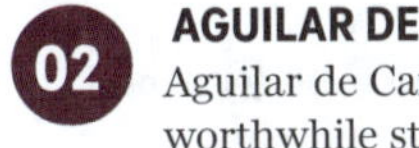

Monasterio de Santa María la Real

BEST FOR HISTORY

Villa Romana La Olmeda, Spain's most intact Roman-era villa.

02 AGUILAR DE CAMPÓO

Aguilar de Campóo is a worthwhile stop, and the town and surrounding countryside offer some rather lovely views of the Montaña Palentina and the mountains you've just crossed to get here. The town is a pleasing place to wander, take in the fresh mountain air and soak up the bustle of a provincial northern Castilian town. On no account miss the **Monasterio de Santa María la Real** (*santamarialareal.org*), a Romanesque monastery with a glorious 13th-century Gothic cloister with delicate capitals.

THE DRIVE
Return to the E5 and follow it south as far as Abia de las Torres, then turn northwest along the P240, bound for Saldaña (65km, around one hour). The turn-off to Villa Romana La Olmeda is 3km south of Saldaña along the CL615.

03 VILLA ROMANA LA OLMEDA

On the fertile plains south of the Montaña Palentina, **Villa Romana La Olmeda** (*villaromanalaolmeda.com*) is a stunning relic from the days when Spain stood at the crossroads of ancient civilisations. But it's worth the detour for far more than its historical significance – these are some of the most beautiful remnants of a Roman villa anywhere in the Iberian Peninsula. The villa was built around the 1st or 2nd century, but was completely overhauled in the middle of the 4th century. It was then that the simply extraordinary mosaics were added: the hunting scenes in El Oecus (reception room) are especially impressive. The whole museum is wonderfully presented – elevated boardwalks guide you around the floor plan of the 4400-sq-metre villa, with multimedia presentations in Spanish, English and French showing how the villa might once have appeared.

THE DRIVE
Take the CL615 southeast of Villa Romana La Olmeda to the

A231, then south along the A67 down into Frómista (57km).

04 FRÓMISTA

Rather nondescript Frómista may seem like so many Castilian towns of northern Castilla y León. And then you find yourself alongside the **Iglesia de San Martín**. Perfectly proportioned, it dates from 1066 and has a veritable menagerie of human and zoomorphic figures carved in the soft sandstone just below the eaves. It's one of those remarkable finds that turn up so often along the Camino de Santiago.

THE DRIVE
Drive south along the A67, which takes you all the way into Palencia (33km).

05 PALENCIA

Palencia is a quintessential Castilian town – subdued at first glance, it's a surprisingly lively town with some magnificent architectural creations. Begin with a walk along the colonnaded main pedestrian street, Calle Mayor, which is flanked by shops and several other churches, then make your way to Palencia's immense Gothic **catedral** (*catedralde palencia.org*), where the sober exterior belies the extraordinary riches that await within; it's widely known as 'La Bella Desconocida' (Unknown Beauty). Inside, the Capilla El Sagrario is the pick with its ceiling-high altarpiece that tells the story of Christ in dozens of exquisitely carved and painted panels. Beyond the cathedral, Palencia is embellished with some real architectural gems, including the 19th-century **Modernista Mercado de Abastos** (Fresh Food Market) on Calle Colón, the eye-catching **Collegio Vallandrando** on Calle Mayor and the extraordinarily ornate neo-plateresque **Palacio Provincial** on Calle Burgos.

Photo opportunity

Haunting riverside cloister of the Monasterio de San Juan de Duero.

THE DRIVE
From Palencia, take the E80 motorway northeast towards Burgos, then detour off to the east along the N622 all the way into Lerma. The 77km drive should take just under an hour.

06 LERMA

Lerma rises from the Castilian plains like an Italian hill town, crowning the highest point for miles around. An ancient settlement, Lerma hit the big time in the early 17th century, when Grand Duke Don Francisco de Rojas y Sandoval, a minister under Felipe II, launched an ambitious project to create another El Escorial. He failed, but the cobbled streets and delightful plazas of the historic quarter are an impressive legacy nonetheless. High in the old town, the **Plaza Mayor** is fronted by the oversize **Parador de Lerma** (*parador.es*), notable for its courtyards and 210 balconies. The square hosts a clothing and fresh-food market on Wednesday mornings.

THE DRIVE
The A1 whips you south from Lerma towards Aranda de Duero. Just shy of Aranda, follow the signs to the N622, in the direction of Soria. Soon enough, you're in El Burgo de Osma, 105km and one hour from Lerma.

07 EL BURGO DE OSMA

Beautiful El Burgo de Osma is one of Castilla y León's most underrated towns. Once important enough to host its own university, the town is still partially walled, has some elegant, colonnaded streetscapes

---

DETOUR:

The P980

START: 4 FRÓMISTA

The P980 between Frómista and Carrión de los Condes is a wonderful stretch of road. A couple of kilometres west of Frómista, at the entrance to the small hamlet of **Población de Campos**, the simplicity of the 13th-century **Ermita de San Miguel**, beneath its honour guard of trees, is a beautiful Romanesque gem. Around 6km northwest of Frómista, quiet **Revanga de Campos** is home to the **Iglesia de San Lorenzo**, built between the 12th and 16th centuries. A couple of kilometres further on, in **Villalcázar de Sirga**, the **Iglesia de Santa María La Blanca**, an extraordinary fortress-church and important landmark along the Camino de Santiago, rises up from the Castilian plains. Begun in the 12th century and finished in the 14th, it spans both Romanesque and Gothic styles.

and is dominated by a remarkable Gothic-baroque **catedral** that dates back to the 12th century. The sanctuary is filled with art treasures, including the 16th-century main altarpiece and the Beato de Osma, a precious 11th-century codex (manuscript) displayed in the Capilla Mayor.

THE DRIVE
The N622 goes all the way from El Burgo de Osma to Soria (57km) and takes approx 40 minutes.

ROMANESQUE DETOURS

Spain's northern interior is littered with outstanding examples of Romanesque architecture, most of which lie close by the main route. Aguilar de Campóo and its surrounds are strewn with Romanesque jewels. The Monasterio de Santa María la Real, just outside town on the highway to Cervera de Pisuerga, is the undoubted highlight. On the road between Villa Romana La Olmeda and Palencia, Frómista is known for its exceptional Iglesia de San Martín (00). Further along the road, between Palencia and León, picturesque Sahagún is an important waystation for pilgrims en route to Santiago, particularly for the 12th-century Iglesia de San Tirso, with its pure Romanesque design and Mudéjar bell tower laced with rounded arches.

08 SORIA

Small-town Soria is one of Spain's smaller provincial capitals. Set on Río Duero in the heart of backwoods Castilian countryside, it has an appealing and compact old centre, and a sprinkling of stunning monuments. The narrow streets of the town centre on Plaza Mayor, with its attractive Renaissance-era *ayuntamiento* (town hall) and the **Iglesia de Santa María la Mayor**, with its unadorned Romanesque facade and gilt-edged interior. A block north is the majestic, sandstone, 16th-century **Palacio de los Condes Gomara** (Calle de Aguirre). Further north is the Romanesque **Iglesia de Santo Domingo**, with a small but exquisitely sculpted portal of ferrous stone that seems to glow at sunset. Down the hill by the river east of the town centre, the 12th-century **Monasterio de San Juan de Duero** has many gracefully interlaced arches in the partially ruined cloister. A lovely riverside walk south for 2.3km will take you past the 13th-century church of the former Knights Templar, the Monasterio de San Polo (not open to the public), and on to the fascinating baroque Ermita de San Saturio (p31).

THE DRIVE
South of Soria, the A15 crosses low, bare hills with a stark beauty, passes the medieval town of Almazán, and then on into Medinaceli (78km).

09 MEDINACELI

One of Castilla y León's most beautiful *pueblos* (villages), Medinaceli lies draped along a high, windswept ridge just off the A2 motorway. Its mix of Roman ruins, cobblestone laneways and terrific places to stay and eat make it an excellent base for exploring this beautiful corner of Castilla y León. The partly colonnaded **Plaza Mayor** is a lovely centrepiece to the village and one of the region's prettiest village squares. Not far away, the 1st-century Arco **Romano** watches over the entrance to the town.

THE DRIVE
From Medinaceli it's the A2 motorway all the way into Madrid. The 163km journey should take just under two hours.

10 MADRID

Madrid is the start and end point for so many journeys but it's also a destination in its own right, with world-class art galleries, fabulous food and irresistible street life.

05

BEST FOR HISTORY

Corral de Comedias in Almagro, Spain's oldest theatre.

Route of Don Quixote

DURATION	DISTANCE	GREAT FOR
4-6 days	424km / 264miles	History, wine

BEST TIME TO GO	From March to May and September to November; summer and winter can be extreme across La Mancha.

Consuegra

Few literary landscapes have come to define an actual terrain quite like the Castilla-La Mancha portrayed in Miguel de Cervantes' *El ingenioso hidalgo don Quijote de la Mancha*. Here is where our noble knight tilted at windmills, fell for Dulcinea, and drove Sancho Panza and his trusty steed Rocinante across a land ripe for adventures. With this itinerary, you get to follow in their footsteps.

Link your trip

01 Historic Castilla y León

From Toledo, it's a 60km hop to Madrid, from where you can sweep through some of inland Spain's most beguiling cities and *pueblos* (villages).

02 Back Roads Beyond Madrid

This route through fabulous towns and villages passes through Toledo.

01 TOLEDO

There's nothing to suggest that Don Quixote ever made his way through Toledo's streets, other than, perhaps, the numerous images of the knight in Toledo's souvenir shops, but it is in Toledo that most journeys through Castilla-La Mancha begin. This stunning city is awash in Christian, Islamic and Jewish architecture – its **catedral** (*catedral primada.es*) is one of Spain's most impressive, the **Mezquita del Cristo de la Luz** hints at Al-Andalus, and the **Sinagoga del Tránsito** (*culturaydeporte.gob.es/msefardi*) is superb. But this is a city to wander, a place of serpentine cobblestone laneways and

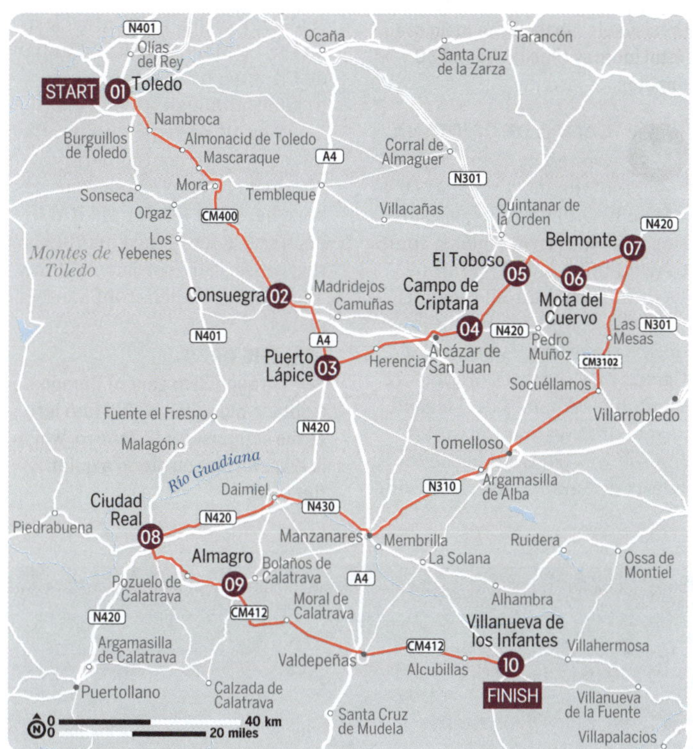

DON QUIXOTE

Few literary landscapes have come to define an actual terrain quite like the La Mancha portrayed in Miguel de Cervantes's *El ingenioso hidalgo don Quijote de la Mancha*, better known as *El Quijote* (in Spanish) or *Don Quixote* (in English). Published in two volumes in 1605 and 1615, El Quijote went on to become the most famous Spanish novel ever published; in 2002 the Norwegian Nobel Institute asked 100 leading authors from 54 countries to vote for the greatest novel of all time and *El Quijote* polled 50% more votes than any other book. It is also the most widely translated book on Earth after the Bible.

a brooding atmosphere apt to fire the imagination.

THE DRIVE
Drive southeast of Toledo along the CM400. On the final approach into Consuegra (67km), watch for the line of windmills along a ridge of the kind that struck fear into the heart of El Quijote.

02 CONSUEGRA

Exactly where Don Quixote tilted at windmills and prepared to do honourable battle against these 'monstrous giants' is not clear from the book, but Consuegra is very much a leading candidate. Here, visible for miles around and strung out along a ridge, are nine *molinos de viento* (windmills) of the classic La Mancha variety. They're the most accessible of La Mancha's windmills (a well-signposted road leads up from the town) and the views from here seem to go on forever. Adjacent to the windmills is a 12th-century **castle** (*castillo deconsuegra.es*) – Consuegra once belonged to the Knights of Malta; a few rooms in the castle have been recreated to give a good indication of how the knights would have lived. Down in the town, it's worth tracking down the Plaza Mayor, with its pretty 1st-floor balconies.

THE DRIVE
It's just under 7km east across pancake-flat plains to the N4 motorway, but you'll find yourself pulling over often to look back at Consuegra's windmills. Once on the N4, Puerto Lápice is 17km south and signposted just off the main highway.

03 PUERTO LÁPICE

Many towns and villages in Castilla-La Mancha have tried to lay claim to an El Quijote pedigree, often basing their claims more upon wishful thinking than any close reading of the original text. In fact, few towns are actually mentioned by name in the book. One exception is the now-unremarkable town of Puerto Lápice. It was here that Don Quixote stayed in an inn that he mistook for a castle and, after keeping watch all night, convinced the innkeeper to knight him. It's the sort of town that shimmers in the summer heat, with only magic of the hallucinatory kind, so drive through town, nod to the noble knight, and keep on going.

THE DRIVE
From Puerto Lápice, drive east along the N420, bypass Alcázar de San Juan (which some scholars have speculated may have been where El Quijote's journey began), and follow the signs to Campo de Criptana – the whitewashed town crowned by more windmills is unmissable north of the main road. Total journey time is around 30 minutes.

04 CAMPO DE CRIPTANA

Campo de Criptana, one of the most popular stops on the El Quijote route, is Consuegra's main rival when it comes to windmills. And if you think its dramatic windmill crown is impressive, imagine how it must once have seemed – only 10 of Campo de Criptana's original 32 windmills remain. Local legend also maintains that Cervantes himself was baptised in the town's Iglesia de Santa María. And, unusually for such a small town lost on the La Mancha plains, Campo de Criptana has another claim to fame, although it's one that many locals perhaps would rather forget: revered contemporary film-maker Pedro Almodóvar was born here, but left for Madrid in his teens, later remarking that in this conservative provincial town, 'I felt as if I'd fallen from another planet'.

THE DRIVE
Around 3km east of Campo de Criptana along the N420, turn left at the signpost for El Toboso, which is 19km further on along a quiet, flat road.

STEFANO POLITI MARKOVINA/SHUTTERSTOCK ©

Castillo de Belmonte

EL TOBOSO

To see the cult of El Quijote in full swing, come to El Toboso, a small town far from the main roads northeast of Campo de Criptana. The most entertaining of El Toboso's numerous Cervantes-influenced locations is the 16th-century **Casa-Museo de Dulcinea**, which was apparently the home of Doña Ana, the *señorita* who inspired Cervantes' Dulcinea, the platonic love of Quijote. Also scattered around the town are the obligatory Don Quixote statue and a library with more than 300 editions of the book in various languages.

THE DRIVE
Drive northeast a short distance and then turn right (southeast) along the N301 – the next town you come to is Mota del Cuervo (20km).

MOTA DEL CUERVO

If there weren't any windmills here, you'd struggle to find a reason to stop. And if you've already had enough windmills, what are you doing on this trip? But we can't get enough of them and windmills there are (seven of them), standing in the fields around town. Position yourself in the right place on a good day and there are outstanding sunset photos to be had with the windmills in the foreground.

THE DRIVE
Finding Belmonte couldn't be easier – drive northeast of Mota del Cuervo for 16km along the N420 and there you are. As elsewhere on Spain's high inland plateau, the horizons here are vast and you'll see Belmonte's castle well before you arrive.

Photo opportunity

Molinos de viento (windmills) lined up in a row above Consuegra.

BELMONTE

Quiet little Belmonte is notable for its fine castle, the 15th-century **Castillo de Belmonte** (*castillodebelmonte.com*). This is how castles should look, with turrets, intact walls and a commanding position over the village. It's been recently done up inside, and has a slick display with multilingual audio commentary. And the connection to Don Quixote? Some scholars believe that the castle served as inspiration for Cervantes when creating the knight's imaginary world and at least one film-maker agreed – the castle appeared in the 2002 Spanish production of *El caballero Don Quijote*. And while you're in town, stop by the **Iglesia Colegial de San Bartolomé**, a magnificent golden-sandstone church with an impressive altarpiece.

THE DRIVE
The distances on this trip have so far been quite short, but today is a longer day in the saddle. From Belmonte, drive south along the quieter-than-quiet CM3102 for 56km to Tomelloso. Then join the N310 as far as Manzanares (42km), before changing to the N430 to Ciudad Real (55km).

CIUDAD REAL

Despite being the one-time royal counterpart of Toledo, these days Ciudad Real is an unspectacular Spanish working town. The town centre has a certain charm with its pedestrianised shopping streets and distinctive Plaza Mayor, complete with carillon clock (topped by Cupid), flamboyant neo-Gothic town-hall facade and modern tiered fountain. The main reason to visit is to track down the museum-library, the **Museo del Quijote y Biblioteca Cervantina**. The museum has audiovisual displays, while the Cervantes library is stocked with 3500 Don Quixote books, including some in Esperanto and Braille, with most of them now digitised, and some dating back to 1724. It helps if you speak Spanish. Entry is by guided tour every half-hour.

THE DRIVE
Head south of Ciudad Real along the N412 and Almagro is just 28km southeast down a road that crosses the flat La Mancha plains.

ALMAGRO

Not even the marketing departments of local tourist authorities can come up with a Quijote connection for Almagro, but it's one of Castilla-La Mancha's prettiest towns and we recommend that you visit for that reason alone. The jewel in Almagro's crown is the extraordinary 16th-century Plaza Mayor, with its wavy tiled roofs, stumpy columns and faded bottle-green porticoes. Right on the square, the **Corral de Comedias** (*corraldecomedias.com*) showcases a literary heritage of a different kind: this is the oldest theatre in Spain, an evocative 17th-century stage with rows of wooden balconies facing the original stage, complete with dressing rooms. Performances are still held here in July during the **Festival Internacional de Teatro Clásico** (*festivaldealmagro.com*). Just around the corner is the **Museo Nacional de Teatro** (*museoteatro.mcu.es*), which has exhibits on Spanish theatre from the golden age of the 17th century displayed in rooms surrounding a magnificent 13th-century courtyard. Otherwise, the town is a delight to wander around, although it can be deathly quiet in the depths of winter.

THE DRIVE
Return to the N412, turn southeast and, 34km later, you'll cross the N4 motorway, pass the wine centre of Valdepeñas and continue east. Some 34km east of Valdepeñas is Villanueva de los Infantes.

10 VILLANUEVA DE LOS INFANTES

'In a village in La Mancha whose name I cannot recall, there lived long ago a country gentleman...' Thus begins the novel and thus it was that the village where our picaresque hero began his journey had always remained a mystery. That was, at least, until 10 eminent Spanish academics marked the 400th anniversary of the book's publishing in 1605 by carefully following the clues left by Cervantes. Their conclusion? That Villanueva de los Infantes, now with an ochre-hued Plaza Mayor surrounded by wood-and-stone balconies and watched over by the 15th-century Iglesia de San Andrés, was Don Quixote's starting point. It's also the end point of our journey, unless, of course, you wish to retrace your steps and set out to follow once again the path trod by Spain's most quixotic knight.

Museo Nacional de Teatro

06

MADRID & CENTRAL SPAIN

Ancient Extremadura

BEST FOR FAMILIES

Wandering slowly through the Ciudad Monumental in Cáceres.

DURATION	DISTANCE	GREAT FOR
5–7 days	520km / 323 miles	History

BEST TIME TO GO	
	From March to May or September to October, when you should enjoy milder weather.

Teatro Romano, Mérida

Extremadura is one of Spain's least-visited corners, but that would surely change if only people knew what was here. This is a land where the stories of ancient civilisations, the golden age of Spanish exploration and untold medieval riches are written in stone, with so many magnificent old cities and villages strung out across a splendid terrain of rolling hills and big horizons.

Link your trip

03 The Forgotten West

Begin in Cáceres then disappear off the map through some of the loveliest, least-known villages in the country.

29 Medieval Jewels in the Southern Interior

It's a 110km drive northwest from Zafra to Elvas, where you'll find striking landscapes and medieval lore in Portugal's southern interior.

01 MÉRIDA

Mérida, capital of Extremadura, is a marvellous place to begin your journey, home as it is to the most impressive set of Roman ruins in all Spain. Once capital of the Roman province of Lusitania, Emerita Augusta (the Roman forerunner to Mérida) has so much to turn the head. The glittering jewel is the 1st-century-BCE **Teatro Romano**, a classical theatre still used for performances during the summer **Festival del Teatro Clásico** (*festivaldemerida.es*), and the adjacent **Museo Nacional de Arte Romano** (*culturaydeporte.gob.es/mnromano/home.html*). But in Mérida such splendours are just

the beginning. There's the 60-arch **Puente Romano** that spans the Río Guadiana, the **Templo de Diana** (Calle de Sagasta) that rises improbably from the modern city centre, and the **Alcazaba**, a fortress that has been occupied by just about everyone down through the ages, from Visigoths and Romans to the enlightened Muslims of Al-Andalus.

THE DRIVE
Getting from Mérida to Trujillo couldn't be easier – take the N5 motorway heading northeast of the city and Trujillo lies just 94km up the road.

02 TRUJILLO

The core of Trujillo is one of the best-preserved medieval towns in Spain. It begins in the Plaza Mayor, which is surrounded by towers and palaces. The splendour continues up the hillside with a labyrinth of mansions, leafy courtyards, churches and convents all enclosed within 900m of walls circling the upper town and dating back to the 16th century when Trujillo's favourite sons returned home as wealthy conquistadors. At the top of the hill, Trujillo's impressive **Alcazaba** has 10th-century Muslim origins. Patrol the battlements for magnificent 360-degree sweeping views. From just about any vantage point up here, whether bathed in the warm light of a summer sunset or shrouded in the mists of winter, Trujillo can feel like a magical place.

THE DRIVE
The A58 connects Trujillo with Cáceres, just 46km to the west.

03 CÁCERES

The old core of Cáceres, its Ciudad Monumental (Old Town), is truly extraordinary. Narrow cobbled streets twist and climb among ancient stone walls lined with palaces and mansions, while the skyline is decorated with turrets, spires, gargoyles and enormous storks' nests. Protected by defensive walls, it has survived almost intact from its 16th-century heyday and so much of the monumental beauty is clustered around three connected squares, the Plaza de Santa María, Plaza de San Jorge, and the Plaza de San Mateo. At dusk or after dark, when the crowds have gone, you'll feel like you've stepped back into the Middle Ages. Stretching at the feet of the old city, the lively and arcaded Plaza Mayor is one of Spain's finest public squares.

THE DRIVE
Drive 13km west of Cáceres along the N521, then turn right (northwest) onto the EX207 (the sign will say Arroyo de la Luz). Some 17km further on, turn left onto the EX207 – Alcántara is 26km away to the northwest.

04 ALCÁNTARA

Out in Extremadura's wild, remote and rarely travelled west, Alcántara is best known for its magnificent Roman bridge. The bridge – 204m long, 61m high and much reinforced over the centuries – spans the Río Tajo below a huge dam. The town itself retains old walls, a ruined castle, several imposing mansions and the enormous Renaissance **Convento de San Benito**. The highlights of the down-at-heel monastery, built in the 16th century to house the Orden de Alcántara (an order of Reconquista knights), include the Gothic cloister and the perfectly proportioned three-tier loggia. Admission is by free hourly guided visits.

THE DRIVE
Leaving Alcántara, return along the EX207 for around 6km, then take the EX117. Where that road ends, just after Membrío, turn right onto the N521. Just when you think you're headed for Portugal, Valencia de Alcántara appears up ahead. Total distance: 60km.

05 VALENCIA DE ALCÁNTARA

Not many travellers stop out here, 7km from the Portuguese border, and its well-preserved old centre is a curious labyrinth of whitewashed houses and mansions. One side of the old town is watched over by

Photo opportunity

On stage at Mérida's Teatro Romano.

the ruins of a medieval castle and the 17th-century **Iglesia de Rocamador**. The surrounding countryside is known for its cork industry and some 50 ancient dolmens (stone circles of prehistoric monoliths).

THE DRIVE
Unless you plan on crossing the border, return a few clicks back up the N521 heading northeast, then turn right (southeast) onto the EX110 along which, 32km later, you'll encounter Alburquerque.

06 ALBURQUERQUE

Looming large above this small town, 38km north of Badajoz, is the intact **Castillo de Luna**. The centrepiece of a complex frontier defence system of forts, the castle was built on the site of its Islamic antecedent in the 13th century and subsequently expanded. From the top, views take in the Portuguese frontier (the Portuguese actually took the town for a few years in the early 18th century).

THE DRIVE
Head roughly south along the EX110, shadowing the Portuguese border, crossing low hills and quiet farmlands all the way into Badajoz. This provincial capital has little to recommend it – carry right on through, looking for the EX107 and the signs to Olivenza. The journey is 72km.

07 OLIVENZA

Pretty Olivenza, 24km south of Badajoz, clings to its Portuguese heritage – it has only been Spanish since 1801. The cobbled centre is distinctive for its whitewashed houses, typical turreted defensive walls and penchant for blue-and-white ceramic tile work. Smack-bang in its centre is the 14th-century castle, dominated by the **Torre del Homenaje**, 36m high, from which there are fine views. The most impressive section of the original defensive walls is around the 18th-century Puerta del Calvario, on the western side of town.

THE DRIVE
It's 29km east-southeast along the EX105 to the N435 at Barcarrota – after all this time in the backblocks, the sudden rush of traffic may come as a surprise. From there it's 25km south into Jerez de los Caballeros

08 JEREZ DE LOS CABALLEROS

Walled and hilly Jerez de los Caballeros was a cradle of conquistadors. It has a 13th-century castle that was built by

DETOUR:

Guadalupe

START: 2 TRUJILLO

Guadalupe's revered **Real Monasterio de Santa María de Guadalupe** (*monasterioguadalupe.com*) is located, according to legend, on the spot where a shepherd found an effigy of the Virgin, hidden years earlier by Christians fleeing the Muslims. A sumptuous church-monastery (complete with works attributed to El Greco, Goya, Zurbarán and even Michelangelo) was built on the site and this is still one of Spain's most important pilgrimage sites. Hour-long guided tours leave every half-hour. While the monastery is the obvious highlight, take some time to wander the picturesque streets off the Plaza Mayor.

the Knights Templar. You can wander around at will, but it's basically just the impressive walls that are preserved. There are several handsome churches scattered across the town, three with towers emulating the Giralda in Seville.

THE DRIVE
Take the N435 southeast to Fregenal de la Sierra, then the EX201, then the EX103 over the hills, watching for signs to Monesterio (and black pigs fattening up in stone-walled fields). It's a 66km journey from Jerez de los Caballeros.

09 MONESTERIO

Since the completion of the A66 motorway, many bypassed towns have disappeared into quiet obscurity, but not Monesterio, because this is one of Spain's (and certainly Extremadura's) most celebrated sources of *jamón*. Occupying pride of place at the southern end of the town is the outstanding **Museo del Jamón** (*museodeljamon demonesterio.com*), arguably the best of its kind in Spain. Its exhibits take visitors through the process of *jamón* production, from ideal pig habitats, to the *matanza* (killing of the pigs) right through to the finished product.

THE DRIVE
It's 40km north from Monesterio to Zafra, either along the motorway or the quieter N630 that shadows it.

ZAFRA

Looking for all the world like an Andalucian *pueblo blanco* (white town), gleaming-white Zafra is a serene, attractive place to rest at journey's end. Originally a Muslim settlement, Zafra's narrow streets are lined with baroque churches, old-fashioned shops and traditional houses decorated by brilliant red splashes of geraniums. Zafra's 15th-century castle, a blend of Gothic, Mudéjar and Renaissance architecture, is now a *parador* and dominates the town's roofscape. Plaza Grande and the adjoining Plaza Chica, arcaded and bordered by bars, are the places to see Zafra life. The southern end of the Plaza Grande, with its palm trees, is one of Extremadura's prettiest corners.

Roman bridge, Alcántara

ATLANTIC OCEAN
Bay of Biscay
Cabo Ortegal
Punta da Estaca de Bares
O Barqueiro
Ferrol
A Coruña
Valdoviño
Baio
Betanzos
San Cosme
Ribadeo
Navia
Avilés
Gijón
Oviedo
Vilalba
Santiago de Compostela
Lugo
Cangas del Narcea
San Antolín de Ibias
Arriondas
R badesella
Parque Natural de Redes
Parque Natural de Somiedo
Parque Nacional de los Picos de Europa
Potes
Fontibre
Reinosa
Parque Natural Saja-Besaya
Torrelavega
Santander
Santoña
Castro Urdiales
Bermeo
San Sebastián
Irún
Bayonne
Dax
FRANCE
Bilbao
Tolosa
Beasain
Vitoria
Miranda de Ebro
Haro
Estella
Pamplona
Roncesvalles
Sarria
Ribeira
Monforte de Lemos
Pedrafita do Cebreiro
La Magdalena
Ponferrada
León
Guardo
Aguilar de Campóo
Pontevedra
Baiona
Vigo
Ourense
A Rúa
Astorga
Sahagún
Osorno
Burgos
Santo Domingo de la Calzada
Logroño
Arnedo
Parque Natural de las Bárdenas Reales
Tudela
Tarazona
Río Ebro
Zaragoza
A Guarda
A Gudiña
Puebla de Sanabria
Río Porma
Verín
Viana do Castelo
Chaves
Bragança
Benavente
Palencia
Lerma
Salas de los Infantes
Soria
Braga
Mirandela
Miranda do Douro
Valladolid
Aranda de Duero
SPAIN
Vila Real
Zamora
Tordesillas
Porto
Río Duero
Paracuellos de Jiloca
Medinaceli
PORTUGAL
Río Tormes
Salamanca
Segovia
Viseu
Águeda
Guarda
Ciudad Rodrigo
Ávila
Colmenar Viejo
Coimbra
Covilhã
MADRID
Guadalajara
A8
A6
AP66
A67
A231
A1
A12
N232
AP68
A15
A52
A62
N122
N234
N111
A2
A23
13
12
09
10
11
08
C7
0
100 km
0
50 miles

Palacio Real (p88), Olite

Northern Spain & the Basque Country

Explore

Northern Spain & the Basque Country

Spain's north is the lesser-known alter ego to the bright lights of the country's sometimes overrun Mediterranean coast. Cities adorned with churches and historic architecture share the north with rolling vineyards, glorious cliffs and beaches, fishing villages, and a reputation for culinary excellence unmatched by many regions in Europe. Connecting these world-class attractions are country byways and the Camino de Santiago, a pilgrimage route across the north that just as many will walk as will drive. You could easily spend weeks exploring the region, but these road trips may be the start of a lifelong love affair with this special place.

Santiago de Compostela

Perched on northwestern Spain's Atlantic rim, Santiago de Compostela is a handsome, church-studded city that calls to pilgrims and architecture buffs alike. There's an unmistakeable grandeur to the place, one that befits its importance as the final destination along the Camino de Santiago. But the tangle of narrow medieval streets that fan out from the city's spiritual core are also filled with tapas bars and excellent restaurants. The result is a fine embodiment of that very Spanish combination of the sacred and the ability to have a very good time.

Bilbao

This once working-class city has been transformed in recent decades and is now a standard bearer for the Basque Country's modern appeal. At one level, Bilbao has come to embrace all that is new and creative, an attitude encapsulated by the Museo Guggenheim, one of Spain's most storied architectural showpieces. Alongside this and other museums and architectural prizes, the city has deep roots in its traditions, with markets, fabulous food and warm Basque hospitality.

Logroño

One of Spain's smallest provincial capitals, Logroño lies along the Camino de Santiago and at the heart of the fabled La Rioja wine region. As the latter suggests, the city has a reputation among Spaniards for gastronomic excellence. With tourists yet to discover the place

WHEN TO GO

Summer (June to August) promises the best weather, although rain is possible at any time; July and August can get really busy. Winter (December to February) can be cold and wet, especially in Galicia, and snow is possible at any time at higher altitudes, especially the Picos de Europa. Spring and autumn are generally mild, if a little unpredictable.

in large numbers, it's a predominantly local crowd that fills its inner-city laneway bars, tapas haunts and restaurants. One particular street, Calle Laurel, is the place to begin.

León

Bathed in the clear light of the north, León is a gem among Spanish cities. Boasting a luminous cathedral at its heart – León's cathedral has some of the finest stained-glass windows anywhere in Europe – the city has a superb medieval centre. Away from the grand monuments, exploring the Barrio Humedo is like immersing yourself in the Spanish love of the good life, with bars, restaurants and traditional shops lining laneways that lead to magnificent public squares.

Oviedo

Oviedo is another of those Spanish cities away from the coast that's beloved by locals but less known by international visitors. As the capital of Asturias, it combines a proudly Spanish history – a story told through its architecture – with a riotous celebration of local food traditions. The variant here is the *sidra* (cider) bars, where locally made cider, poured straight from the barrel by expert bartenders, fuels a passionate city determined to enjoy itself.

TRANSPORT

Along the coast and its hinterland, the challenging terrain can make for slow travel – but that's not always a bad thing. Although motorways connect most major towns, east-west rail services generally lack the high-speed possibilities on offer elsewhere in Spain. The region otherwise has decent connections by road and rail.

WHAT'S ON

Batalla del Vino

On 29 June the wine town of Haro in La Rioja has a wine fight to celebrate yet another premier harvest.

Festival Ortigueira

In July Galicia celebrates its Celtic roots with a bagpipe- and fiddler-filled music fest.

Fiestas del Apóstol Santiago

The Día de Santiago on 25 July marks the day of Spain's national saint (St James) and is spectacularly celebrated in Santiago de Compostela.

WHERE TO STAY

All of northern Spain's cities and towns have a good selection of accommodation choices to suit a wide range of budgets and styles. Santiago de Compostela has the widest selection, and anywhere along the Camino de Santiago there's a mix of traditional accommodation and basic *albergues* (pilgrim hostels). Despite the unreliable summer weather, accommodation can be difficult to find along the coasts of the Basque Country, Cantabria, Asturias and Galicia in July and August. The same can apply to anywhere along the Camino (also in summer) or in the Picos de Europa (in both summer and winter).

Resources

Camino de Santiago (*santiago-compostela.net*) Extensive information on the various routes, with maps.

Asturias (*asturias.com*) Plan your visit and discover why Spaniards love this northern region.

Galicia (*turismo.gal*) Learn what magical experiences await you along Spain's most northwesterly shore.

La Rioja (*lariojaturismo.com*) Map out your trip through this premier wine region.

07

NORTHERN SPAIN & THE BASQUE COUNTRY

Northern Spain Pilgrimage

BEST FOR A SENSE OF ACHIEVEMENT

Reaching Santiago de Compostela

DURATION	DISTANCE	GREAT FOR
5-7 days	786km / 488 miles	History, nature

BEST TIME TO GO	From April to June for fields of poppies, September and October for golden leaves.

Pamplona

For over a thousand years pilgrims have marched across the top of Spain on the Camino de Santiago (Way of St James) to the tomb of St James the Apostle in Santiago de Compostela. Real pilgrims walk, but by driving you'll enjoy religious treasures, grand cathedrals, big skies and wide open landscapes – and no blisters.

Link your trip

13 Coast of Galicia

With the Camino de Santiago ticked off, carry on to Fisterra and a spectacular trip along Galicia's awe-inspiring coast.

01 Historic Castilla y León

From Burgos you can head south to discover the rich heritage of the cities of the Spanish plain.

01 RONCESVALLES

History hangs thick in the air of the **Roncesvalles monastery complex** (*roncesvalles.es*), where pilgrims give thanks for a successful crossing of the Pyrenees. The monastery contains a number of different buildings of interest, including the 13th-century Gothic **Real Colegiata de Santa María** (*roncesvalles.es*) which houses a much-revered, silver-covered statue of the Virgin beneath a modernist-looking canopy. Also of interest is the cloister, containing the tomb of King Sancho VII (El Fuerte) of Navarra, leader of one of the victorious Christian armies in the battle of Las Navas de Tolosa, fought against the Muslims in 1212.

THE DRIVE

It's 49km (one hour) basically downhill to Pamplona – a pretty drive along the N135 through mountainscapes, forests and gentle farmland. Innumerable hamlets and villages are painted in the red and white Basque colours and centred on old stone churches, many of them crammed with religious treasures

02 PAMPLONA

Renowned across the world for the Sanfermines festival (6 to 14 July), when bulls tear through the streets at 8am causing chaos as they go (and alcohol-fuelled revellers cause chaos for the remainder of the day – and night), Pamplona (Iruña in Basque) is a quiet, low-key city at any other time of the year. Animal welfare groups condemn the bull-running as a cruel tradition. Pamplona's history stretches back to Roman times, and is best traced in the fantastic **Museo de Navarra** (*navarra.es*), whose highlights include huge Roman mosaics. Another Pamplona highlight is the tour of the **catedral** (*catedraldepamplona.com*), a late-medieval Gothic gem with a neoclassical facade. The tour takes you into the cloisters and a museum displaying the remains of a Roman-era house and the skeleton of a seven-month-old baby. The 11.15am tour also goes up the bell tower to see (and possibly hear) the second-largest church bell in Spain.

THE DRIVE

Take the A12 southwestward. After about 10 minutes take exit 9 onto the driver-friendly NA1110. Drive through Astraín and continue along this country road for 15 minutes to Legarda and Muruzábal, then it's 2km southeast to Santa María de Eunate. Total 22km; about 40 minutes.

03 SANTA MARÍA DE EUNATE

Surrounded by cornfields and brushed by wildflowers, the near-perfect octagonal Romanesque chapel of **Santa María de Eunate** (*santamariadeeunate.es*) is one of the most picturesque churches along the Camino. It dates from around the 12th century but its origins – and the reason why it's located in the middle of nowhere – are a mystery.

THE DRIVE
From the chapel it's just a 5km drive along the NA6064 and NA1110 to gorgeous Puente la Reina.

04 PUENTE LA REINA

The chief calling card of Puente la Reina (Basque: Gares) is the spectacular six-arched **medieval bridge** dominating the western end of town, but Puente la Reina rewards on many other levels. A key stop on the Camino de Santiago, the town's pretty streets throng with the ghosts of a multitude of pilgrims. Pilgrims' first stop here is the late-Romanesque **Iglesia del Crucifijo**. Erected by the Knights Templar, it contains one of the finest Gothic crucifixes in existence.

THE DRIVE
The fastest way between Puente la Reina and Estella is on the A12 (20km, 20 minutes), but the more enjoyable drive is along the slower, more rural, NA1110, taking about half an hour. You'll probably spy a few Camino pilgrims striding along.

05 ESTELLA

Estella (Basque: Lizarra) was known as 'La Bella' in medieval times because of the splendour of its monuments and buildings, and though the old dear has lost some of its beauty to modern suburbs, it still has charm. During the 11th century, Estella became a main reception point for the growing flood of pilgrims along the Camino. Today most visitors are continuing that same tradition. The attractive old quarter has a couple of notable churches, including the 12th-century **Iglesia de San Pedro de la Rúa**, whose cloisters are a fine example of Romanesque sculptural work. Across the river and overlooking the town is the **Iglesia de San Miguel**, with a fine Romanesque north portal. The countryside around Estella is littered with monasteries. Two of the most impressive are **Monasterio de Iratxe**, 2.5km southwest near Ayegui, and **Monasterio de Irantzu**, 11km north near Abárzuza.

THE DRIVE
It's a 40km (50 minute) drive to Viana. Take the A12 westward and turn onto the NA1110 at junction 58. Follow the NA1110 through the sleepy villages of Los Arcos, Sansol and Torres del Río. In hillside Torres you'll find a remarkably intact eight-sided Romanesque chapel, the Iglesia del Santo Sepulcro.

TOP TIP:

Fuente del Vino (Fountain of Wine)

Opposite the Monasterio de Iratxe is the well-known local wine producer, **Bodegas Irache** (*irache.com*). For the benefit of Camino de Santiago pilgrims, the winery has installed two taps providing free liquid. From one flows water; from the other, wine – 100L per day.

06 VIANA

Overlooked by many non-pilgrim tourists, Viana, the last town in Navarra, started life as a garrison town defending the kingdom of Navarra from Castilla. The old part of the town, which sits atop a hill, is still largely walled and is an interesting place to wander about for a couple of hours. Work started on the **Iglesia de Santa María** in the 13th century and it's one of the more impressive religious structures on this eastern part of the Camino. Viana's former **bullring** is now a plaza in the middle of town, where children booting footballs are considerably more common than bulls.

THE DRIVE
It's 10km to Logroño. The first half of the drive is through open, big-sky countryside; the last part through the city suburbs. There's a large car park under Paseo del Espolón on the south edge of Logroño's old town.

07 LOGROÑO

Logroño, capital of La Rioja – Spain's wine-growing region par excellence – doesn't feel the need to be loud and brash. Instead it's a stately town with a heart of tree-studded squares, narrow streets and a monumentally good selection of *pintxos* (tapas) bars. It's the sort of place where you can't help feeling contented. And it's not just the wine. The superb **Museo de la Rioja** (*museodelarioja.es*) in the centre takes you on a wild romp through Riojan history and culture, from the days when dinner was killed with arrows to recreations of the kitchens that many a Spanish granny grew up using. The other major attraction is the **Catedral de Santa María de la Redonda** (*laredonda.org*); it started life as a Gothic church before maturing into a full-blown cathedral in the 16th century.

THE DRIVE
For the 45km (35-minute) hop to Santo Domingo de la Calzada, the Camino walking trail parallels – mostly at a respectful distance – the fast, and dull, A12. There's not much reason for you to veer off the motorway (none of the quieter roads really follow the Camino).

08 SANTO DOMINGO DE LA CALZADA

Santo Domingo is small-town Spain at its very best. A large number of the inhabitants still live in the partly-walled old quarter, a labyrinth of medieval streets where the past is alive and the sense of community is strong. The **Catedral de Santo Domingo de la Calzada** (*catedral santodomingo.com*) and its attached museum glitter with the gold that attests to the great wealth the Camino has bestowed on otherwise backwater towns. The cathedral's most eccentric feature is the white rooster and hen that forage in a glass-fronted cage opposite the entrance to the crypt. Their presence celebrates a long-standing legend, the Miracle of the Rooster, which tells of a young man who was unfairly executed only to recover miraculously, while the broiled cock and hen on the plate of his judge suddenly leapt up and chickened off, fully fledged.

THE DRIVE
It's 68km (one hour) to Burgos. Again, you're sort of stuck with using the main road, the N120.

MARBOM/SHUTTERSTOCK ©

Walking the Camino de Santiago

WHAT IS THE CAMINO DE SANTIAGO?

The Camino de Santiago (Way of St James) originated as a medieval pilgrimage. For more than a millennium, people have taken up the challenge of the Camino and walked to Santiago de Compostela. It all began in the 9th century when a remarkable event occurred in the poor Iberian hinterlands: following a shining star, a religious hermit named Pelayo unearthed the tomb of St James the Apostle (Santiago in Spanish). The news was confirmed by the local bishop, the Asturian king and later the pope.

Compostela became the most important destination for Christians after Rome and Jerusalem. Its popularity increased with an 11th-century papal decree granting it Holy Year status: pilgrims could receive a plenary indulgence (a full remission of your life's sins) during a Holy Year. These occur when Santiago's feast day (25 July) falls on a Sunday: the next is 2027 – but driving there doesn't count...

The 11th and 12th centuries marked the heyday of the pilgrimage. The Reformation was devastating for Catholic pilgrimages and by the 19th century the Camino had nearly died out. In its startling late-20th-century reanimation, which continues today, it's equally popular as a personal and spiritual journey of discovery as for primarily religious motives. These days over 350,000 people a year arrive in Santiago on foot, or sometimes bicycle and occasionally horseback, having completed one of the many Caminos de Santiago that lead to the city from all points of the Iberian Peninsula and beyond. The most popular route has always been the Camino Francés, which in its full extent crosses some 770km of northern Spain from the Pyrenees, and attracts walkers of all backgrounds and ages from across the world. For pilgrims, it's equal to visiting Jerusalem, and by finishing it you can expect a healthy chunk of time off purgatory.

09 BURGOS

On the surface, conservative Burgos seems to embody all the stereotypes of a north-central Spanish town, with sombre grey stone architecture, the fortifying cuisine of the high *meseta* (plateau) and a climate of extremes. But Burgos is a city that rewards. The historic centre is austerely elegant, guarded by monumental gates and with the **cathedral** (p30) as its centrepiece – a World Heritage–listed masterpiece that started life as a modest Romanesque church, but over time became one of the most impressive cathedrals in a land of impressive cathedrals. Read more about Burgos in Trip 1: Historic Castilla y León.

THE DRIVE
It's 48km (45 minutes) to castle-topped Castrojeriz. Head southwest on the A62 to junction 32 and turn off northwest along the minor BU400.

10 CASTROJERIZ

With its mix of old and new buildings huddled around the base of a hill that's topped with what's left of a crumbling castle, Castrojeriz is a typical small *meseta* town. It's worth a climb up to the castle if only for the views. The town's church, **Iglesia de San Juan**, is worth a look as well.

THE DRIVE
From Castrojeriz it's 26km (30 minutes) along the BU403 and P432 to Frómista. The scenery is classic *meseta* and if you're lucky you'll catch a glimpse of such evocative sights as a flock of sheep being led over the alternately burning or freezing plateau by a shepherd.

11 FRÓMISTA

The main (and some would say only) reason for stopping here is the village's exceptional **Iglesia de San Martín**. Dating from 1066 and restored in the early 20th century, this harmoniously proportioned church is one of the premier Romanesque churches in rural Spain, adorned with human and animal forms below the eaves. The capitals within are also richly decorated.

THE DRIVE
Take the P980 (the Camino runs alongside it) to Carrión de los Condes, then the more major A231 west to Sahagún (56km; 45 minutes).

WHY I LOVE THIS TRIP

John Noble, writer

Millions of people following the Camino de Santiago over 1200 years have given rise to an unrivalled heritage of monumental cathedrals, tiny chapels, ancient inns and other landmarks. To follow the pilgrims' path today is to breathe the aura of countless journeys and to sense the excitement of those doing it on foot. You might even be inspired to come back and walk it yourself one day!

Photo opportunity

Standing outside the Cathedral of Santiago de Compostela.

12 SAHAGÚN

Despite appearances, Sahagún was an immensely powerful and wealthy Benedictine centre by the 12th century. The brick Romanesque churches, some with later Mudéjar additions, merit a visit.

THE DRIVE
The 60km (50-minute) stretch from Sahagún to León along the A231 and A60 isn't a memorable drive. Still, you have to feel for those walking the Camino: some pilgrims bus between Burgos and León because so much of the route is next to busy roads.

13 LEÓN

León is a wonderful city, combining stunning historical architecture with an irresistible energy. Its standout attraction is the 13th-century **catedral** (*catedraldeleon.org*), one of the most beautiful cathedrals in Spain and arguably the country's premier Gothic masterpiece. Whether spotlit at night or bathed in glorious sunshine, it exudes an almost luminous quality. The showstopping facade has a radiant rose window, three richly sculpted doorways and two muscular towers. Inside, an extraordinary gallery of stained-glass windows awaits. The even older **Real Basílica de San Isidoro** provides a stunning Romanesque counterpoint to the cathedral's Gothic strains. Fernando I and Doña Sancha founded this church in 1063 to house the remains of San Isidoro, and of themselves and 21 other early Leonese and Castilian monarchs. The main basilica is a hotchpotch of styles, but the two main portals on the southern facade are pure Romanesque. The attached **Real Colegiata de San**

Isidoro (*museosanisi dorodeleon.com*) houses royal sarcophagi, which rest with quiet dignity beneath a canopy of some of the finest Romanesque frescoes in Spain. Motif after colourful motif of biblical scenes drench the vaults and arches of this extraordinary hall.

THE DRIVE
Taking the N120 to Astorga will keep you on the route of the Camino, which runs alongside the road for long stretches. It's a 50km (one-hour) drive. The AP71 is much faster, but what's the point in coming all this way to drive on a road like that?

14 ASTORGA

Perched on a hilltop on the frontier between the bleak plains of northern Castilla and the mountains that rise west towards Galicia, Astorga is a fascinating small town with a wealth of attractions way out of proportion to its size. The most eye-catching sight is the **Palacio Episcopal**, a rare flight of fancy in this part of the country, designed by Antoni Gaudí. There's also a smattering of Roman ruins (Astorga was once an important Roman settlement called Astúrica Augusta), a fine Gothic and plateresque **catedral** and even a **Museo del Chocolate**, dedicated to the town's long chocolate-making tradition. Less sinfully, the town sees a steady stream of pilgrims passing through along the Camino de Santiago.

THE DRIVE
It's just 8km (15 minutes) along the rural LE142 to Castrillo de los Polvazares. Non-residents are not allowed to drive into Castrillo, so park in one of the parking areas on the edge of the village.

WHO WAS ST JAMES THE APOSTLE?

St James, or James the Greater, was one of the 12 disciples of Jesus. He may even have been the first disciple. He was also probably the first to be martyred, by King Herod in 44 CE. So, if St James was living in the Holy Lands 2000 years ago, an obvious question persists: what were his remains doing in northwest Spain 800 years later? The legend (and we're not standing by its historical accuracy) suggests that two of St James' own disciples secreted his remains on a stone boat which sailed across the Mediterranean and passed into the Atlantic to moor at present-day Padrón (Galicia). After various trials and tribulations, they buried his body in a forest named Libredón (present-day Santiago de Compostela). All was then forgotten until about 820 CE, when a religious hermit found the remains. Further legends attest that during his lifetime, St James preached in various parts of Spain, including Galicia, which might explain why his remains were brought here.

15 CASTRILLO DE LOS POLVAZARES

One of the prettiest villages along the Camino – if a little twee – is Castrillo de los Polvazares. It consists of little but one main cobbled street, a small church and an array of well-preserved 18th-century stone houses. If you can be here before the tour buses arrive, or after they have left, then it's an absolute delight of a place and one in which the spirit of the Camino can be strongly felt.

THE DRIVE
Continue along the LE142 to Ponferrada (53km, 1¼ hours). It runs pretty much beside the Camino and you'll pass through attractive stone villages, most of which have churches topped with storks' nests. Rabanal del Camino, with its 18th-century church Ermita del Bendito Cristo de la Vera Cruz, is worth a quick stop.

16 PONFERRADA

Ponferrada is not the region's most enticing town, but its castle and remnants of the old town centre (around the stone clock tower) make it worth a brief stop. Built by the Knights Templar in the 13th century, the walls of the fortress-monastery **Castillo Templario** rise high over the Río Sil with a lonely and impregnable air, and its square, crenellated towers ooze romance and history.

THE DRIVE
If you're not in a huge hurry, take the NVI to Villafranca del Bierzo (24km, 30 minutes). It's slower but gentler than the A6 motorway.

17 VILLAFRANCA DEL BIERZO

Villafranca del Bierzo has a very well preserved old core and a number of interesting churches and other religious buildings. Chief among these are **San Nicolás El Real**, a 17th-century convent with a baroque altarpiece, and the 12th-century **Iglesia de Santiago**. The northern doorway of this church is called the 'door of forgiveness'. Pilgrims who were sick, or otherwise unable to continue to Santiago de Compostela, were granted the same godly favours as if they'd made it all the way.

THE PÓRTICO DE LA GLORIA

Santiago cathedral's artistically unparalleled **Pórtico de la Gloria** features 200 Romanesque sculptures by Maestro Mateo, who was placed in charge of the cathedral-building programme in the late 12th century. These detailed and remarkably lifelike sculptures add up to a comprehensive review of major figures and scenes from the Bible. The Old Testament and its prophets (including a famously smiling Daniel) are on the north side; the New Testament, Apostles and Last Judgement are on the south; and glory and resurrection are depicted in the central archway.

Visits are limited to 25 people at a time. Spanish-language **guided visits** are given several times daily, with tickets sold up to 90 days ahead through the cathedral website or on the same day (if available) at the **Pazo de Xelmírez** adjoining the cathedral, where the visit starts. Fifteen-minute **unguided visits** happen from 7pm to 8pm Monday to Saturday; 50 tickets for these (free) are given out between 7pm and 8pm the day before at the Fundación Catedral office in the **Casa do Deán** (Rúa do Vilar 3). For Monday visits go on Saturday. Take your ID document.

THE DRIVE
It's 32km (45 minutes) uphill to O Cebreiro using the NVI, or a bit quicker via the A6. On the NVI you can admire or pity the pilgrims making the Camino's longest, hardest climb, right beside the road on several stretches. Turn off at Pedrafita do Cebreiro and take the LU633 for the last 4km.

18 O CEBREIRO

O Cebreiro, 1300m high, is the first village in Galicia on the Camino. It's an atmospheric and picturesque little place, busy with pilgrims happy to have completed the climb from Villafranca. O Cebreiro con-

JOSE ARCOS AGUILAR/SHUTTERSTOCK ©

Santiago de Compostela

tains several *pallozas* (circular, thatched dwellings known in Galicia since pre-Roman times). A former village priest here, Elías Valiño (1929–89), is considered to have been the driving force behind the revival of the Camino de Santiago in the late 20th century.

THE DRIVE
The marvellous 33km drive to Samos winds down the LU633 through refreshingly green countryside with great long-distance views, frequently criss-crossing the Camino.

19 SAMOS

A pretty village in the Río Sarria valley, Samos is built around the very fine Benedictine **Mosteiro de Samos** (*abadiadesamos.com*). This monastery has two beautiful big cloisters – one Gothic, with distinctly unmonastic Greek nymphs adorning its fountain, the other neoclassical and filled with roses.

THE DRIVE
Follow the LU633 and N547 to stay fairly close to the Camino and pass through attractive villages and small towns such as Portomarín. There's no avoiding the A54 motorway to get past Santiago airport. Follow 'Centro Histórico' signs towards the city centre (137km, 2¾ hours from Samos). Private vehicles are barred from the Old Town; underground car parks around its fringes charge around €15 per 24 hours. Cheaper are Aparcadoiro Xoan XXIII (€11) and open-air Aparcadoiro Belvís (€7.50).

20 SANTIAGO DE COMPOSTELA

This, then, is it. The end of The Way. And what a spectacular finish. Santiago de Compostela, with its granite buildings and frequent drizzle, is one of the most beautiful, fascinating cities in Spain. With more than 350,000 pilgrims arriving annually, Santiago has a busy, festive atmosphere throughout the warmer half of the year (May to October). The magnificent **Catedral de Santiago de Compostela** (*catedraldesantiago.es*) soars above the city centre in a splendid jumble of spires and statues. Its beauty is a mix of the original Romanesque structure (built between 1075 and 1211) and later Gothic and baroque flourishes. The tomb of Santiago beneath the main altar is a magnet for all who arrive. The artistic high point is the **Pórtico de la Gloria** inside the west entrance. Grand Praza do Obradoiro, in front of the cathedral's west facade, is traffic- and cafe-free and has a unique atmosphere. From here you can start exploring Santiago's other fine squares and churches. At the square's northern end, the **Hostal dos Reis Católicos** (*parador.es*) was built in the 16th century as a refuge for exhausted pilgrims. Today it's a *parador* (luxurious state-owned hotel), but its four courtyards are open to visitors.

DETOUR:

Cabo Fisterra

START: 20 SANTIAGO DE COMPOSTELA

This spectacular, cliff-girt, wave-lashed cape has, in popular imagination, long been considered the western edge of Spain, and in days way before satnav it was believed to be the very end of the world. The name Fisterra (Finisterre in Castilian Spanish) means 'Land's End'. In fact, Spain's real westernmost point is Cabo Touriñán, 20km north, but that doesn't lessen Fisterra's magnetic appeal. The end point of a highly popular extension to the Camino de Santiago, the cape is an 82km, 1½-hour drive west from Santiago. Camino pilgrims ritually burn smelly socks, T-shirts and the like on the rocks just past the lighthouse. Many people come for sunset but it's a magnificent spot at any time (unless shrouded in fog or rain). Fisterra town, 3.5km before the cape, is a fishing port with a picturesque harbour and some beautiful beaches nearby.

08

NORTHERN SPAIN & THE BASQUE COUNTRY

Roving La Rioja Wine Region

BEST FOR FOOD

Logroño has some of the best tapas bars in Spain.

DURATION	DISTANCE	GREAT FOR
2-3 days	145km / 90 miles	Wine, history

BEST TIME TO GO	September and October when the grapes are being harvested.

Vineyards, La Rioja

La Rioja is home to the best wines in Spain, and on this short and sweet road trip along unhurried back roads, you'll enjoy gorgeous vine-striped countryside and asleep-at-noon villages of honey-coloured stone. But the overriding interest is reserved for food and drink: winery tours, cutting-edge museums and some of the best tapas in Spain make this drive an essential for any food and wine lover.

Link your trip

07 Northern Spain Pilgrimage

Follow the path of pilgrims on the road to Santiago de Compostela. You can join The Way in Logroño.

11 Along the Río Ebro

From Logroño you can join this tour and explore deserts and Islamic palaces, churches carved into rock and castles with hanging gardens.

01 LOGROÑO

Small, low-key Logroño is the capital of La Rioja. The city doesn't receive all that many tourists and there aren't all that many things to see and do, but the historic centre makes for pleasant strolling and there is a monumentally good selection of *pintxos* (tapas) bars. In fact, Logroño is quickly gaining a culinary reputation to rival anywhere in Spain. **Rioja Trek** (*riojatrek.com*), based 2.5km southeast of the city centre, offers a wide range of customisable winery tours (which can include visiting a traditional vineyard and bodega and even doing some wine-making yourself), as well as wine

tastings, tapas tours, hikes along some of La Rioja's fabulous mountain trails and activities for families with children.

THE DRIVE
It's only a short drive of 28km (25 minutes) from Logroño to Nájera, starting along the LO20, which transforms into the A12 motorway around the halfway point.

02 NÁJERA

The main attraction of this otherwise unexciting town, which lies on the Camino de Santiago, is the Gothic **Monasterio de Santa María la Real** and, in particular, its fragile-looking, early-16th-century cloisters. The monastery was built in 1032, but was significantly rebuilt in the 15th century.

THE DRIVE
The dry landscapes around Nájera become greener and more rolling as you head southwest along the LR113 and LR205 for 18km (20 minutes) to San Millán de Cogolla. In the far distance rise the 2000m-plus mountains of the Sierra de la Demanda – snow-capped in winter.

03 SAN MILLÁN DE COGOLLA

The hamlet of San Millán de Cogolla is home to two remarkable monasteries, which between them helped give birth to the Castilian (Spanish) language.

THE WEALTH OF THE GRAPE

La Rioja, and the surrounding areas of Navarra and the Basque province of Álava, comprise Spain's best-regarded wine-producing region. The principal grape is the tempranillo and the first taste is of leather and cherries, and lingers on the tongue. The Riojans have had a long love affair with wine. There's evidence that both the Phoenicians and the Celtiberians produced and drank wine here and the earliest written evidence of grape cultivation in La Rioja dates to 873 CE. Today, some 250 million litres of wine burst forth from the grapes of La Rioja annually. Almost all of this is red wine, though some quality whites and rosés are also produced. In the town of Haro they even have a fiesta devoted to wine. It culminates with a 'wine battle', in which thousands of litres of wine gets chucked around, turning everyone's clothes red. This takes place on 29 June.

How to find a good bottle? Spanish wine is subject to a system of classification, similar to the ones used in France and Italy. La Rioja is the only wine region in Spain classed as Denominación de Origen Calificada (DOC), the highest grade and a guarantee that any wine labelled as such was produced according to strict standards. The best wines are often marked with the designations 'Crianza' (aged more than two years, with at least one year in an oak barrel), 'Reserva' (aged for three years, one of them in an oak barrel) or 'Gran Reserva' (aged for two years in an oak barrel and three years in the bottle).

On account of their linguistic heritage and artistic beauty, they have been recognised by Unesco as World Heritage sites. The **Monasterio de Yuso** (*monasterio desanmillan.com/yuso*) contains numerous treasures in its museum. You can only visit as part of a guided tour (in Spanish, with English and French information sheets available). Tours last 50 minutes and run every half-hour or so. A short distance away is the **Monasterio de Suso** (*monasterio desanmillan.com/suso*). It's believed that in the 13th century, a monk named Gonzalo de Berceo wrote some of the first Castilian words here. Again, it can only be visited on a guided tour. Tickets include a short bus ride up to the monastery from the Monasterio de Yuso, whose reception area sells them; you can't arrive independently.

THE DRIVE
It's a 20km (20-minute) drive along the delightfully quiet LR206 and LR204 to Santo Domingo de la Calzada. The scenery is a mix of vast sunburnt fields, red-tinged soils, vineyards and patches of forest.

Photo opportunity

Waving at the camera from in front of the Hotel Marqués de Riscal.

04 SANTO DOMINGO DE LA CALZADA

The small, walled old town of Santo Domingo is the kind of place where you can be certain that the baker knows all his customers by name and that everyone will turn up for María's christening. Santiago-bound pilgrims have long been a part of the fabric of this town, and that tradition continues to this day, with most visitors being foot-weary pilgrims. All this helps to make Santo Domingo one of the most enjoyable places in La Rioja. The biggest attraction in town, aside from the very worthwhile pursuit of just strolling the streets and lounging in the main old-town plaza, is a visit to the monumental **catedral** (*catedral-santodomingo.com*).

THE DRIVE
The LR111 (becoming the N126) goes in an almost ruler-straight line across fields of crops and under a big sky to the workaday town of Haro (20km, 20 minutes).

05 HARO

Despite its fame in the wine world, there's not much of a heady bouquet to Haro, La Rioja's premier wine-producing town. But it has a cheerful pace, and the compact old quarter, leading off Plaza de la Paz, has some intriguing alleyways with bars and wine shops aplenty. There are plenty of wine bodegas in the vicinity of the town, some of which are open to visitors (but almost always with require reservation). One of the more receptive to visitors is **Bodegas Muga** (*bodegasmuga.com*), which is just after the railway bridge on the way out of town to the north. It gives guided tours and tastings, in Spanish and English, daily except Sunday.

THE DRIVE
Briones is almost within walking distance of Haro. It's just 9km away (10 minutes) along the N124 and N232.

06 BRIONES

One man's dream has put the small, obscenely quaint village of Briones firmly on the Spanish wine and tourism

TAPAS IN LOGROÑO

Make no mistake about it: Logroño is an eater's delight. There are several very good restaurants, and then there are the tapas (which here are often called by their Basque name, *pintxos*). Few cities have such a dense concentration of excellent tapas bars. Most of the action takes place on Calle Laurel and Calle San Juan. *Pintxos* cost around €2 to €4, and most of the bars are open from about 8pm to midnight Tuesday to Sunday. Here are some of our favourites:

Bar Torrecilla The best *pintxos* in town? You be the judge. Go for the melt-in-your-mouth foie gras or the mini-burgers, or anything else that takes your fancy, at this modern bar on buzzing Calle Laurel.

Tastavin (*facebook.com/tastavinbardepinchos*) On *pintxos* bar-lined San Juan, stylish Tastavin whips up some of the tastiest morsels in town, including smoked trout and lemon cream cornets, fried artichokes, tuna tataki and braised oxtail. The wines are outstanding.

Bar Soriano This venerable bar has been serving just one tapa, a mushroom stack topped with a prawn, since 1972.

map. The sunset-gold village crawls gently up a hillside and offers commanding views over the surrounding vine-carpeted plains. It's on these plains where you will find the fantastic wine museum **Vivanco** (*vivancoculturadevino.es*). Over several floors you will learn all about the history and culture of wine and the various processes that go into its production. All of this is done through interesting displays brought to life with computer technology. The treasures on display include Picasso-designed wine jugs, Roman and Byzantine mosaics, and gold-draped, wine-inspired religious artefacts. Various guided tours take you behind the scenes of the winery and include tastings.

THE DRIVE
It's 23km (30 minutes) along the N232, LR211 and A3210 to Elciego. The scenery, which is made up of endless vineyards, will delight anyone who enjoys wide open spaces (and vine leaves). In the distance are strange, sheer-faced, table-topped mountains.

07 ELCIEGO

Rioja wine's most flamboyant flourish lurks in the village of Elciego (Eltziego in Basque) in the show-stopping form of the **Hotel Marqués de Riscal** – not unlike a rainbow-hued Guggenheim museum (not surprising, perhaps, as both buildings were designed by Canadian Frank Gehry). Casual visitors are not welcome at the hotel, but if you want to see it, you have three options. The easiest is to join one of the **Marqués de Riscal winery tours** (*marquesderiscal.com*) – there's at least one English-language tour a day, but it's best to book in advance. You won't get inside the building, but you will get to see its exterior from some distance. A much closer look can be obtained by reserving a table at one of the two superb in-house restaurants: the Michelin-starred Restaurante **Marqués de Riscal** (*restaurantemarquesderiscal.com*) or the **1860 Tradición** (*hotel-marquesderiscal.com*). For the most intimate look at the building, you'll need to reserve a hotel room for the night.

THE DRIVE
It's only 10 minutes (7km) along the A3210 from Elciego to wonderful Laguardia, which rises up off the otherwise flat, vine-striped countryside.

DETOUR:
Bodegas Ysios

START: 08 LAGUARDIA

Just a couple of kilometres north of Laguardia is **Bodegas Ysios** (*bodegasysios.com*), architecturally perhaps the most gobsmacking bodega in Spain. Designed by Santiago Calatrava as a 'temple dedicated to wine', it features a cedar exterior with an aluminium wave for a roof that matches the flow of the rocky mountains behind it – and looks best after dark when pools of light flow out of it. Tours provide an insight into wine production; book ahead.

WHY I LOVE THIS TRIP

John Noble, writer

How can anyone not love an area sloshing in wine, and with fine restaurants and plenty of tempting tapas bars too? There's a soothingly slow pace and sense of space that adds an extra dimension to touring La Rioja, Spain's premier wine-producing region, with broad, vine-carpeted plains, big skies, sleepy honey-toned *pueblos* (villages) and plenty of sunshine, even in winter when the distant hills are capped with snow.

08 LAGUARDIA

It's easy to spin back the wheels of time in the medieval fortress town of Laguardia, or the 'Guard of Navarra' as it was once appropriately known, sitting proudly on its rocky hilltop. As well as memories of long-lost yesterdays, the town further entices visitors with its wine-producing present. **Bodegas Palacio** (*bodegaspalacio.com*), just 800m south of Laguardia, arranges tours and tastings by appointment. Check the website for details of its wine-appreciation courses (from €35 for one hour). On the southeast edge of town is the **Centro Temático del Vino Villa Lucía** (*villa-lucia.com*), a wine museum and shop selling high-quality wine from a variety of small, local producers. Museum visits are by guided tour only and finish with a 4D film and wine tasting.

THE DRIVE
From Laguardia, it's a short 18km (20 minutes) down the A124 back to Logroño where you started this tour.

09

BEST FOR ADRENALINE RUSH

Swaying in the breeze on the Teleférico de Fuente Dé.

NORTHERN SPAIN & THE BASQUE COUNTRY

Lofty Roads: the Picos de Europa

DURATION	DISTANCE	GREAT FOR
2-4 days	183km / 114 miles	Nature, families

BEST TIME TO GO	From June and September have the best combination of reliable(ish) weather and fewer crowds.

Puente Romano, Cangas de Onís

Rising snow-capped and majestic off the coastal plain, the Picos de Europa mark the greatest, most dramatic heights of the Cordillera Cantábrica. The awe-inspiring mountainscapes make this not just some of Spain's finest hill-walking country but also some of its most exciting for car touring. You can drive along precipitous gorges and up to alpine lakes, and when the road runs out you never have to walk far for magnificent vistas.

Link your trip

10 Cantabria's Eastern Valleys

Rural paradise your thing? After finishing this trip, head to Santander and start meandering Cantabria's eastern valleys.

12 North Coast Beaches & Culture

Swap the mountains for the allure of golden beaches and cultured cities. Join the coastal route anywhere between Santander and Ribadesella.

01 ARRIONDAS

The little town of Arriondas, on the northwest fringe of the Picos de Europa, is the starting point for hugely popular and fun canoe trips down the tree-lined Río Sella (7km to 15km, 1½ to four hours). Numerous agencies hire out canoes and gear, show you how to paddle and bring you back to Arriondas at the end. The river has a few entertaining minor rapids, but isn't a serious white-water affair. Anyone from about eight years old can enjoy the outing. The standard charge, including a picnic lunch, is €25/15 per adult/child. You can normally start any time between 11am and 1.30pm. Bring a change of clothes. Just don't

come on the first Saturday after 2 August, when tens of thousands of people converge for the **Descenso Internacional del Sella** (*descensodelsella.com*), an international canoeing event that sees 1000-plus serious paddlers racing off downriver to Ribadesella at noon.

THE DRIVE
It's a simple 8km journey southeast along the N625 to Cangas de Onís.

02 CANGAS DE ONÍS

This largely modern town bustles with Picos-related tourism activity throughout the summer months. It's a decent base for Picos explorations, with plenty of accommodation and eating options in and around the town. If you want organised activities, numerous agencies will take you hiking, climbing, canoeing, rafting, horse riding or canyoning. The so-called **Puente Romano** (Roman Bridge) spans the Río Sella, arching like a cat in fright. In fact there's nothing Roman about it – it was built in the 13th century – but it's no less beautiful for that. From it hangs a copy of the Cruz de la Victoria, the symbol of Asturias that resides in Oviedo's cathedral.

THE DRIVE
It's just 9km (15 minutes) along the AS114 and AS262 to Covadonga, with the scenery becoming increasingly impressive.

GARGANTA DEL CARES WALK

Ten kilometres of well-maintained path (the PRPNPE3) high above the Río Cares between Poncebos and Caín constitutes the **Garganta del Cares walk**, the most popular mountain walk in Spain. In August the experience can feel like Saturday morning on London's Oxford St, but this is still a spectacular – and at times vertiginous – excursion along the gorge separating the Picos' western and central massifs. It's possible to walk the whole 10km and return in one longish day's outing of six to seven hours plus stops. There are restaurants in Caín where you can lunch before heading back (though you can't be sure to find anything open from November to February). There's no drinkable water along the route, so bring your own. A number of agencies in Picos towns offer transport support, such as a drive back from Caín to Poncebos for around €30 per person.

The beginning of the walk from Poncebos involves a steady climb in the gorge's wide, mostly bare early stages; you're over the highest point after about 3km. As you approach the regional boundary with Castilla y León, the gorge becomes narrower and its walls thick with vegetation, creating greater contrast with the alpine heights above. The last stages of the walk are possibly the prettiest and, as you descend nearer the valley floor, you pass through a series of low, wet tunnels to emerge at the end of the gorge in Caín.

03 COVADONGA

The importance of the tiny village of Covadonga lies in what it represents rather than what it is. Somewhere hereabouts, in approximately 722 CE, the Muslim invaders suffered their first defeat in Spain, at the hands of the Visigothic nobleman Pelayo – an event considered to mark the beginning of the 800-year Reconquista. The place is an object of pilgrimage, for in a cave here, the **Santa Cueva**, the Virgin supposedly appeared to Pelayo's warriors before the battle. On weekends and in summer, long queues of the faithful and curious line up to enter the cave, now with a chapel installed. The cave's two tombs are claimed to contain the remains of Pelayo and several of his family members including son-in-law Alfonso I of Asturias. The **Fuente de Siete Caños** spring, by the pool below the cave, supposedly ensures marriage within one year to women who drink from it. Landslides destroyed much of Covadonga in the 19th century and the main church, the **Basílica de Covadonga** (*santuariodecovadonga.com*), is a neo-Romanesque affair built between 1877 and 1901.

WEATHER WARNING

The weather in and around the Picos can change very fast, and sudden bouts of mist, rain, cold and snow are common. If you're motoring around higher roads anytime between late October and early May, be prepared for sudden snowfall, which can block routes and even leave you stranded. If you get out on foot, go properly equipped for sudden weather changes. For mountain weather forecasts, see *mountain-forecast.com* (select 'Cantabrian Mountains'), or *aemet.es/en/eltiempo/prediccion/montana*.

Basílica de Covadonga

THE DRIVE

It's 12km (30 minutes) up a narrow, winding and scenic mountain road to the main car park at the Lagos de Covadonga. For three weeks over Easter and from June to September, and on the early November and early December holiday weekends, private vehicles may only continue past Covadonga before 8.30am or after 9pm, but can drive back down at any time. A shuttle bus runs from Cangas de Onís and three car parks along the Cangas–Covadonga road

04 LAGOS DE COVADONGA

Summer crowds don't distract from the beauty of these two little lakes. Most of the trippers don't get past snapping selfies near the water, so walking here is as nice as anywhere else in the Picos. **Lago de Enol** is the first lake you reach, with the main car park just past it. It's linked to **Lago de la Ercina**, 1km away, not only by the paved road but also by a footpath via the **Centro de Visitantes Pedro Pidal**, which has displays on Picos flora and fauna. There are rustic restaurants near both lakes (closed in winter). A marked circuit walk, the **Ruta Lagos de Covadonga**, takes in the two lakes, the visitors centre and an old mine, the Minas de Buferrera. Other trails will take you further afield. When mist descends, the lakes, surrounded by the green pastures and bald rock that characterise this part of the Picos, take on an eerie appearance.

THE DRIVE

After you've finished delighting in the lakes, backtrack all the way down to the AS114 and head east along the northern fringe of the Picos to Arenas de Cabrales (45km, one hour). The drive is through rollicking farmland with a daunting mountain backdrop.

05 ARENAS DE CABRALES

Arenas lies at the confluence of the bubbling Ríos Cares and Casaño. The busy main road is lined with hotels, restaurants and bars, and just off it lies a little tangle of quiet squares and back lanes, with several more local *sidrerías* (cider bars). You can learn all about and sample the fine, smelly, blue Cabrales cheese at Arenas' **Cueva del Queso de Cabrales** (*fundacioncabrales.com*), a cheese-cave museum on the Poncebos road 500m from Arenas' centre. There are 45-minute guided visits in Spanish. Working hours may be shorter from November to Easter.

THE DRIVE

Head south for 6km (10 minutes) along the AS264 to Poncebos.

06 PONCEBOS

Poncebos, a tiny straggle of buildings at the northern end of the incredible Cares gorge, is set amid already spectacular scenery. A side road uphill from here leads 1.5km to the hamlet of **Camarmeña**, where there's a lookout with views to the gigantic rock pillar El Naranjo de Bulnes in the Picos' central massif. The **Garganta del Cares Walk** is one of the most spectacular day walks in Spain. Even if you don't like to get out of the car, this one's well worth the huff and puff.

THE DRIVE

From Poncebos the minor CA1 winds its way 11km (20 minutes) up to small and often chilly Sotres.

07 SOTRES

If you want a room with a view, then Sotres, the highest village in the Picos (altitude: 1045m) and the starting point for a number of good walks, is where you should head to. The setting, under a shaft of bare limestone mountain peaks, is breathtaking. Many walkers head west along the PRPNPE21 trail to the **Collado de Pandébano** pass (1212m), a 4km walk (one to 1½ hours). At Pandébano, the massive rock pillar **El Naranjo de Bulnes** comes into view and you can continue up to its base in 2½ to three hours. Another popular walking route goes east to the village of Tresviso and on down to Urdón in the Desfiladero de la Hermida gorge on the Potes–Panes road. As far as Tresviso (11km) it's a paved road, but the final 6km is a dramatic walking trail, the Ruta Urdón-Tresviso (PRPNPE30), snaking 825m down to the floor of the gorge.

SPOTTING PICOS WILDLIFE

Although a few wolves survive in the Picos and the odd brown bear might wander through, you stand a much better chance of spotting the *rebeco* (chamois), some 6000 of which skip around the rocks and steep slopes. Deer, badgers, wild boar, squirrels, foxes, genets and martens, in various numbers, inhabit wooded areas. Otters, trout and salmon swim in the rivers.

Eagles, hawks and other raptors soar in the Picos' skies. Keep your eyes peeled for the majestic *águila real* (golden eagle) and the huge scavenging *buitre leonado* (griffon vulture). The even bigger, bone-eating *quebrantahuesos* (lammergeier; bearded vulture), extinct in the Picos since the mid-20th century, is being very slowly reintroduced.

THE DRIVE
Head back to Arenas de Cabrales and follow the AS114 east to its junction with the north–south N621 at the humdrum town of Panes. South of Panes, the N621 to Potes follows the Río Deva upstream through the impressive Desfiladero de la Hermida gorge before reaching the turn-off to Lebeña (1km). Total journey distance 60km (1¼ hours).

08 LEBEÑA

The fascinating little **Iglesia de Santa María de Lebeña** dates back to the 9th or 10th century. The horseshoe arches in the church are a telltale sign of its Mozarabic style, rarely seen this far north in Spain. The floral motifs on the columns are Visigothic, and a Celtic engraved stone supports the altarpiece with its 15th-century image of the breastfeeding Virgen de la Buena Leche (Virgin of the Good Milk). Outside the church stands the stump of a beloved, centuries-old yew tree destroyed by a storm in 2007. A sapling grown from a cutting from the tree was planted beside it in 2017.

THE DRIVE
Keep following the N621 south to Potes for 9km (10 minutes).

Photo opportunity

The gorgeous blue Lagos de Covadonga.

09 POTES

Potes is a popular staging post on the southeastern edge of the Picos, with the range's eastern massif rising close at hand. The Quiviesa and Deva rivers meet here and the heart of town is a cluster of bridges, towers and back streets restored in traditional slate, wood and red tile after considerable damage during the civil war. Christian refugees, fleeing from Muslim-occupied Spain to this remote Christian enclave in the 8th century, brought with them the **Lígnum Crucis**, purportedly the single biggest chunk of Jesus' cross. The **Monasterio de Santo Toribio de Liébana** (*santotoribiodeliebana.org*), 3km west of Potes, has housed this holy relic ever since, making it a significant pilgrimage goal. The monastery is also famous as the home of medieval monk and theologian Beato de Liébana, celebrated across Europe for his Commentary on the Apocalypse. You can drive 500m past the monastery to the tiny **Ermita de San Miguel**, a chapel with great valley and Picos views.

THE DRIVE
It's a beautiful 23km (30 minutes) along the CA185 to Fuente Dé, following the Río Deva upstream through several small villages – some of them, such as Cosgaya and Espinama, with attractive sleeping and eating options. This route is best outside high summer, when you can really get a better feel for the majesty of the Picos.

10 FUENTE DÉ

At 1078m, Fuente Dé lies at the foot of the southern wall of the Picos' central massif. In four minutes the dramatic (and frankly rather terrifying!) **Teleférico de Fuente Dé cable car** (*cantur.com*) whisks people 753m up to the top of that wall, from where walkers and climbers can make their way deeper into the mountains. It's an easy 3.5km, one-hour walk from the top of the *teleférico* to the Hotel Áliva, open from June to mid-October, where you can get refreshments. From here several other walks of varying length will reveal the beauty of the mountains. You can walk back down to Fuente Dé by the PRPNPE24 Puertos de Áliva trail, through landscapes of stark limestone peaks and lush alpine pastures. It starts off along the track that goes down to Espinama on the CA185, then branches off about halfway down to reach Fuente Dé (11km, about 3½ hours from the hotel). Be warned that during the high season (especially August) you can wait an hour or more for a place in the cable car, going up or down. Good job the scenery is worth lingering for.

POTES FIREWATER

The potent liquor *orujo*, made from grape pressings, is drunk throughout northern Spain and is something of a Potes speciality, often made using traditional copper stills. People here like to drink it as an after-dinner aperitif as part of a herbal tea called *té de roca* or *té de puerto*. Plenty of shops around town sell *orujo*, including varieties flavoured with honey, fruits and herbs, and most will offer you tastings if you're thinking of buying. Potes' jolly **Fiesta del Orujo** (*facebook.com/fiestaorujo*) happens on the second weekend in November, with practically every bar in town setting up a stall selling *orujo* shots for a few cents. The proceeds go to charity. Of course, you'll have to decide in advance whose turn it is to drive...

Teleférico de Fuente Dé cable car

10

BEST FOR ANCIENT ART

The prehistoric paintings of Cueva de Covalanas.

NORTHERN SPAIN & THE BASQUE COUNTRY

Cantabria's Eastern Valleys

DURATION	DISTANCE	GREAT FOR
2-4 days	245km / 152 miles	Nature, families, history

BEST TIME TO GO	In May, June and September, temperatures are up, rainfall and prices are down, and crowds are away.

Palacio de la Magdalena

This route is one for art lovers. Nature itself has painted a grand canvas of brilliantly green river valleys reaching up to panoramic passes and down to a coast where pretty beaches alternate with wave-lashed cliffs. Humanity has added a sprinkling of stone-and-terracotta villages that enhance the landscape's charms. This is also where people did some of their first painting, depicting prehistoric animals on cave walls tens of thousands of years ago.

Link your trip

11 Along the Río Ebro

It's simple enough to join this trip up with the leisurely drive along the mighty Río Ebro.

09 Lofty Roads: the Picos de Europa

Mountainscapes – and driving routes – don't get much more dramatic than those found on the Picos de Europa drive.

01 SANTANDER

Cantabria's busy capital enjoys a superb setting along the northern side of the Bahía de Santander, and has good city beaches, a heaving bar and restaurant scene, and some intriguing cultural attractions. On the waterfront, the futuristic-looking **Centro Botín** (*centrobotin.org*) arts centre opened in 2017. Designed by Italian Renzo Piano, it includes 2500 sq metres of exhibition space and a bright cafe where you can stop in for a drink or bite to eat. The parklands of the **Península de la Magdalena**, 3km east of the centre, are perfect for a stroll. Kids will enjoy the seals and penguins and the little train that

choo-choos around the headland. The English-inspired **Palacio de la Magdalena** (*palaciomagdalena.com*) was built between 1908 and 1912 as a gift from Santander to Spain's royal family: you can get inside on 45-minute Spanish-language guided tours.

THE DRIVE
It's 27km (40 minutes, depending on the traffic leaving Santander) along the busy S10 and the less hectic N623 to Puente Viesgo. Once you reach the town, turn right at the 'Cuevas del Monte Castillo' sign and go 1.5km uphill.

02 CUEVAS DE MONTE CASTILLO

The valley town of Puente Viesgo lies at the foot of the conical Monte Castillo. Part way up this hill is the **Cuevas de Monte Castillo** (*cuevas.culturadecantabria.com*), a series of caves frequented by humans since 150,000 years ago. Four of them are World Heritage–listed and two of these, **El Castillo** and **Las Monedas**, are open for 45-minute guided visits (in Spanish). Booking ahead is highly advisable, especially for the more spectacular El Castillo, whose 275 paintings and engravings of deer, bison, horses, goats, aurochs, handprints, mysterious symbols and a mammoth (very rare) date from around 39,000 to 11,000 BCE. One red symbol, believed to be 40,800 years old, is Europe's oldest known cave art. Las Monedas has less art (black animal outlines from around 10,000 BCE) but contains an astounding labyrinth of stalactites and stalagmites.

THE DRIVE
Turn east off the N623 3km south of Puente Viesgo and follow the CA270 and CA142 southeast to Selaya. Here, turn right on the CA625 and follow signs 800m to Quesería La Jarradilla. Total distance 21km.

03 QUESERÍA LA JARRADILLA

Milk from cattle grazed on the rich green pastures of northern Spain is made into a wide variety of tasty cheeses. The cheeses of the Valles Pasiegos (the parallel valleys of the Ríos Pas, Pisueña and Miera) are notably young, soft and creamy – the damp climate means they can't mature. At the family-run dairy **Quesería La Jarradilla** (*quesoslajarradilla.com*), just outside Selaya in the Pisueña valley, you can taste, buy and find out all about these tempting cheeses. The shop opens daily except Sunday; tours (free) run once weekly (occasionally in English, depending on demand), usually with an extra one at 5pm Wednesday or Thursday from July to September.

THE DRIVE
From Selaya follow the CA262 south for 16km to Vega de Pas. The views from the Puerto de la Braguía pass are stunning – pull over by the bus stop to admire them. This is a popular cycling route.

04 VEGA DE PAS

Vega de Pas is the 'capital' of the Valles Pasiegos (*vallespasiegos.org*), which are among Cantabria's (and therefore Spain's) most traditional rural areas. The small town has a handsome central plaza of stone houses with wooden galleries and flowery window boxes. Look for shops advertising *quesadas* and *sobaos*, two local food specialities that are favourites throughout Cantabria. *Quesadas* are a kind of dense cheesecake; *sobaos* are rich sponge cakes prepared with lots of butter. The countryside is outrageously picturesque: it's all deep greens and steep-sided hills with minuscule villages of stone houses. There are plenty of opportunities to get out for a walk all around here.

THE DRIVE
Climb southeast for 14km on the CA631 up the lovely, green Yera valley with a few switchbacks to the Puerto de las Estacas de Trueba.

05 PUERTO DE LAS ESTACAS DE TRUEBA

Stop to take in the panoramas from this 1154m-high pass where your route leaves Cantabria and enters Castilla y León. It's a lonely but exhilarating spot with a few scattered stone barns and the cliffs of Castro Valnera (1718m) looming over to the east.

THE DRIVE
Continue into Castilla y León on the BU570. Turn north just after Las Machorras onto the BU571, which heads up to the Puerto de la Sía (19km, 30 to 40 minutes).

06 PUERTO DE LA SÍA

Wonderful views of green Cantabrian valleys open out below you as you cross the 1200m Puerto de la Sía mountain pass back into Cantabria.

THE DRIVE
Zigzag down into Cantabria on the CA665. At a T-junction after 9km, go left for 3km to the viewpoint over the Nacimiento del Río Asón.

ANTONIO LOPEZ VELASCO/SHUTTERSTOCK ©

Valleys near Vega de Pas

07 NACIMIENTO DEL RÍO ASÓN

The Río Asón, the main river of Cantabria's easternmost reaches, begins life as a 50m waterfall pouring straight out of a cliff into a deep, thickly wooded valley – a beautiful sight easily taken in from the mirador (viewpoint) across the valley on the CA265.

THE DRIVE
Head 3km back up the CA265 to the T-junction where it meets the CA665, and continue 2km straight on to La Gándara on the CA256.

08 LA GÁNDARA

La Gándara is a scattered high-valley village with mountain vistas all around, and a couple of restaurant-bars for refreshments. The **Centro de Interpretación Collados del Asón** (*redcantabrarural.com/naturea-3*) offers information on this upland area (protected as a parque natural). A 400m walk behind the office leads to a viewpoint over the Cascada La Gándara waterfall.

TOP TIP:

Weather Wisdom

Check the weather before setting out on this drive. You'll be crossing mountain passes where cloud or fog sometimes make the going difficult, and snow occasionally makes it impossible.

Photo opportunity

Snap the breathtaking views from the Puerto de la Sía pass.

THE DRIVE
Continue 10km down the CA256 to Regules.

09 REGULES

In a lovely, tranquil spot beside the tree-lined Río Gándara, Regules is a mere pinprick on many a map. The country around here provides lots of opportunities for walking and generally moseying about at a slow pace. There's also a wonderful hotel beside the bridge, with a good restaurant.

THE DRIVE
Head on down the CA256, which feeds into the marginally more major N629 for the final couple of kilometres into Ramales de Victoria (10km, 15 minutes from Regules).

10 RAMALES DE LA VICTORIA

The easy going small valley town of Ramales de la Victoria is the 'capital' of the Alto Asón district, which stretches from the mountains almost to the coast and claims more than half of Cantabria's 9000 known caves. There are two outstanding visitable caves here. The **Cueva de Cullalvera** (*cuevas.culturadecantabria.com/cullalvera-2*) is a jaw-droppingly vast cavity but its prehistoric art is off-limits. The **Cueva de Covalanas** (*cuevas.culturadecantabria.com/covalanas-2*), 2km up the N629 south from Ramales, then 650m up a footpath, is World Heritage–listed for its stunning depictions of deer and other animals, executed around 20,000 BCE using an unusual dot-painting technique. Visits to either cave are guided and last 45 minutes; it's advisable to book ahead online. Ramales' **tourist office** (*cantabriaorientalrural.es/turismo*) can tell you all about the area's attractions.

THE DRIVE
From Ramales head 18km north down the N629, then go 13km east along the A8 motorway to junction 160, from which it's a 1.5km drive down to Playa Oriñón – 30 to 40 minutes total.

11 PLAYAS DE ORIÑÓN & SONABIA

After your mountain wanderings it's time for the beach! The broad sandy strip of **Playa de Oriñón** is set deep between protective headlands, making the water calm and comparatively warm. The settlement here consists of ugly holiday flats and caravan parks. For a smaller but wilder strand continue 1km past Oriñón to the hamlet of Sonabia, and turn left 100m after the church to reach a parking area. It's then a 200m walk down to **Playa de Sonabia**, a little, clothing-optional beach tucked into a rock-lined inlet beneath high crags, above which huge griffon vultures circle the sky. There are a couple of seasonal bar-restaurants by the car park.

THE DRIVE
It's 15km (15 minutes) along the A8 to Laredo.

12 LAREDO

Laredo's very long, sandy and normally very calm beach is backed by ugly 20th-century blocks. But at the east end of town, the cobbled streets of the old **Puebla Vieja** slope down from the impressive 13th-century **Iglesia de Santa María**, with the remains of the 16th-century **Fuerte del Rastrillar** fortress spread over the scenic La Atalaya hill above. The Puebla Vieja has a lively food and drinks scene.

THE DRIVE
It's a 20-minute (15km) hop around the bay on the A8 and CA241 to Santoña. Alternatively, between March and November, park near El Puntal, the northwestern end of Laredo's beach, and take the Excursiones Marítimas passenger ferry to Santoña (one-way/return €2/3.50, five minutes) and explore on foot.

13 SANTOÑA

The engaging fishing port of Santoña is famed for its anchovies, which are bottled or tinned here, with olive oil to preserve them, and sold all over town. At the eastern end of the seafront promenade and also at the foot of the hilly headland **Monte Buciero** are two old fortresses: the **Fuerte de San Martín** and, further along, the abandoned **Fuerte de San Carlos**. Monte Buciero has five hiking paths for a stretch of the legs. You could also head 2.5km north along the CA141 and CA907 to **Playa de Berria**, a magnificent sweep of sand and surf on the open sea.

THE DRIVE
To get back to Santander, head along the A8 and S10 for 47km (40 minutes).

GREENS AND BLUES/SHUTTERSTOCK ©

Laredo

PAZ

11

NORTHERN SPAIN & THE BASQUE COUNTRY

Along the Río Ebro

BEST FOR KNIGHTS IN ARMOUR

Rescuing a princess from the castle of Olite.

DURATION	DISTANCE	GREAT FOR
2-4 days	482km / 300 miles	History, wine, nature

BEST TIME TO GO	In May when the poppies are in bloom and the weather pleasing.

Nacimiento del Río Ebro

Stand on top of a castle turret in Olite and think back over everything you have seen – and will see – on this stunning drive and you'll probably end up agreeing that this is perhaps the single most diverse and fascinating drive you can cover in northern Spain. Just look at what there is: mountain springs and deserts, underground churches and Islamic palaces, wine and superb tapas. This is a drive you won't forget.

Link your trip

08 Roving La Rioja Wine Region

Once you hit Logroño, take a couple of days to enjoy the gift of the grape on the La Rioja Wine Region drive.

19 Barcelona to Valencia

Head on south from Zaragoza to uncover more of Aragón's unsung secrets.

01 FONTIBRE

Where else to start your Ebro odyssey but at the **Nacimiento del Río Ebro**, where the baby Ebro spills out of a rock to begin its 930km meander from the remote hills of southern Cantabria to the Mediterranean. Five kilometres west of the area's main town, Reinosa, this is a stunningly serene spot in its own tree-shaded park, with a big pool of deep-turquoise water, a tiny shrine and a few ducks splashing around. Wander up into the village to scrutinise a large open-air map-model of the river's entire course.

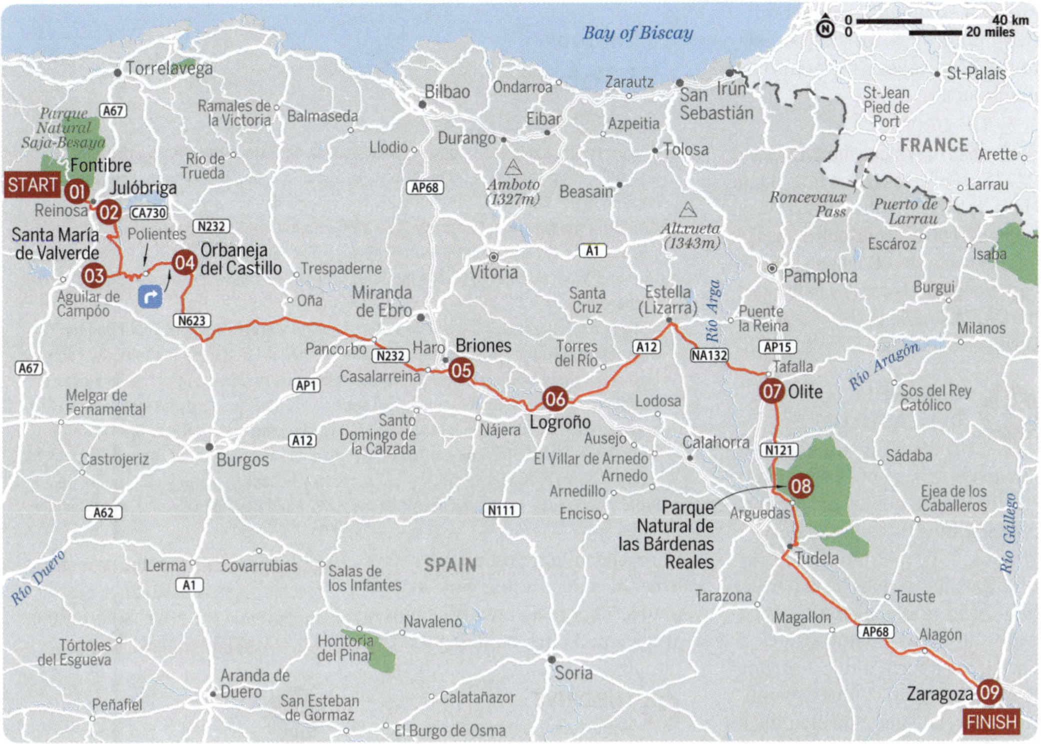

THE DRIVE

It's just 10km east to Julióbriga but navigation round Reinosa needs attention. Entering Reinosa on the CA183, go left at a roundabout following 'A67 Santander Palencia' signs. After 2km go right at another roundabout (CA171 Requejo). Turn left CA171 Corconte after 500m, then right (CA731 Bolmir) after 1km. In Bolmir (1.5km) go left on the CA730. After 500m take the Julióbriga turn-off for the final 1km.

02 JULIÓBRIGA

On the edge of the hamlet of Retortillo, you'll discover the remains of Cantabria's most significant Roman town, **Julióbriga** (*centros.culturadecantabria.com*). Hourly guided visits (45 minutes, in Spanish) lead you through the Museo Domus, a full-scale recreation of one of Julióbriga's houses. You're free to explore independently the excavated parts of the town (about 10% of the total), with a 12th-century Romanesque church built over the Roman forum.

THE DRIVE

It's 45km through woodlands and countryside to Santa María de Valverde, with the now much Ebro your companion. From Julióbriga head back to the CA730, go 7.5km east to Arroyo, then 4km south along the CA735 to turn right onto the CA741. Head 9km along this to meet the CA272. Turn left and go 13km to a roundabout, then 9km west along the CA273.

03 SANTA MARÍA DE VALVERDE

The beautiful little **Iglesia Rupestre de Santa María de Valverde**, hewn out of solid rock, is the most impressive of several remarkable *iglesias rupestres* (rock-cut churches) along the Ebro valley in the extreme south of Cantabria. The churches date from the 7th to 10th centuries, the early days of Christianity in the region. Santa María retains a magical beauty, with irregular stone arches and rough-cut stone floors suffused in ghostly subterranean light. Visits are in conjunction with visits to the adjacent **Centro de Interpretación del Rupestre**, which gives an excellent introduction (with photos, videos and maps) to the Ebro valley's rock church phenomenon.

THE DRIVE
Head east along the CA273 and CA272 to Polientes (22km from Santa María de Valverde), the biggest village in this part of the world and a possible refreshments stop. Continue 18km east along the Ebro valley following the CA274, CA275 and BU643 to Orbaneja del Castillo.

04 ORBANEJA DEL CASTILLO

The quaint stone-and-terracotta village of Orbaneja is the first settlement that the Ebro reaches after threading a deep gorge as it flows from Cantabria into Castilla y León. It's a perfect halt for its gorgeous multi-tailed waterfall, views of fantastic karstic rock formations and, not least, some good country restaurants specialising in grilled meats and *cocidos* (meat-bean-sausage stews).

THE DRIVE
Continue 6km southeast on the BU643 to meet the N623 and follow this south for 27km, between imposing rock-topped bluffs, then turn east along the CL633. Crossing mostly flatter, more arable land, this becomes the CL663 leading to Cornudilla. From Cornudilla head east on the more major N232 for 58km to Briones – altogether 123km (about two hours) from Orbaneja.

05 BRIONES

Even without the marvel that is the Vivanco wine museum (p73), Briones, in the heart of La Rioja's world-renowned wine-growing country, would be worth a stop. From its hillside perch above a loop of the Ebro, the village commands views over the surrounding vine-striped plains. There's a cute little church and a small park built around the remains of a castle.

THE DRIVE
Seeing as the navigator is likely to have tried to satisfy their wine cravings in Briones, you'll probably be pleased to know that it's just a straightforward 36km cruise down the N232 to the capital of Spain's wine country: Logroño. Lucky navigator!

06 LOGROÑO

Logroño, the capital of La Rioja, is one of those towns that on the surface doesn't have much to attract visitors, yet everyone who comes here does seem to end up having a good time. The food (p72) and, of course, the wine are exceptional, and there's a superb museum (p64) in the attractive old centre.

THE DRIVE
With the navigator now likely singing songs about wine in the seat next to you, they won't be disappointed to know there's a fermented-grape-juice theme at the next stop, too. It's an easy 86km drive east across wine and crop country via the A12, NA132 and N121 to Olite.

07 OLITE

The turrets and spires of Olite are filled with stories of kings and queens, brave knights and beautiful princesses – it's as if it has burst off the pages of a fairy tale. This honey-coloured village was once the home of the royal families of Navarra, and the walled old quarter is crowded with their memories. It's Carlos III that we must thank for the exceptional **Palacio Real** (*guiartenavarra.com*), which towers over the village. Back in Carlos' day, the castle's inhabitants included not just princes and jesters but also lions and other exotic pets, as well as Babylon-inspired hanging gardens. Don't miss the **Museo de la Viña y el Vino de Navarra**, a fascinating journey through wine and wine culture.

DETOUR:

El Tobazo

START: 03 SANTA MARÍA DE VALVERDE

The pretty little riverside village of **Villaescusa de Ebro** is the starting point for an exhilarating short hike up to **El Tobazo**, one of the smallest but most superbly located of the Ebro rock-cut churches. The village sits just across the Ebro from the CA275 on the way from Santa María de Valverde to Orbaneja del Castillo.

Eleven kilometeres past Polientes there's a sizeable parking area on the left side of the road. Walk across the bridge into Villaescusa and follow 'El Tobazo' signs up out of the village.

It's 1km gradually uphill to the top of a beautiful **waterfall**, where you'll find the **cave-church** (three small caves) and some natural caves behind the falls. Just above is the *surgencia* (spring) where the crystal-clear stream flows out of the rock before tumbling down the hillside – a magical spot where you can easily imagine a few *anjanas*, Cantabria's legendary water nymphs, skipping around the rocks. Heading back down, after 200m you can take the path signed 'Cascada del Tobazo Zona Inferior' down to the **lower falls**, then return to Villaescusa along an Ebro-side track. From Villaescusa, continue 7km along the CA275 and BU643 to Orbaneja del Castillo.

THE DRIVE Start dressing like Lawrence of Arabia as you head south along the N121 to Arguedas on the edge of the semidesert Parque Natural de las Bárdenas Reales. It's a pleasant 42km drive.

08 PARQUE NATURAL DE LAS BÁRDENAS REALES

In a region largely dominated by fertile farmland and wet mountain slopes, the last thing you'd expect is a sunburnt desert, but in the Bárdenas Reales a desert is exactly what you'll find. The weirdly eroded sandstone hills and snakelike gorges may look like an almost pristine wilderness, but it's actually a human creation: the Bárdenas Reales were once forest, but people chopped it all down and let their livestock eat all the lower growth. There are a couple of dirt motor tracks and numerous hiking and cycling trails, but most people come to drive the park's 34km loop road. The **park information office** (*bardenasreales.es*), on the main route into the park from Arguedas, can supply information.

Photo opportunity

Framing a Wild West backdrop in the Parque Natural de las Bárdenas Reales.

THE DRIVE Head south to Tudela (its old quarter is worth a quick stop if time allows) and join the A68 then the AP68 tollway for the final push to Zaragoza. Total distance: 100km (1¼ hours).

09 ZARAGOZA

Few foreign tourists find their way to Zaragoza, which is a real pity for them but a bonus for those who do, because this city with 11 bridges straddling the Ebro is truly one of the most interesting and beautiful in northern Spain. For more on Zaragoza, see Trip 19: Barcelona to Valencia (p134).

Olite

12

BEST FOR FOODIES

San Sebastián's *pintxos* (Basque tapas) bars.

NORTHERN SPAIN & THE BASQUE COUNTRY

North Coast Beaches & Culture

DURATION	DISTANCE	GREAT FOR
4-6 days	551km / 348 miles	History, wine, nature

BEST TIME TO GO July and August have the most sunshine and a festive atmosphere; June and September have decent weather and fewer crowds.

Casco Viejo Bilbao

Just turn off the A8 motorway and you're straight on to rural lanes winding down through green countryside to hundreds of sandy strands that alternate with the high rocky capes and cliffs of this surprisingly untamed coast. You'll discover breathtaking ocean-facing expanses like Playa Oyambre, perfect headland-bounded crescents like Playa de Torimbia, and places of awe-inspiring geology like the rock 'cathedrals' of Praia As Catedrais.

Link your trip

08 Roving La Rioja Wine Region

Treat yourself to a couple of days' touring Spain's premier wine region.

09 Lofty Roads: the Picos de Europa

Head inland to explore the most spectacular of the mountains lining the southern horizon.

01 SAN SEBASTIÁN

With golden beaches, a world-famous culinary scene and a packed cultural calendar, San Sebastián may well tempt you to reschedule the following stages of your trip. When it comes to cooking, no other city quite compares, whether you're snacking on delectable *pintxos* (Basque tapas) in the Parte Vieja, or lingering over a multicourse feast in a Michelin-starred dining room. **Playa de la Concha** is a 1.5km stretch of golden sands curving gently around a protected bay. Complete with calm seas, a picturesque promenade and wonderful vistas, it's

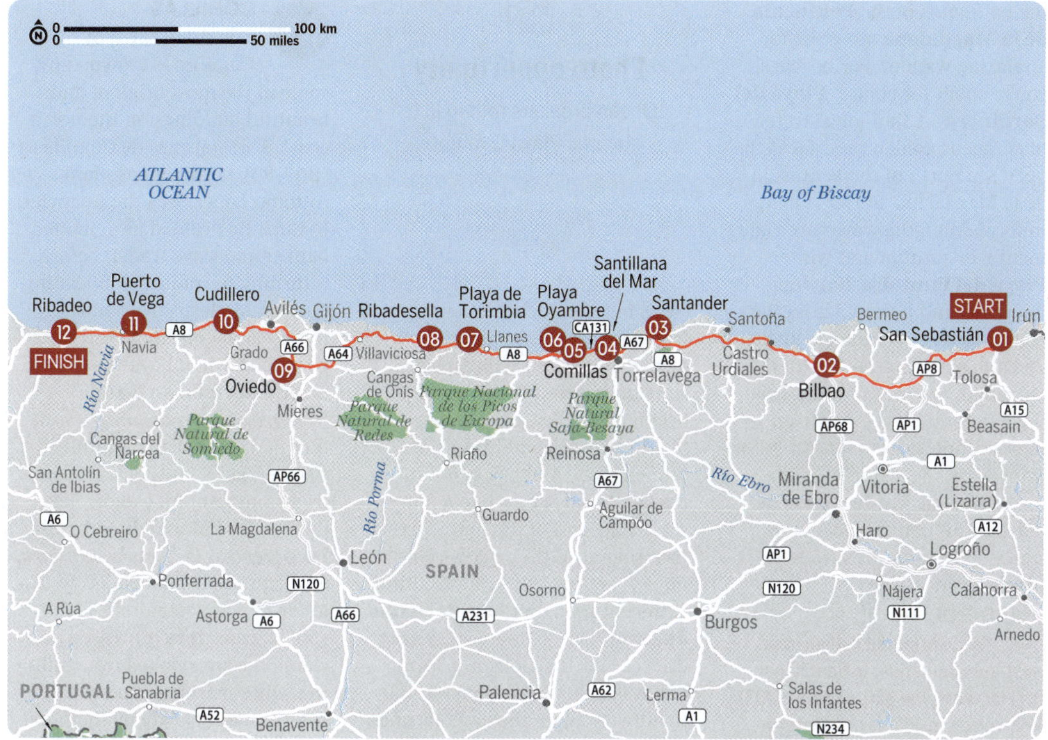

one of Europe's most perfect city beaches. Behind the beach and the *pintxos* bars stands a city of great design. Elegant art-nouveau buildings, ornate bridges and beautifully manicured parks and plazas are an integral part of San Sebastián. The showpiece cultural attraction is **San Telmo Museoa** (*santelmomuseoa.eus*), a thought-provoking collection that explores Basque history and culture in all its complexity.

THE DRIVE
It's a straight-forward 102km, mostly along the AP8 motorway, from San Sebastián to Bilbao (about 1½ hours, depending on traffic, from city centre to city centre).

02 BILBAO

The Basque Country's biggest city is famed for its contemporary architecture and enjoys a dining scene just as varied and mouth-watering as San Sebastián's. Buzzing *pintxos* bars, venerable family-run restaurants and temples of fine dining offer endless different takes on Basque cuisine, especially in the cobbled lanes of the atmospheric **Casco Viejo** (Old Town). Frank Gehry's shimmering titanium **Museo Guggenheim** (*guggenheim-bilbao.eus*), itself a byword for contemporary architecture, is packed with art treasures inside and out, and has lost none of its ability to captivate more than two decades after its opening. Today it stands among other great architectural works, like the nearby **Zubizuri**, a soaring bridge designed by Santiago Calatrava.

THE DRIVE
Hop on to the A8 motorway for the 100km drive to the north's next major city – Santander. The drive should take about 1¼ hours, traffic permitting.

03 SANTANDER

Capital of the Cantabria region, Santander has a fabulous setting along the north side of the broad Bahía de Santander. The waterfront arts centre, the Centro Botín (p80), is the city's latest showpiece, while the parklands of the **Península de la Magdalena** are great for a relaxing wander. For beaches, you're spoilt for choice. **Playa del Sardinero**'s 1.5km-long stretch of gorgeous golden sand faces the open sea north of the Península de la Magdalena. Surfers emerge in force when the waves are right, mainly in autumn and winter. **Playa del Puntal**, a 2km-long finger of sand jutting across the bay towards Santander, is idyllic on calm days (but beware of the currents). Ferries sail there from the city through the day from May or June to October. An 18km drive west, the exquisite, 3km-long **Playa de Valdearenas** has a delightful natural feel and is hugely popular with surfers and beach-lovers alike.

THE DRIVE
It's 30km (about half an hour) west from Santander to Santillana del Mar, along the S20, A67 and CA131. Only village residents or guests in hotels with garages may take vehicles into the old heart of Santillana. Other hotel guests may drive to unload luggage and then return to the car park at the village entrance.

04 SANTILLANA DEL MAR

Despite its name, Santillana is not by the *mar* (sea), but don't let that deter you from visiting this medieval jewel of a village. It's in such a perfect state of preservation with its bright cobbled streets, flower-filled balconies and huddle of tanned stone and brick buildings that it almost seems like a film set. At the end of the main street, past solemn 15th- to 18th-century nobles' houses, rises the beautiful 12th-century **Colegiata de Santa Juliana**. This ex-monastery's big drawcard is the cloister, a formidable storehouse of Romanesque handiwork, with the capitals of its columns finely carved into a huge variety of figures.

THE DRIVE
Drive 16km west along the CA131 through verdant countryside to Comillas.

Photo opportunity
Ocean breakers rolling in to glorious Playa Oyambre.

05 COMILLAS

The small town of Comillas is crowned by some of the most original and beautiful buildings on the north coast. The Marqués de Comillas (1817–83), born here as plain Antonio López, was the financier; in Cuba he profited as a planter, banker and slave trader, before returning to commission leading Catalan Modernista architects to reimagine his home town. A particularly flamboyant example is the **Capricho de Gaudí** (*elcaprichodegaudi.com*), a summer play-pad for the marquis' sister-in-law's brother, designed by a young Antoni Gaudí. Next door is the **Palacio de Sobrellano** (*centros.culturadecantabria.com*), an imposing neogothic affair by Joan Martorell. The spooky **cemetery** (off Paseo de Garelly) is overlooked by a chilling white-marble statue of the exterminating angel by sculptor Josep Llimona.

THE DRIVE
Continue west on the CA131, then turn north on the CA236 to reach Playa Oyambre, 5km from Comillas.

06 PLAYA OYAMBRE

The 2km-long, soft-blonde Playa Oyambre, 5km west of Comillas, is a sandy dream protected by the Parque Natural Oyambre. It has surfable waves and a dash of intriguing history as the emergency landing spot of the first ever USA–Spain flight (1929) – commemorated by the Pájaro Amarillo (Yellow Bird) monument towards the beach's west end. Waves and wind can be strong: swim only when the green flags fly.

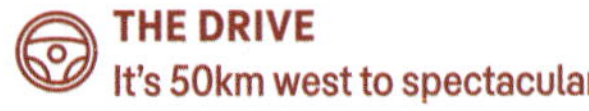

THE DRIVE
It's 50km west to spectacular

ALTAMIRA

Spain's finest prehistoric art, the wonderful carbon-and-ochre paintings of bison, horses, deer and other animals in the Cueva de Altamira, 2.5km from Santillana del Mar, was discovered in 1879 by Cantabrian historian and scientist Marcelino Sanz de Sautuola and his eight-year-old daughter María Justina. By 2002, Altamira had attracted so many visitors that the cave was closed to stop deterioration of the art. Today, a replica cave in the **Museo de Altamira** (*culturaydeporte.gob.es/mnaltamira*) enables everyone to appreciate the inspired, 13,000- to 35,000-year-old paintings. The museum is incredibly popular, so you should book well ahead online, especially from Easter to September.

Playa de Torimbia, about a 40-minute drive if you use the A8 motorway, approached through San Vicente de la Barquera. Exit at junction 300 and go southwest to Balmori. Here turn right to follow the LLN11 to Niembro, from where it's 2km (signposted) to the beach car park.

07 PLAYA DE TORIMBIA

A beautiful gold crescent bounded by rocky headlands and a bowl of green hills, clothing-optional Torimbia is truly spectacular. You have to walk the last kilometre or so to reach it, which keeps the crowds down. A 1km walk back over the headland from Torimbia (or 500m from Niembro village) brings you to the also attractive **Playa de Toranda**, 250m of sand backed by green fields and a forested headland. Both beaches have appealing *chiringuitos* (informal seasonal bar-restaurants) serving drinks and food from about mid-June to early September.

THE DRIVE Head back to Niembro then west on the LLN11 to join the A8 westbound at junction 303. Exit at junction 319 on to the N632, which follows the Río Sella into Ribadesella (23km, about 30 minutes).

08 RIBADESELLA

This low-key fishing town and seaside resort straddles the estuary of the Río Sella. The western part (with most of the best hotels) has an expansive golden beach, **Playa de Santa Marina**, lined by handsome early-20th-century *casas de indianos* (houses built by emigrants returned from the Americas). To see some of Spain's finest prehistoric cave art, including superb horse paintings probably done between 15,000 and 10,000 BCE, book ahead for Ribadesella's World Heritage–listed **Cueva de Tito Bustillo** (*centrotitobustillo.com*). The one-hour visits are guided in Spanish. If you miss the cave itself, the displays of the adjacent **Centro de Arte Rupestre Tito Bustillo** (*centrotitobustillo.com*) are well worth your time. The broad, 1.5km-long sands of **Playa de Vega**, 8km west of Ribadesella, are among the least known of northern Spain's finest beaches. There are three or four relaxed restaurant-bars (most closed in winter) at the east end, and it's a surfing beach – but it's big enough, and just hard enough to reach, that it never feels crowded. To find it, go west from Ribadesella on the N632, turn off at Km 9.3 and go 1.6km to the beach.

THE DRIVE It's 45km through woodlands and countryside to Santa María de Valverde, with the now much larger Ebro often your companion. From Julióbriga head back to the CA730, go 7.5km east to Arroyo, then 4km south along the CA735 to turn right onto the CA741. Head 9km along this to meet the CA272. Turn left and go 13km to a roundabout, then 9km west along the CA273.

TOP TIP:

Bilbao from Above

Bilbao's setting among rolling green hills comes as a pleasant surprise to many. For a change of pace and mesmerising views, take a ride on the old-fashioned **Funicular de Artxanda.**

09 OVIEDO

Forsake the coastal vistas briefly for a breath of urban sophistication in Asturias' civilised capital. Oviedo is endowed with a lively Old Town of stone-paved, traffic-free streets and plazas, a stash of intriguing sights and some excellent restaurants and bars. The imposing **Catedral de San Salvador** (*catedraldeoviedo.com*) was built mainly in Gothic and baroque styles between the 13th and 18th centuries, but its origins and greatest interest lie in the **Cámara Santa**, a pre-Romanesque chapel begun in the 8th century to house important holy relics. Nearby are two excellent museums, the **Museo Arqueológico de Asturias** (*museoarqueologicodeasturias.com*), which houses the region's archaeological riches, and the **Museo de Bellas Artes de Asturias** (*museobbaa.com*), which features many Spanish greats.

THE DRIVE Make your way out on to the A66 running north past the east side of Oviedo. Branch onto the A8 westbound and follow this to junction 425, where you exit and drive the last 6km down into Cudillero by the N632 and CU2. It's a 60km trip, taking 45 minutes (barring wrong turns when extricating yourself from Oviedo's one-way system).

10 CUDILLERO

Cudillero is the most picturesque fishing village on the Asturian coast, with houses cascading down to a port on a narrow inlet. The main activities in town are watching the fishing boats unload (3pm to 8pm), then sampling fish and crustaceans at local *sidrerías* (cider bars) and restaurants. The coastline is a dramatic sequence of sheer cliffs and fine beaches, with Playa del Silencio (15km west) outstanding for its beauty: a long, silver-sand cove backed by a natural rock amphitheatre. It isn't great for swimming due to underwater rocks, but it's a stunning spot for a stroll and some sunbathing. To find it, take exit 441 off the A8, then head 2.5km west on the N632 to Castañeras, where the beach is signposted. The last 500m is on foot.

THE DRIVE

Leave Cudillero westward by the CU1 to join the A8 westbound. Exit at junction 474 to drive the last 4km down to Puerto de Vega (49km, 40 minutes).

11 PUERTO DE VEGA

Puerto de Vega, 15km west of bigger Luarca, is a lovely fishing village with a colourful harbour and several inviting seafood-focused restaurants. It's also the starting point for scenic walks along the **Senda Costa Naviega** coastal footpath to two beautiful, undeveloped, sandy beaches. **Playa de Barayo**, 5km east of town, stretches along a pretty bay with a river winding through wetlands and dunes. **Playa de Frejulfe**, 4km west (2.5km if you drive), stretches 750m along the ocean shore in front of thick eucalyptus woods. Surfers might catch a wave here in spring or late summer. The pick of the eateries is **Mesón El Centro** (*facebook.com/Meson-El-Centro-303872116336839*), on a tiny plaza just up from the port, preparing good fresh seafood with a touch of flair and without scrimping on the portions.

THE DRIVE

Return to the A8 and head west. Just after crossing the bridge high above the Ría de Ribadeo, exit at junction 506 for the final 2km into Ribadeo town (40km, about 40 minutes).

12 RIBADEO

This lively port town on the Ría de Ribadeo – a sunseeker magnet in summer – is your introduction to Galicia, Spain's northwestern region. The Old Town between the central Plaza de España and the harbour is an attractive mix of handsome old galleried and stone houses. **Praia As Catedrais** (*ascatedrais.gal*), 10km west, is perhaps the north's most spectacular beach and a perfect place to finish your drive. This 1.5km sandy stretch is strung with awesome Gothic-looking rock towers, arches and chambers. Such is As Catedrais' popularity that during Easter week, July, August, September and some holiday weekends, permits (free from *ascatedrais.xunta.gal*) are required to go onto the beach. Avoid the hour or two either side of high tide when the beach is under water.

PRE-ROMANESQUE OVIEDO

Largely cut off from the rest of Christian Europe by the Muslim invasion of 711 CE, the tough and tiny kingdom that emerged in 8th-century Asturias engendered a unique style of art and architecture known as pre-Romanesque. The buildings, taking some inspiration from Roman and Visigothic styles, are typified by straight-line profiles, semicircular arches, and a triple-naved plan for churches.

Of the surviving buildings of the genre, several of the best are found in and near Oviedo. The **Iglesia de San Julián de los Prados**, 1km northeast of the city centre, is the largest remaining pre-Romanesque church, constructed in the early 9th century under Alfonso II. Its interior is covered with wonderfully preserved, brightly coloured frescoes. On the slopes of Monte Naranco, 3.5km northwest of central Oviedo, the **Iglesia de San Miguel de Lillo** and the **Palacio de Santa María del Naranco** were built by Ramiro I (r 842–50 CE). The beautifully proportioned Santa María was probably a royal hunting lodge. Of San Miguel, only the western end remains (the rest collapsed centuries ago), but what's left has a singularly pleasing form. Visits inside all three of these buildings are by guided tour, in Spanish only.

A short walk below Santa María, the **Centro de Interpretación del Prerrománico** (*prerromanicoasturiano.es*) has informative displays on the pre-Romanesque phenomenon.

Iglesia de San Miguel de Lillo

13

NORTHERN SPAIN & THE BASQUE COUNTRY

Coast of Galicia

DURATION	DISTANCE	GREAT FOR
5-7 days	654km / 406 miles	Nature, wine

BEST TIME TO GO	June to September for beach weather (normally!), and November to February for wild storms.

Rocky headlands, winding inlets, small fishing towns, narrow coves, wide sweeping bays and many a sandy beach – this is the beautiful coastline of Galicia and it's a world away from the clichéd images of Spain. Relatively heavily populated in the south (known as the Rías Baixas – Lower Rías), the coast becomes wilder as you work your way north to the Rías Altas (Upper Rías).

Link your trip

07 Northern Spain Pilgrimage

The beaches and cliffs of Galicia's coast are the perfect follow-up to the inland trip along the Camino de Santiago.

30 The Minho's Lyrical Landscapes

The Atlantic beaches, historic cities and verdant landscapes of northern Portugal have a lot in common with Galicia, but also fascinating contrasts.

01 A GUARDA

A fishing port just north of where the Río Miño spills into the Atlantic, A Guarda (Castilian: La Guardia) has a pretty harbour and good seafood restaurants, but its unique draw is the beautiful **Monte de Santa Trega**, whose summit is a 4km drive or 2km uphill walk (the PRG122) from town. On the way up, poke around the partly restored **Castro de Santa Trega** (*castros* were the fortified settlements of circular stone huts inhabited by Galicians' Celtic ancestors). At the top, you'll find a 16th-century chapel, an interesting small **archaeological museum**, a couple of cafes – and truly majestic panoramas up the

TRABANTOS/SHUTTERSTOCK ©

Castro de Santa Trega

BEST FOR GHOSTS

The shipwreck-haunted Costa da Morte (Coast of Death).

Miño, across to Portugal and out over the Atlantic.

THE DRIVE
Follow the PO552 north along its fairly straight coastal route to Baiona (30km, 35 minutes). Enjoy not fighting the steering wheel much – this is almost the last straight stretch of road you're going to encounter!

02 BAIONA

Baiona (Castilian: Bayona) is a popular resort with an inviting *casco histórico* (historic centre) of tangled lanes, and its own little place in history: the shining moment came on 1 March 1493, when one of Columbus' small fleet, the *Pinta*, stopped in for supplies, bearing the remarkable news that the explorer had made it to the (West) Indies. You can't miss the pine-covered promontory **Monte Boi**, dominated by the **Fortaleza de Monterreal**. This fortress is protected by a 3km circle of walls, and an enjoyable 40-minute walking trail loops round the rocky shoreline, which is broken up by small beaches.

THE DRIVE
It's 25km (45 minutes) along the PO552 to Vigo. It's best to use one of the several signposted underground car parks around the centre.

03 VIGO

Vigo is both a historic city and a gritty industrial port that's home to Europe's largest fishing fleet. Its central areas make for good strolling, and it's the main departure point for summer ferries (45 minutes one-way) to the beautiful **Illas Cíes**, the three islands in the mouth of the Ría de Vigo that are home to some of Galicia's most splendid beaches. Vigo's citizens really know how to enjoy life, especially after dark in the many buzzing tapas bars, restaurants and clubs. The Casco Vello (Old Town) climbs uphill from the cruise-ship port; at the heart of its jumbled lanes is elegant **Praza da Constitución**, a perfect spot for a drink. To the east spreads the heart of the modern city, with the parklike **Praza de Compostela** a welcome green space in its midst.

GALICIA SEAFOOD TIPS

Galicia's ocean-fresh seafood, from pulpo á feira (tender, spicy octopus slices) to melt-in-the-mouth lubiña (sea bass), is a reason in itself to come here. In any coastal town or village (and many inland) you can get a meal to remember. Tuck into any of these and you'll never want to eat red meat again.

Pulpo á feira is Galicia's signature dish (known as *pulpo a la gallega* elsewhere in Spain): tender slices of octopus tentacle sprinkled with olive oil and paprika. It's even better when accompanied by *cachelos* (sliced boiled potatoes).

Percebes (goose barnacles) is Galicia's favourite shellfish delicacy, pulled off coastal rocks at low tide (a sometimes dangerous pursuit) and looking like miniature dragon claws. To eat them you hold the 'claw' end, twist off the other end and eat the soft, succulent bit inside.

Shellfish fans will also delight in **ameixas** (clams), **mexillons** (mussels), **vieiras** (scallops), **zamburiñas** (small scallops), **berberechos** (cockles) and **navajas** (razor clams). These will be on the menu in every coastal town.

Other delicacies include **bogavantes** or **lubrigantes**, types of mini-lobster with two outsized claws, and various crabs, from little **nécoras** and **santiaguiños** to huge **centollos** (spider crabs) and the enormous **buey del mar** (ox of the sea).

Shellfish in restaurants is often priced by weight: around 250g per person usually makes a fairly large serving. Simple steaming or hotplate-grilling (*a la plancha*) is almost always the best way to prepare shellfish, maybe with a dash of olive oil, garlic and herbs to enhance the natural flavour.

THE DRIVE
Head east out of central Vigo past Guixar train station, following A9 (or AP9) Pontevedra signs. From the far end of the Puente de Rande bridge (spanning the Ría de Vigo), follow the AG46, CG4.1 and VG4.6 westward. Where the VG4.6 ends at a roundabout, go left. Just after Aldán village, turn right along the narrow EP1008 for 1km to Hío – 33km (40 minutes) from Vigo.

04 HÍO

Little Hío village is home to Galicia's most famous *cruceiro* (carved wayside cross, a traditional Galician art form). The **Cruceiro de Hío**, standing outside the Romanesque San Andrés de Hío church, was sculpted in the 1870s by Ignacio Cerviño. Its delicate, detailed carvings narrate key passages of Christian teachings, from Adam and Eve to the taking down of Christ from the cross.

THE DRIVE
Take the winding EP1006 from Hío through woodlands and Donón village (following occasional signs to Cabo de Home or Facho) until ocean views open out before you, with a couple of cafes on the right. You can park nearby (5km, 10 minutes).

05 CABO DE HOME

Windswept Cabo de Home is a rocky cape with walking trails, three lighthouses and great views of the offshore Illas Cíes. It's an excellent area to spend a few hours exploring. The partly excavated Iron Age *castro* **Berobriga** sits atop panoramic Monte Facho nearby. There are some beautiful beaches in the area as well (some nudist).

THE DRIVE
It's 36km (45 minutes) along the south side of the Ría de Vigo from Cabo de Home to appealing Pontevedra. Return to Aldán, then follow the PO551, VG4.4 and PO12. There's a convenient car park underneath the Mercado Municipal on the northern edge of Pontevedra's Old Town, and plenty of free open-air parking just across the river there.

06 PONTEVEDRA

Back in the 16th century, Pontevedra was Galicia's biggest city. Columbus' flagship, the *Santa María*, may have been built here. Today this is an inviting, small, riverside city that combines history, culture and style into a lively overnight stop. It's a pleasure to wander the narrow, traffic-free streets and the dozen or so small plazas of the Old Town, abuzz with shops, markets, cafes, taverns and tapas bars. The eclectic **Museo de Pontevedra** (*museo.depo.gal*) is scattered over six city-centre buildings. The **Edificio Sarmiento**, in a renovated 18th-century Jesuit college, houses a particularly absorbing collection encompassing Galician Sargadelos ceramics, modern art, prehistoric gold jewellery and much more. The adjoining **Sexto Edificio** has three floors of Galician and Spanish art from the 14th to 20th centuries.

THE DRIVE
Head north on the AP9 then west on the AG41 and VG2 to Cambados (28km, 30 minutes).

07 CAMBADOS

The capital of **albariño wine country**, the pretty little *ría*-side town of Cambados is a delightful stop. Its old streets are lined by stone architecture and dotted with inviting taverns and eateries. Cambados' **tourist office** (*cambados.es*) has details on all visitable wineries. The best-known ones are in the countryside, including the innovative **Mar de Frades** (*mardefrades.es*), 9km east (book visits via the website or by phone). Don't miss **Gil Armada** (*bodegagilarmada.com*) in the town: the handsome 17th-century Pazo de Fefiñáns mansion in which it's housed steals the show here. Pay a visit to the ruined 15th-century church, the **Igrexa de Santa Mariña Dozo**, now roofless but still with its four roof arches intact. It's surrounded by a well-kept cemetery – particularly atmospheric after dark! The five-minute walk up to the **Mirador de A Pastora**, behind, is well worth it for expansive views over the Ría de Arousa.

THE DRIVE
It's a longish hop to Muros, so it makes sense to take the easiest route. Head east from Cambados to join the AP9 motorway northbound. Exit at junction 93 on to the AG11, then almost immediately turn north on the AC301. This brings you to the CG1.5. Follow this then the AC554 and AC550 to Muros (95km, about 1½ hours from Cambados).

08 MUROS

The small fishing port of Muros is an agreeable halt en route to the Costa da Morte. Behind the bustling seafront extends a web of stone-paved lanes dotted with taverns and lined with dignified stone houses. The medieval **Igrexa de San Pedro** is a fine example of a Galician 'maritime Gothic' church, typified by a single very wide nave.

THE DRIVE
As you leave Muros, the real excitement of this drive begins (can you believe that everything so far was a mere taster?) as you start along the famed Costa da Morte. It's so named because of the number of shipwrecks it has claimed. To get to Carnota follow the AC550 round the coast (17km, 20 minutes).

09 CARNOTA

Carnota village is renowned as home to Galicia's largest *hórreo* (traditional grain store on stilts) – 34.5m long and constructed in an 18th-century *hórreo*-building contest with nearby Lira. However, many people come here not for the grain store but for the spectacular, if exposed, 7km curve of nearby **Praia de Carnota**. The more protected sections are at its south end, signposted (all with separate names) from Lira.

THE DRIVE
Driving to the end of the world has never been so easy. Just follow the AC550 and AC445 to Fisterra (37km, 45 minutes), enjoying some great views over the Ría de Corcubión as you go.

10 FISTERRA

Cabo Fisterra is the western edge of Spain, at least in popular imagination. The real westernmost point is Cabo Touriñán, 20km north, but that doesn't stop throngs of people from heading out to this beautiful, windswept cape, which is also the end point of an 86km extension of the Camino de Santiago. It's crowned by a lighthouse, the Faro de Fisterra. The cape is a 3.5km drive past the town of Fisterra. On the edge of town you pass the 12th-century **Igrexa de Santa María das Areas**. Some 600m past the church, a track signed 'Conxunto de San Guillermo' heads up the hill to the right, Monte Facho. This provides a longer but even more scenic alternative walking route to the cape on which you can visit the mysterious **Ermida de San Guillerme** – a ruined medieval chapel and rock shelter, possibly the location of a legendary pre-Christian *ara solis* (altar of the sun). Fisterra itself is a fishing port with a picturesque harbour. **Praia da Mar de Fora**, over on the ocean side of the promontory, is spectacular but not safe for swimming. For calmer waters, head to sandy, 2km-long **Praia de Langosteira** north of town.

THE DRIVE
Fisterra to Lires is an easy 12km drive. Head north on the AC445 and turn left after 2.5km (500m after Hotel

TOP TIP:

Bring Your Umbrella

Swept by one rainy Atlantic front after another, Galicia has, overall, twice as much rain as the Spanish national average. Galicians have more than 100 words to describe different kinds of rain, from *babuxa* (a variety of drizzle) to *xistra* (a type of shower) and *treboada* (a thunderstorm).

Playa de Langosteira). The rest of the way is along minor country roads, with some glimpses of Praia do Rostro.

11 LIRES

Pretty Lires village sits just inland from the coast, above the little Ría de Lires, amid typically green, wooded Costa da Morte countryside. It's a popular stop for walkers on both the Camino de Santiago and the coastal Camiño dos Faros trail, but with wonderful beaches nearby, it's a fine stop even if you're not following any *camino*. The beautiful, 1.5km sandy curve of **Praia de Nemiña**, stretching north from the mouth of the Ría de Lires, attracts surfers in numbers from roughly April to November. The *ría* mouth can be crossed from Lires at low tide in summer, but otherwise it's a 2.5km walk (or a roundabout drive of 9km) from village to beach. **Praia do Rostro** is a broad 2km stretch of unbroken sand beginning about 4km south of Lires. It's a particularly magnificent sight from the headlands at either end, with the Atlantic surf pouring in. Unfortunately it's not good for swimming, but it's a wonderful walk.

Photo opportunity

Cabo Fisterra – the end of the world.

THE DRIVE
Take the long route to Muxía via scenic Cabo Touriñán, mainland Spain's most westerly point, great for a breezy walk. Follow Touriñán signs off the CP2301 3km east of Lires, and head northwest to the cape through woodlands and Frixe and Touriñán villages. Afterwards, return 5km the way you came, then turn north along the DP5201 for 12km to Muxía. Total distance: 31km (45 minutes' driving).

12 MUXÍA

Muxía is a photogenic little fishing port with a handful of cosy bars and restaurants, and, like Cabo Fisterra, a popular onward destination for pilgrims from Santiago de Compostela. The **Santuario da Virxe da Barca** on the rocky seashore marks the spot where (legend attests) the Virgin Mary arrived in a stone boat and appeared to Santiago (St James) while he was preaching here. Two of the rocks strewn on the foreshore, the **Pedra dos Cadris** and **Pedra d'Abalar**, are, supposedly, the boat's sail and keel. Crawling under the former nine times is said, improbably, to be good for back problems.

THE DRIVE
Camariñas is just 4km northeast of Muxía across the Ría de Camariñas, but 25km (40 minutes) by road. Fortunately it's a pretty drive, via the inviting beach Praia do Lago, the *hórreo*-studded hamlet Leis and the riverside villages of Cereixo and Ponte do Porto.

13 CAMARIÑAS

Wrapped around its colourful fishing harbour, Camariñas is the starting point for the scenic Ruta Litoral drive.

THE DRIVE
The Ruta Litoral to Camelle is one of the most beautiful stretches of the Costa da Morte, but if you don't like the sound of its unpaved sections you can head inland from Camariñas along the AC432, then turn left on to the DP1601 as you leave Ponte do Porto. It's 15km (20 minutes) this way.

14 CAMELLE

Camelle has no outstanding charm, but it does have two touching mementos of 'Man' (Manfred Gnädinger), a long-time German resident who died in 2002, only weeks after the *Prestige* oil tanker went down just offshore. The resulting oil slick devastated this fragile coastline and, some people say, caused Man to die of a broken heart. His hut and quirky sculpture garden made from rocks and ocean bric-a-brac, beside the pier, are now labelled

RUTA LITORAL DRIVE

It takes longer than the inland road but don't miss the scenic coastal route (part paved, part dirt/gravel) from Camariñas to Camelle. You start by going 5km northwest to **Cabo Vilán lighthouse** (with a cafe and an exhibition on shipwrecks and lighthouses), then head east to Camelle, a further 19km. The route winds past secluded beaches, across windswept hillsides and past weathered rock formations, and there are several places to stop along the way. **Praias da Pedrosa, da Balea** and **da Reira** are a picturesque set of short sandy strands a couple of kilometres past Cabo Vilán; then there's the **Ceminterio dos Ingleses** (English Cemetery), the sad burial ground from an 1890 shipwreck that took the lives of 172 British naval cadets. Signposting after the cemetery is poor: go left at forks after 2km and 3km, straight on at the junction after 5.7km, and left at the fork after 8.5km. This takes you into Camelle through pretty Arou village.

the **Museo Xardín de Man** (view from outside only); the **Museo Man de Camelle** (*mandecamelle.com*), back along the waterfront, exhibits some of his sketchbooks, notebooks and objets trouvés. **Praia de Traba**, a little-frequented 2.5km stretch of sand with dunes and a lagoon, is a lovely 4km walk east along the coast.

THE DRIVE
Head inland on the DP1601 and AC432 to Vimianzo, then east along the AC552 and the quick AG55 to A Coruña (85km, 1¼ hours).

15 A CORUÑA

A Coruña (Castilian: La Coruña) is a port city, beachy hot spot and cruise-ship stop; a busy commercial centre and a cultural enclave; a historic city and a modern metropolis. The Ciudad Vieja (Old City) has shady plazas, charming old churches, hilly cobbled lanes and a good smattering of cafes and bars. The Unesco-listed **Torre de Hércules** (*torredeherculesacoruna.com*) sits near the windy northern tip of the city. It was actually the Romans who originally built this lighthouse in the 1st century CE – a beacon on what was then the furthest edge of the 'civilised' world. Kids love the seal colony and the underwater Nautilus room (surrounded by sharks and 50 other fish species) at the excellent **Aquarium Finisterrae** (*coruna.gal/mc2/es/aquarium-finisterrae*) on the city's northern headland. There's a great tapas scene along the streets west of the central Plaza de María Pita – Calles de la Franja, Barrera, Galera, Olmos and Estrella. Moving westward along these lanes the vibe mutates from old-style *mesones* (taverns) to contemporary tapas bars.

THE DRIVE
The straight, yes straight, drive to Betanzos takes just 20 minutes if you're lucky with the traffic. Take the AP9 motorway then the A6, exiting at junction 567.

16 BETANZOS

Once a thriving estuary port rivalling A Coruña, Betanzos is renowned for its welcoming taverns and a well-preserved medieval Old Town that harmoniously combines galleried houses, old-fashioned shops and some monumental architecture. Take Rúa Castro up into the oldest part of town. Handsome **Praza da Constitución** is flanked by a

Torre de Hércules

couple of appealing cafes along with the Romanesque/Gothic **Igrexa de Santiago**. A short stroll northeast, two beautiful Gothic churches, **Santa María do Azougue** and **San Francisco**, stand almost side by side. The latter is full of particularly fine stone carving, including many sepulchres of 14th- and 15th-century Galician nobility.

THE DRIVE
Take the N651 north from Betanzos and join the AP9 motorway after Pontedeume. The AP9 takes you across the Ría de Ferrol; now navigation becomes tricky due to poor signage. Turn north at junction 34F, 2km after the bridge, then go right at a roundabout after 6km, then left at another roundabout after 1.5km. You're now on the AC566, which leads all the way to Cedeira (65km, one hour from Betanzos).

17 CEDEIRA

The fishing port and very low-key resort of Cedeira has a cute little old town sitting on the west bank of the Río Condomiñas, while **Praia da Magdalena** fronts the modern, eastern side of town. Around the headland to the south (a 7km drive) is the wilder **Praia de Vilarrube**, a long, sandy beach with shallow waters between two river mouths, in a protected area of dunes and wetlands. For a nice stroll of an hour or two, walk along the waterfront to the fishing port, climb up to the 18th-century **Castelo da Concepción** above it, and walk out to Punta Sarridal, overlooking the mouth of the Ría de Cedeira.

Weather permitting, you can take a scenic boat trip north past the spectacular Herbeira cliffs and Cabo Ortegal as far as Cariño and back (per person €30, 1¾ hours, adults only) with **Rutas Cedeira** (*facebook.com/rutascedeira*). The ride can be bumpy. A minimum six people are required.

THE DRIVE
This 28km drive is the most spectacular of the whole trip. Heading northeast from Cedeira, take the DP2204 then the DP2205. The road crosses the Serra da Capelada and has incredible views. The Garita de Herbeira lookout, after 4km, is 615m above sea level and the best place to be wowed over southern Europe's highest sea cliffs. Continue to Cariño then north to Cabo Ortegal.

18 CABO ORTEGAL

The Atlantic Ocean meets the Bay of Biscay at the mother of all Spanish capes, Cabo Ortegal, where great stone shafts drop sheer into the ocean from such a height that the waves crashing on the rocks below seem pitifully benign.

DETOUR:

Best Bank of the World

START: 18 CABO ORTEGAL

At Km 63.1 of the AC682, 20km east of Ponte Mera, turn north (signed to Praia do Picón) and go 3km north along narrow country lanes to Picón village, set above a cliff-foot beach. One kilometre west along the clifftops stands the bench that has acquired celebrity status under the English name 'Best Bank of the World' (thanks to a confusion about the Spanish word *banco*, meaning both bench and bank). It affords magnificent panoramas along the jagged coast all the way from Cabo Ortegal to the Punta da Estaca de Bares. From here return to the AC682 and continue towards the Estaca de Bares.

THE DRIVE
Head south to Ponte Mera and turn east along the AC682. At O Barqueiro, after 25km, head north on the AC100. After Vila de Bares (Vares), follow signs to the Faro and/or Estaca de Bares. Park just before the lighthouse and follow the trail to the tip of the peninsula, the Punta da Estaca de Bares (47km, one hour, from Cabo Ortegal).

19 ESTACA DE BARES

The Bares Peninsula is a marvellously scenic spur of land jutting north into the Bay of Biscay, with walking trails, beaches, cliffs and a few delightfully low-key spots to stay over. From the lighthouse near the tip of the peninsula, a 400m path follows the spine of a rock outcrop to the Punta da Estaca de Bares, Spain's most northerly point, a satisfying place to complete your drive, with awe-inspiring cliffs and fabulous panoramas.

Cabo Ortegale

FRANCE
SPAIN
ANDORRA
ANDORRA LA VELLA
Bilbao
San Sebastián
Biarritz
Irún
Bayonne
Aire-sur-l'Adour
Auch
Toulouse
Castres
Mazamet
Béziers
St-Palais
Pau
Tarbes
St-Jean Pied de Port
Montréjeau
Carcassonne
Colombiers
Golfe du Lion
Soraluze
Vitoria
Burguete
Pamplona
Estella
Logroño
Yesa
Sos del Rey Católico
Calahorra
Tudela
Hecho (Echo)
Parque Nacional de Ordesa y Monte Perdido
Jaca
Ayerbe
Huesca
Alquézar
Barbastro
Benabarre
Vielha
Sort
Tremp
Foix
Ax-les-Thermes
Perpignan
Adrall
Ripoll
Figueres
Cadaqués
Olot
Girona
Vic
Cardona
Manresa
Sant Celoni
Palamós
Tossa de Mar
Barcelona
Igualada
Lleida
Soria
Zaragoza
Sariñena
Bujaraloz
Paracuellos de Jiloca
Azaila
Río Ebro
Medinaceli
Daroca
Alcañiz
Móra la Nova
Reus
Tarragona
Cambrils
Vilanova i la Geltrú
Molina de Aragón
Caminreal
Alcorisa
Utrillas
Tortosa
Sant Carles de la Ràpita
Balearic Sea
Albarracín
Teruel
Mora de Rubielos
Peníscola
Cuenca
Benicàssim
Castellón de la Plana
Río Júcar
Sagunto
Valencia
Aldaya
Golfo de Valencia
Alginet
Sueca
Munera
Albacete
Xàtiva
Gandia
Almansa
Ontinyent
Dénia
Villena
Alcoy
Calpe (Calp)
Ibi
Benidorm
Elda
Novelda
Alicante
Elche
Parque Natural Sierras de Cazorla, Segura y las Villas
Hellín
Río Segura
Cieza
Puebla de Don Fadrique
Alhama de Murcia
Murcia
Torrevieja
San Pedro del Pinatar
Los Alcázares
Cartagena
Huéscar
Lorca
Puerto Lumbreras
Cúllar
Huércal-Overa
Águilas
Mojácar
Inca
Artà
Mallorca
Palma de Mallorca
Manacor
Ibiza
Ibiza Town
Formentera
Mediterranean Sea
A15
A1
N135
AP15
N240
N260
N111
AP68
A23
N240
AP2
A2
N211
A2
N211
A23
N420
N420
AP7
A3
N420
A23
A3
AP36
N330
A31
A31
A7
A30
AP7
A7
AP7
A7
AP7
14
15
16
17
18
19
0 100 km
0 50 miles

LOUIELEA/SHUTTERSTOCK ©

Basílica de Nuestra Señora del Pilar (p136), Zaragoza

Barcelona & Eastern Spain

Explore

Barcelona & Eastern Spain

There are times when Catalonia and the surrounding areas feel like worlds unto themselves, with a strong cultural identity and an iconic mix of Mediterranean coast and Pyrenean highlands. This is a region of fabulous cities – Barcelona, Girona, Valencia and even Donostia-San Sebastián over in the Basque Country on the Bay of Biscay. The landscapes here are just as appealing, from high mountain valleys to storied beaches and hidden forested coves. And the entire region is a culinary superstar – travelling here means sampling one divine local speciality after another, which will add a whole new dimension to your trip.

Barcelona

Welcome to one of the world's coolest cities. Barcelona has so many things going for it, from the zany architecture of Antoni Gaudí to the fabulous food of restaurants, tapas bars and the Mercat de la Boquería to a string of Mediterranean beaches. But the city also has that intangible something – a joic de vivre, a feeling on the streets that this is the way that life should be lived. Dive right in and you'll very quickly fall in love.

Girona

Girona is a glorious bastion of Catalan culture, a provincial city with a fascinating history and superb medieval architecture. It's also known for its culture of culinary excellence, as well as being a much more manageable size than Barcelona or Madrid. It's an easy city to get around on foot, and is perfectly placed for exploring one of Catalonia's most intriguing corners.

Valencia

Gorgeous Valencia with its clutch of first-rate beaches is the kind of place where you'll end up envying those who live here. The city is also the true home of paella – lining up along the beachfront (and elsewhere) are restaurants serving nothing but Spain's most famous rice dish, cooked to perfection. Its City of Arts and Sciences is a daringly designed complex, at once an icon of contemporary architecture and a fascinating collection of attractions. Near-perfect

WHEN TO GO

Summer offers perfect beach weather and the best conditions for hiking in the Pyrenees. However, anywhere along the coast, especially Barcelona, can get very crowded; June or September may be better choices. Winters are generally mild along the coast, but snowfalls are common in the Pyrenees – good for the region's ski resorts, less so for mountain driving.

weather and a stunning old quarter, the Barrio del Carmen, round out a wonderful experience.

Cartagena

Sitting pretty where the province of Murcia meets the Med, Cartagena is an appealing small city with an attractive waterfront and a slew of Roman and pre-Roman ruins scattered around the town – the place was named after the ancient Phoenician capital of Carthage. Cartagena's traffic-free centre makes it an eminently walkable place to explore, and you can enjoy its fresh seafood while overlooking the water.

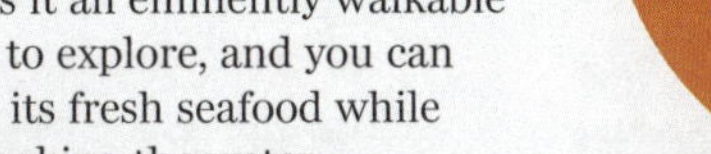

Zaragoza

The capital of Aragón, a modern region that arose from some of Spain's most powerful ancient kingdoms, Zaragoza has a little bit of everything. Start with the Roman ruins, visit La Aljafería (one of Spain's finest examples of Islamic architecture outside Andalucía) and watch in awe the fervour with which Catholic pilgrims travel to and from the city's cathedral. And when that's all done, go on a tapas crawl and dance the night away in the historic centre of town.

TRANSPORT

Excellent rail and road networks connect towns in northeastern Spain. Roads hug the coast and also fan out across the coastal hinterland. Where trains don't go, local buses take up the slack. Wherever there are mountains, such as anywhere near the Pyrenees, the going will be much slower and public transport less frequent.

WHAT'S ON

Carnaval

Riotously fun, Carnaval involves fancy-dress parades and festivities that end 47 days before Easter Sunday. It's wildest in Sitges.

Las Fallas de San José

Held in March, this festival involves all-night dancing and drinking, first-class fireworks and the ritual burning of effigies in the streets, most famously in Valencia.

La Tomatina

Buñol's massive tomato-throwing festival, held in late August, takes place near Valencia.

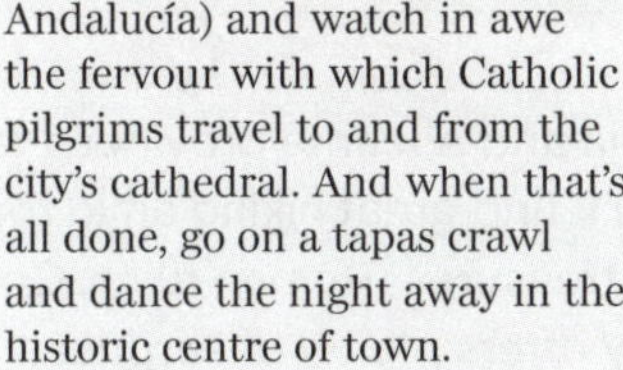

WHERE TO STAY

There's no shortage of accommodation anywhere in this region. Barcelona is one of the most visited cities in Europe (this is especially apparent on weekends and in summer), and the Catalan coast all the way down past Cartagena is replete with hugely popular tourist destinations that fill with holidaymakers whenever the weather is warm. Book well in advance, or plan your visit for spring or autumn. If you arrive in Barcelona without a reservation – what were you thinking? – head for the tourist office to see what's possible. Ski resorts in the Pyrenees get busy in winter.

Resources

Barcelona (*barcelonaturisme.com*) Get ready to explore this wonderful city.

Salvador Dalí (*salvador-dali.org*) Get a primer on Dalí's life and work and how to see some of it while you're in Catalonia.

Catalonia (*catalunya.com*) Discover the magic of northeastern Spain in all its online glory.

14

BARCELONA & EASTERN SPAIN

Unsung Wonders of Murcia & Alicante

DURATION	DISTANCE	GREAT FOR
2-4 days	402km / 241 miles	Nature, history

BEST TIME TO GO	From March to June or September to November to escape the heat and crowds.

This winding route through Murcia and Alicante provinces takes you to some of the unsung wonders of southeast Spain. You'll find great hiking amid rocky forests, striking coastal scenery and a trove of historical treasures (Roman ruins, Gothic cathedrals and Modernista architecture). This 402km journey offers plenty of surprises, from strolling among ancient groves of date palms to swimming in untouched coves in the Mediterranean.

Link your trip

19 Barcelona to Valencia

From Villena, take the A7 90km north to Valencia, to hook up with this memorable route between two great cities.

20 Mediterranean Meander

For a longer drive, join up with this trip at Cartagena, and take in the splendour of coastal Spain.

01 MURCIA

Bypassed by most tourists and treated as a country cousin by many Spaniards, this laid-back provincial capital nevertheless more than merits a visit. Murcia's most striking site is the **Real Casino de Murcia** (*realcasinomurcia.com*), which first opened as a gentlemen's club in 1847. Painstakingly restored to its original glory, the building is a fabulous combination of historical design and opulence. A few blocks south, the **Catedral de Santa María** (*catedral murcia.com*) was built in 1394 on the site of a mosque. It has a stunning facade facing onto Plaza Belluga. North of the centre, the **Museo Arqueológico**

TRABANTOS/SHUTTERSTOCK ©

Real Casino de Murcia

BEST FOR WILDLIFE

Spotting birds in the lagoons of the Salinas de San Pedro.

(*museosregiondemurcia.es*) has exceptionally well-laid-out and well-documented exhibits spread over two floors, focusing mostly on prehistory. The trendy cafe with pleasant outdoor seating is a popular spot.

THE DRIVE
It's a short and easy 37km drive west along the toll-free A7 from Murcia to Alhama de Murcia, gateway to the national park.

02 PARQUE NATURAL DE SIERRA ESPUÑA

The Sierra Espuña is an island of pine forest and limestone formations rising high above an ocean of heat and dust down below. The natural park that protects this fragile and beautiful environment has more than 250 sq km of unspoilt highlands covered with trails and is popular with walkers and climbers. Access to the park is best via Alhama de Murcia. The informative Ricardo Codorniu Visitors Centre is located in the heart of the park. A few walking trails leave from here, and it can provide good maps for picturesque hikes.

THE DRIVE
It's a straight shot (30 minutes or so) along the A7 from Alhama de Murcia to Lorca, 36km to the southwest.

03 LORCA

The market town of Lorca has long been known for its historic centre crowned by a 13th-century castle and for hosting one of Spain's most flamboyant Holy Week celebrations. Among the highlights is **Castillo de Lorca** (*lorcatallerdeltiempo.com*), the castle that looms high over Lorca. In the old town, take a stroll through the **Plaza de España**. It's surrounded by a group of baroque buildings, including the Pósito, a 16th-century former granary, and the golden limestone **Colegiata de San Patricio**. Peculiar to Lorca are various small museums exhibiting the magnificent Semana Santa costumes. The big two are the **Museo de Bordados del Paso Azul** (*museoazul.com*), which competes in splendour with the **Museo de Bordados del Paso Blanco** (*mubbla.org*).

THE DRIVE
The journey takes you from the southern slopes of the Sierra del Caño down to to the coast. It's a speedy 37km ride along the RM11 from Lorca to Águilas.

04 ÁGUILAS

This easy-going waterfront town is beautiful, and still shelters a small fishing fleet. Town beaches are divided from each other by a low headland topped by an 18th-century fortress. The real interest, though, are the Cuatro Calas a few kilometres south of town. These four coves are largely unmolested by tourist development (though they get very busy in summer) and have shimmering waters that merge into desert rock. Take RM33 to get there.

THE DRIVE
Take the Carretera de Lorca (RM11) 2.5km northward, then head east some 70km along the toll-road AP7. Take exit 815 towards Cartagena Oeste and continue onto RM332.

Photo opportunity

Limestone cliffs in Parque Natural de Sierra Espuña.

05 CARTAGENA

Inhabited for over 2000 years, Cartagena wears its history with pride. From ancient Roman ruins to Modernista architecture, the city has a dazzling array of eye candy, made all the more photogenic against its magnificent mountain-fringed harbour. Set alongside the Molinete hill, the **Barrio del Foro Romano** (*cartagenapuertodeculturas.com*) are the evocative remains of a whole town block and street linking the port with the forum, dating from the 1st century BCE.

THE DRIVE
From Paseo Alfonxo XIII, take the A30 towards Murcia. After 3km, take exit 190 onto CT32. Continue for 5km then take Autovía de La Manga/RM12 20km east. It's a 30-minute drive in total.

ADDING COLOUR TO SEMANA SANTA

In Lorca, locals tend to see things in blue and white – the colours of the two major brotherhoods that have competed every year since 1855 to see who can stage the most lavish Semana Santa display.

Lorca's Easter parades move to a different rhythm, distinct from the slow, sombre processions elsewhere in Murcia. While still deeply reverential, they're full of colour and vitality, mixing Old Testament tales with the Passion story.

If you hail from Lorca, you're passionately *Blanco* (White) or *Azul* (Blue). Each brotherhood has a statue of the Virgin (one draped in a blue mantle, the other in white, naturally), a banner and a spectacular museum. The result of this intense and mostly genial year-round rivalry is just about the most dramatic Semana Santa you'll see anywhere in Spain.

06 CABO DE PALOS

The Mar Menor is a 170-sq-km saltwater lagoon. Its waters are a good 5°C warmer than the open sea and excellent for water sports. Cabo de Palos, at the southern base of a narrow 22km peninsula, is delightful with a picturesque small harbour filled with pleasure boats. The waters around the tiny protected Islas Hormigas (Ant Islands) are great for scuba diving and the harbour is lined with dive shops.

THE DRIVE
Start off this 50km journey by retracing your route (heading west) along RM12. After 20km, take exit 1 onto AP7. After 25km take exit 774 toward San Pedro del Pinatar. Go straight through the roundabout as it leads you down to Lo Pagán.

07 LO PAGÁN

At the northern end of the lagoon, Lo Pagán is a mellow, low-rise resort with great water views, a long promenade, pleasant beach, and plenty of bars and restaurants. Get locals to show you where to walk out on jetties for natural mud treatments.

THE DRIVE
It's just 2.5km up to the salt pans. Take Carretera Quintín north and turn right on Avenida de las Salinas.

08 SALINAS DE SAN PEDRO

Just east of Lo Pagán lie the Salinas de San Pedro (San Pedro salt pans), where you can follow the well-signposted Sendero de El Coterillo. This relatively easy walk of just under 4km passes by a lagoon favoured by various bird species (including flamingos), dunes and a pristine beachfront.

THE DRIVE

Skip the high-speed AP7 and take the more scenic coastal route (60km in total). Head back to San Pedro del Pinatar and take the N332 north. You'll pass sea-fronting but overdeveloped beach towns such as Torrevieja on the way. A few kilometres after the Dunas de Guadamar (a fine beach for swimming), exit onto CV853 and follow signs north to Elche.

09 ELCHE

Thanks to Moorish irrigation, Elche (Valenciano: Elx) is an important fruit producer and also a Unesco World Heritage site twice over: for the Misteri d'Elx, its annual mystery play, and for its extensive palm groves, Europe's largest, planted by the Phoenicians. The palms, the mosque-like churches, and the historic buildings in desert-coloured stone give it a North African feel. Around 200,000 palm trees, each with a lifespan of some 250 years, make the heart of this busy industrial town a veritable oasis. A 2.5km walking trail leads from the **Museu del Palmerar** through the groves.

THE DRIVE

Take Calle San Fulgencio west and turn right onto CV8510. Merge onto AP7 and after 3.5km take A31 north towards Alicante. Take exit 185 towards Villena. The 55km drive takes about 45 minutes.

10 VILLENA

Villena, between Alicante and Albacete, is the most attractive of the towns along the corridor of the Val de Vinalopó. Plaza de Santiago is at the heart of its old quarter. Perched high above the town, the 12th-century Castillo de Atalaya (*turismovillena.com*) is splendidly lit at night.

Cartagena

15

BARCELONA & EASTERN SPAIN

Artistic Inspiration on the Costa Brava

DURATION	DISTANCE	GREAT FOR
2-4 days	160km / 99 miles	Nature, history, families

BEST TIME TO GO	May or September for beach weather with fewer crowds.

Just north of Barcelona, the Costa Brava has long captivated visitors with its beautiful bays, dramatic headlands and quaint, cobblestone villages just inland from the surf. Great views aside, there's much to do in this picturesque corner of Catalonia: you can visit ancient Roman ruins, clamber around medieval castles, go eye-to-eye with marbled rays off the Iles Mendes, and wander wide-eyed through fantastical Salvador Dalí creations.

Link your trip

16 Central Catalonia's Wineries & Monasteries

After ending in Figueres, travel 44km south to Girona to the start of this scenic drive around Catalonia's interior.

18 The Pyrenees

From Figueres it's just 25km west to Besalú, where you can drive the Pyrenees trip in reverse, travelling across the mountains to San Sebastián.

01 TOSSA DE MAR

Curving around a boat-speckled bay and guarded by a headland crowned with impressive defensive medieval walls and towers, Tossa de Mar is a picturesque village of crooked, narrow streets onto which tourism has tacked a larger, modern extension. The deep-ochre, fairy-tale walls and towers on the pine-dotted headland, **Mont Guardí**, at the end of the main beach, were built between the 12th and 14th centuries. The area they girdle is known as the Vila Vella – or Old Town – full of steep little cobbled streets and picturesque whitewashed houses, garlanded with flowers.

KAVALENKAVA/SHUTTERSTOCK ©

Tossa de Mar

BEST FOR FAMILIES

Playing in the sand on pretty Llafranc beach.

THE DRIVE
A snaking road hugs the ups and downs of the Costa Brava for the 23km from Tossa de Mar to Sant Feliu de Guíxols with – allegedly – a curve for each day of the year. From Tossa de Mar take Carretera Blanes a Sant Feliu and stick to the shoreline.

02 SANT FELIU DE GUÍXOLS

Sant Feliu has an attractive waterside promenade and a handful of curious leftovers from its long past, the most important being the so-called **Porta Ferrada** (Iron Gate): a wall and entrance, which is all that remains of a 10th-century monastery. The gate lends its name to an annual music festival held here every July since 1962. Just north along the coast is **S'Agaró**, with each of its Modernista houses designed by Gaudí disciple Rafael Masó. Leave your wheels behind and walk the shoreline Camí de Ronda to **Cala Sa Conca** – one of the most attractive beaches in the area.

THE DRIVE
Take the Carretera de Palamós (located just a few blocks north of the marina) east. After 1.5km take the Carretera Castelo d'Aro and follow this north onto C31. After 17km on C31, take exit 331. Continue through the historic village of Mont-Ras, skirting the southern edge of bigger Palafrugell. Then take Avinguda del Mar into Calella de Palafrugell. It takes about a half-hour to do the 28km drive.

03 CALELLA DE PALAFRUGELL

Halfway up the coast from Barcelona to the French border begins one of the most beautiful stretches of the Costa Brava. Start off in Calella, the southernmost of Palafrugell's crown jewels. The settlement is strung Aegean-style around a bay of rocky points and small, pretty beaches, with a few fishing boats still hauled up on the sand. The seafront is lined with year-round restaurants serving the fruits of the sea. Perched high above the sea, 2.5km from the centre, the verdant **Jardins de Cap Roig** (*fundacionlacaixa.org/ca/centros/jardines-de-cap-roig*) contain some 1000 floral species, set around an early-20th-century castle-palace. From mid-July to late August, the gardens host over two dozen open-air concerts, featuring big-name performers (tickets from €30).

THE DRIVE The next stop is barely 2km northeast of Calella. If you need to stretch your legs, you can also walk to Llafranc along coastal footpaths. Driving, take Avinguda Joan Pericot i García east. Go straight through the roundabout at Plaça Doctor Trueta, then veer to the right on Carrer de Lluís Marquès Carbó.

04 LLAFRANC

Llafranc has a smaller bay but a longer, handsome stretch of sand, cupped on either side by pine-dotted craggy coastline. Above the east side of town, the **Cap de Sant Sebastià** is a magical spot that offers fabulous views in both directions and out to sea. There's a lighthouse and an excellent restaurant here, as well as a defensive tower and chapel now incorporated into a hotel. You can also check out the ruins of a pre-Roman Iberian settlement with multilingual explanatory panels. It's a 40-minute walk up: follow the steps from the harbour and the road up to the right.

THE DRIVE From Llafranc, head north along Cami de la Font d'En Xecu towards Palafrugell and follow the signs to Tamariu. You'll pass through piney forest on the way. Again, if you'd prefer to walk, it's a magnificent (but hilly) 4km walk along the coast.

05 TAMARIU

Tamariu is a small, crescent-shaped cove redolent with the scent of pine. Its beach has some of the most translucent waters on Spain's Mediterranean coast. The gently sloping sands and shallow waters are a great place for small children to play.

THE DRIVE It's around 8km to Begur. Take narrow Carrer Aigublava north on a scenic forested uphill journey, then turn right on GIP6531 and follow this to Begur.

06 BEGUR

Attractive little Begur, with its quaint cobblestone lanes, is dotted with tempting restaurants and cafes, and topped by a 10th-century *castell* (castle) towering above the village. The sublime coastline around Begur, with its pocket-sized coves hemmed in by pine trees and subtropical flowers and lapped by azure water, is magical. There are some lovely **walking trails** around Begur, including to several attractive beaches and an 11.5km hike south to Tamariu (five hours) along GR92.

THE DRIVE Head west out of Begur along GI653. In Regencós, take C31, then a few kilometres north of the village of Pals, turn left onto GI651. Drive time to Peratallada is about 20 minutes.

WHY I LOVE THIS TRIP

Regis St Louis, writer

As a lifelong admirer of the strange and captivating works of Salvador Dalí, I've always felt a deep affinity for the wild coastal scenery around Cadaqués where Dalí spent his formative (and later) years. Yet the whole Costa Brava easily passes for artistic inspiration, with its serene bays, rugged headlands and golden beaches. This coastal drive is pure magic.

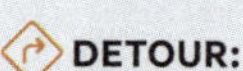

DETOUR:

Castell de Púbol

START: 07 PERATALLADA

Northwest of Peratallada, the **Castell de Púbol** (*salvador-dali.org*) forms the southernmost point of the 'Salvador Dalí triangle', other elements of which include the Teatre-Museu Dalí (p116) in Figueres and his home in Portlligat (p116). Having promised to make his wife, Gala, his muse and the love of his life, 'queen of the castle', in 1969 Dalí finally found the ideal residence to turn into Gala's refuge, since at the age of 76 she no longer desired Dalí's hectic lifestyle – a semi-dilapidated Gothic and Renaissance stronghold, which included a 14th-century church in the quiet village of Púbol.

The sombre castle, its stone walls covered with creepers, is almost the antithesis to the flamboyance of the Teatre-Museu Dalí or Dalí's seaside home: Gala had it decorated exactly as she wished and received only whom she wished. Legend has it that Dalí himself had to apply for written permission to visit her here.

The interior reflects her tastes, though Dalí touches creep in here and there. In the dining room is a replica of *Cua d'oreneta i violoncels* (Swallow's Tail and Cellos) – his last painting, completed here in 1983 during the two years of mourning following Gala's death.

The Castell is 2km from the village of La Pera, just south of the C66 and 15km northwest of Peratallada.

07 PERATALLADA

One of Catalonia's most gorgeous villages, Peratallada is blessed with beautifully preserved narrow lanes, heavy stone arches, a 12th-century Romanesque church and an 11th-century castle-mansion (now a luxury hotel and restaurant). It's a wonderfully characterful spot, particularly at night.

THE DRIVE
Get back on GI651 and retrace the drive to C31. But this time turn north onto C31 and continue for 6km. You'll cross the attractive medieval town of Torroella de Montgrí, then continue on Carretera de L'Estartit. At the roundabout continue straight, along GI641. The 18km drive takes about 25 minutes.

08 L'ESTARTIT

L'Estartit has a long, wide beach of fine sand but it's the diving that stands out. The protected **Illes Medes**, a spectacular group of rocky islets barely 1km offshore, are home to some of the most abundant marine life on Spain's Mediterranean coast. Eateries serving fresh seafood as well as standard Spanish fare are plentiful along the seafront.

THE DRIVE
Retrace the drive back through Torroella de Montgrí, then continue onto C31 northwest. After about 3km turn right onto GI632, which leads straight into town (depositing you at the town hall if you so wish). The 19km drive takes about 22 minutes.

09 L'ESCALA

Travel back millennia to the ancient Greco-Roman site of **Empúries** (*mac.cat*), set behind a near-virgin beach facing the Mediterranean. Its modern descendant, L'Escala, 11km north of Torroella de Montgrí, is a sunny and pleasant medium-sized resort on the often-windswept southern shore of the Golf de Roses. The Empúries is a picturesque two-part site that was an important Greek, and later Roman, trading port, though the site was originally used by Phoenicians. There are fine pieces – including mosaics – in the museum here, which gives good background information. Empúries is 2km northwest of the L'Escala town centre along the coast.

Castell de Púbol

THE DRIVE
Start this half-hour drive by taking Carretera Sant Martí d'Empúries to Sant Pere Pescador. After crossing a small river, look for GIV6216 leading north. From here, it's a straight shot 8km or so to Castelló d'Empúries.

10 CASTELLÓ D'EMPÚRIES

This well-preserved ancient town was once the capital of Empúries, a medieval Catalan county that maintained a large degree of independence up to the 14th century. Today it makes a superb base for birdwatching at the nearby **Parc Natural dels Aiguamolls de l'Empordà** (*gencat.cat/parcs/aiguamolls_emporda*), as well as a number of wind-blown but peaceful beaches. The park lies 4km to the northeast along Carretera Castelló d'Empúries. Away from the avian allure of the natural park, architectural beauty can be found in the town centre's 14th-century **Basílica de Santa Maria**. A short stroll southwest of there, the **Museu d'Historia Medieval de la Cúria-Presó** provides fascinating insight into Castelló's medieval history (with centuries-old graffiti in a few creepy prison cells).

Photo opportunity
The weird and wonderful Teatre-Museu Dalí in Figueres.

THE DRIVE
It's 23km to Cadaqués – a 30-minute trip, though you could take much longer, with stops to admire the panoramic views on this stunning drive. From Castelló d'Empúries, take Carrer Santa Clara to C260. Pass through La Garriga and get on curvy, narrow GI614, which will take you the rest of the way.

11 CADAQUÉS

A whitewashed village around a rocky bay, Cadaqués' narrow, hilly streets are perfect for wandering. The iconic town and its surrounding area have a special magic – a fusion of wind, sea, light and rock – that isn't dissipated even by the throngs of summer visitors. A portion of that magic owes itself to Salvador Dalí, who spent family holidays here during his youth, and lived much of his later life at Portlligat, 1km northeast of Cadaqués: there the **Casa Museu Dalí** (*salvador-dali.org*) is a mishmash of cottages and sunny terraces, linked by narrow labyrinthine corridors and an assortment of offbeat Dalí-esque flourishes. Access is by semi-guided eight-person tour; it's essential to book well ahead.

THE DRIVE
Backtrack to Castelló d'Empúries. Stay on C260 as it skirts the southern edge of town, and follow it all the way to Figueres. Total drive time is about 45 minutes for the 35km drive.

12 FIGUERES

Twelve kilometres inland, Figueres is a busy town with a French feel and an unmissable attraction: Salvador Dalí. The artist was born in Figueres in 1904 and although his career took him to Madrid, Barcelona, Paris and the USA, he remained true to his roots. In the 1960s and '70s, he created here the extraordinary **Teatre-Museu Dalí** (*salvador-dali.org*) – a monument to surrealism and a legacy that outshines any other Spanish artist, both in terms of popularity and sheer flamboyance. This red castle-like building, topped with giant eggs and studded with plaster-covered croissants, is an entirely appropriate final resting place for the master of surrealism. 'Theatre-museum' is an apt label for this trip through the incredibly fertile imagination of one of the great showmen of the 20th century. The inside is full of surprises, tricks and illusions, and contains a substantial portion of Dalí's life's work.

Teatre-Museu Dalí

THE COSTA BRAVA WAY

The 255km-long stretch of cliffs, coves, rocky promontories and pine groves that make up the signposted Costa Brava Way, stretching from Blanes to Colliure in France, unsurprisingly offers some of the best walks in Catalonia, ranging from gentle rambles to high-octane scrambles (or one long, demanding hike if you want to do the whole thing).

For the most part, the trail follows the established GR92, but also includes a number of coastal deviations. A choice route runs from Cadaqués to Cap de Creus Lighthouse (2½ hours each way). This relatively easy 7km walk from the centre of Cadaqués passes Portlligat before continuing along windswept, scrub-covered, rocky ground past several isolated beaches before it reaches the lighthouse – there's an appealing restaurant-cafe (Bar Restaurant Cap de Creus) next door.

16

BARCELONA & EASTERN SPAIN

Central Catalonia's Wineries & Monasteries

BEST FOR HISTORY

Strolling the medieval Jewish quarter in Girona.

DURATION	DISTANCE	GREAT FOR
2-4 days	380km / 236 miles	History, wine

BEST TIME TO GO	Any time, but March to November for warmer days.

Castell de Cardona

You'll experience many of Catalonia's lesser known charms on this memorable inland drive. The wonderful medieval town of Girona is crammed with historic sites, while a wander along Vic's cobblestone streets reveals countless architectural treasures. You'll find a photogenic castle in Cardona and atmospheric monasteries along the Cistercian route. The trip ends at the town of Vilafranca del Penedès, in the heart of magnificent wine country.

Link your trip

19 Barcelona to Valencia

After finishing this trip, head 56km west to Lleida for historic villages and outdoor adventures.

20 Mediterranean Meander

From the last monastery, drive 64km south on C14 to Tarragona for a highlight-filled drive along Spain's south coast.

01 GIRONA

Northern Catalonia's largest city, Girona is a tight huddle of ancient arcaded houses, grand churches and climbing cobbled streets. It's home to Catalonia's most extensive and best-preserved medieval Jewish quarter, all enclosed by defensive walls, with the lazy Río Onyar meandering along the edge of town. The excellent **Museu d'Història dels Jueus de Girona** (*girona.cat/call*) shows genuine pride in Girona's Jewish heritage. Nearby, the stunning 800-year-old **catedral** (*catedraldegirona.cat*) provides a window into medieval Christendom.

THE DRIVE

From Girona, it's about one hour (70km) to Vic. Take Carrer del Carme east out of town. At the roundabout (2.7km further), turn onto GIV6703. Merge onto the N11. Take exit 702 onto the C25. Follow this 50km through lush mountainous scenery, before taking exit 187 onto N141, which takes you into Vic.

02 VIC

Vic is one of Catalonia's gems. The enchanting old quarter is crammed with Roman remnants, medieval leftovers, a grand Gothic cloister, an excellent art museum and a glut of good-value restaurants. **Plaça Major**, the largest of Catalonia's central squares, is lined with medieval, baroque and Modernista mansions. It's still the site of the huge twice-weekly market (Tuesday and Saturday mornings). Around it swirl the narrow serpentine streets of medieval Vic, lined by mansions, churches, chapels, a Roman temple and a welcoming atmosphere. The **Museu Episcopal** (*museu episcopalvic.com*) holds a marvellous collection of Romanesque and Gothic art, including works by key figures like Lluís Borrassà and Jaume Huguet.

THE DRIVE

From Vic, take a northern, slightly longer, route to Cardona for stunning mountain scenery. Take C25 west from town. After about 6km, take exit 170 onto C651, then take C62. Around La Plana, take E9 north, then take the C26 southwest. Stay on this until the B420, and follow the signs to Cardona.

03 CARDONA

Long before arrival, you spy in the distance the outline of the impregnable 18th-century fortress high above Cardona, which itself lies next to the Muntanya de Sal (Salt Mountain). The castle – follow the signs uphill to the Parador de Cardona, a lovely place to stay overnight – was built over an older predecessor. The single-most remarkable element of the buildings is the elegant Romanesque **Canònica de Sant Vicenç**.

THE DRIVE

It's a one-hour drive south to Montserrat. The scenic route along C55 passes over forested slopes and around the old village of Manresa (a pilgrimage site). About 20km south of there, take BP1121 and follow the signs to Montserrat.

04 MONTSERRAT

Montserrat is a spectacular 1236m-high mountain of strangely rounded rock pillars, shaped by wind, rain and frost. With the historic Benedictine Monestir de Montserrat, this is one of Catalonia's most important shrines. Its caves and many mountain paths offer spectacular rambles, reachable by funiculars. You can explore the mountain above the monastery on a web of paths leading to some of the peaks and to 13 empty hermitages. The **Funicular de Sant Joan** (*cremallerademontserrat.cat*) will carry you up the first 250m from the monastery. To see the chapel on the spot where the holy image of the Virgin was discovered, it's an easy walk down, followed by a stroll along a precipitous mountain path with fabulous views.

THE DRIVE
The drive from the monastery offers magnificent views from clifftop heights, particularly along BP1103, which merges onto B110. A few kilometres further, take the ramp onto A2 and stay on it for 9km. Take exit 559 towards Vilafranca del Penedès, then take C15 south, and BP2151 into Sant Sadurní d'Anoia.

05 SANT SADURNÍ D'ANOIA

Some of Spain's finest wines come from the Penedès plains southwest of Barcelona. Sant Sadurní d'Anoia, located about a half-hour west of Barcelona, is the capital of cava, a sparkling, champagne-style wine popular worldwide, and drunk in quantity in Spain over Christmas. The headquarters of **Codorníu** (*visitascodorniu.com*) are in a beautiful Modernista cellar at the entry to Sant Sadurní d'Anoia. Next to the Sant Sadurní train station, **Freixenet** (*freixenet.es*) is the biggest cava-producing company in Penedès. Visits include a tour of its 1920s cellar, a spin on the tourist train around the property and samples of its cava. Chocolate lovers shouldn't miss a visit to **Espai Xocolata Simón Col** (*simoncoll.com*), a family-run, bean-to-bar chocolate maker, which has been going strong since 1840.

Photo opportunity

Montserrat against its dramatic mountainous backdrop.

THE DRIVE
It's an easy 15km drive to the next stop. To avoid the AP7 toll road, take the Rambla de la Generalitat southwest and follow it onto C243a. Stay on this all the way to Vilafranca del Penedès.

06 VILAFRANCA DEL PENEDÈS

Vilafranca del Penedès is an attractive historical town and the heart of the Penedès Denominación de Origen (DO; Denomination of Origin) region, which produces noteworthy light white wines and some very tasty reds. Vilafranca has appealing narrow streets lined with medieval mansions. The mainly Gothic **Església de Santa Maria** stands at the heart of the old town. Nearby, you can delve into the history and cultural significance of wine at the **Vinseum** (*vinseum.cat*), housed in the medieval Palau Reial. Admission includes an audio guide and a glass of wine in the attached bar.

THE DRIVE
Leave town via Avinguda de Tarragona. Follow this onto the AP7. Take the E90/AP2 exit towards Lleida. After 17km on this road, take exit 11 and get onto TP2002, which leads up to Santes Creus. All told it's about a 45-minute drive.

07 REIAL MONESTIR DE SANTES CREUS

Cistercian monks settled here in the 12th century and from then on this **monastery** (*larutadelcister.info*) developed as a major centre of learning and a launch pad for the repopulation of the surrounding territory. Behind the Romanesque and Gothic facade lies a glorious 14th-century sandstone cloister, austere chapter house, cavernous dormitory and royal apartments where the count-kings often stayed when they popped by during Holy Week.

THE DRIVE
Take TP2002 south and turn onto C51 about 7km south of Santa Creus. Stay on C51 for a few kilometres before taking N240. Fine views await as you cross the Tossal Gros mountain, part of Catalonia's pre-coastal range. Exit onto TV7001 towards L'Espluga de Francolí. You'll pass through this small town along T700 en route to the monastery.

08 REIAL MONESTIR DE SANTA MARIA DE POBLET

This fortified **monastery** (*poblet.cat*), now a Unesco World Heritage site, was founded in 1150. It became Catalonia's most powerful

DETOUR:

Torres

START: 06 VILAFRANCA DEL PENEDÈS

Just 3km northwest of Vilafranca del Penedès on the BP2121, **Torres** (*torres.es*) is the area's premier winemaker, with a family winemaking tradition dating from the 17th century and a strong emphasis on organic production and renewable energy. Apart from a shop, tasting room and high-end restaurant, there's also a small (free) museum containing ancient amphorae, a massive wine press and videos on the craft of barrel making. Tours in various languages explore the vineyards and several bodegas. Reserve ahead.

Reial Monestir de Santa Maria de Vallbona de les Monges

monastery and the burial place of many of its rulers. Poblet was sacked in 1835 by marauding peasants as payback for the monks' abuse of their feudal powers, which included imprisonment and torture. High points include the mostly Gothic main cloister and the alabaster sculptural treasures of the Panteón de los Reyes (Kings' Pantheon). The raised alabaster sarcophagi contain eight Catalan kings, including such greats as Jaume I (the conqueror of Mallorca and Valencia) and Pere III.

THE DRIVE
The last stop is another 30km north. You'll take the T700 back through L'Espluga de Francolí, then hop onto the T232. You'll take the L220 as you reach Els Omells de na Gaia. Follow this north, about another 1km, then look for the signed right turn leading to Valbona de les Monges.

09 REIAL MONESTIR DE SANTA MARIA DE VALLBONA DE LES MONGES

This **monastery** (*monestirvallbona.cat*) was founded in the 12th century and is where a a handful of *monges* (nuns) still live and pray. The monastery has undergone years of restoration, which has finally cleared up most of the remaining scars of civil war damage. Visits are by hourly 40-minute guided tour (Spanish or Catalan).

17

BEST FOR OUTDOORS

White-water rafting from Llavorsí to Rialp.

BARCELONA & EASTERN SPAIN

Peaks & Valleys in Northwest Catalonia

DURATION	DISTANCE	GREAT FOR
2-4 days	258km / 160 miles	Nature, history

BEST TIME TO GO	
	From May to October for hiking and rafting.

Parc Nacional d'Aigüestortes i Estany de Sant Maurici

This zigzagging journey through northwest Catalonia takes you back through the centuries, as you roll through stone villages and past Romanesque churches sitting pretty against a backdrop of pine-covered peaks. This is also a major draw for adventure lovers, with white-water rafting along the pristine Riu Noguera Pallaresa and scenic walks amid wildflower-strewn valleys, craggy summits and one breathtaking river gorge.

Link your trip

16 Central Catalonia's Wineries & Monasteries

From Taüll it's about 185km south to Monestir de Santa Maria de Vallbona, where you can make this memorable drive in reverse.

18 The Pyrenees

At the trip's end in Taüll, drive 58km back to Vielha to intersect with the magnificent drive across the Pyrenees.

01 LA SEU D'URGELL

The lively valley town of La Seu d'Urgell (la *say*-oo dur-*zhey*) has an attractive medieval centre, watched over by a Romanesque cathedral. When the Franks evicted the Muslims from this part of the Pyrenees in the 9th century, they made La Seu a bishopric and capital of the counts of Urgell; it remains an important market town. Much of the town is dominated by the 19th-century seminary above the cathedral. On the southern side of Plaça dels Oms, the 12th-century **Catedral de Santa Maria** is one of Catalonia's outstanding Romanesque buildings, with a gorgeous cloister full of characterful carved capitals.

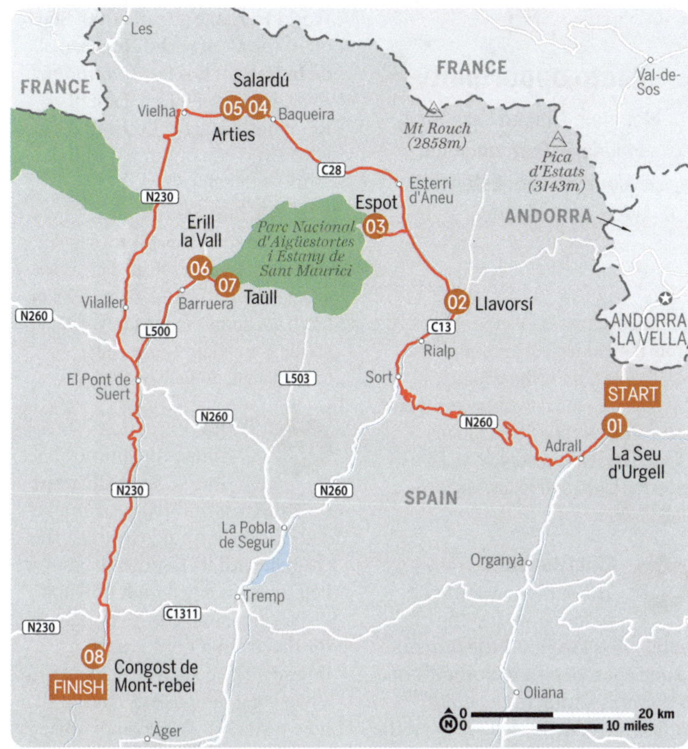

THE DRIVE

Get ready for magnificent mountain scenery on this winding 66km drive. From La Seu take the N260 about 51km northwest to Sort. From there, switch to the C13 for the final 15km. It will take you straight in to Llavorsí.

02 LLAVORSÍ

The Riu Noguera Pallaresa, running south through a dramatic valley about 50km west of La Seu d'Urgell, is Spain's best-known white-water river. The village of Llavorsí (along with Rialp and Sort) is a good place to organise a white-water trip. The Riu Noguera Pallaresa's grade-IV drops attract a constant stream of white-water fans between mid-March and mid-October. It's usually at its best in May and June. The best stretch is the 12km from Llavorsí to Rialp, on which the standard raft outing costs around €45 per person for two hours. In town, there are several rafting operators, including **Rafting Llavorsí** (*raftingllavorsi.cat*). Longer rides to Sort and beyond will cost more, and Sort is the jumping-off point for the river's tougher grade-IV rapids. You can also arrange other summer activities including kayaking, canyoning, horse riding, rock climbing and canoeing.

THE DRIVE

More lush scenery including rolling pine-dappled hillsides spread beneath you on this easy 20km drive. From Llavorsí go 12km north along C13. At the tiny stone village of Berrós Jussà, switch to the winding LV5004 for the final 7.5km.

03 ESPOT

Espot is a principal gateway to the stunning **Parc Nacional d'Aigüestortes i Estany de Sant Maurici**, Catalonia's only national park. Although small – just 20km east to west, and 9km north to south – the rugged terrain positively sparkles with more than 400 lakes and countless streams and waterfalls. This combined with a backdrop of pine and fir forests, and open bush and grassland, bedecked with wildflowers in spring, creates a wilderness of rare splendour. Created by glacial action over two million years, the park is essentially two east–west valleys at 1600m to 2000m altitudes lined by jagged 2600m to 2900m peaks of granite and slate. The park is crisscrossed by paths. Numerous good walks of three to five hours return will take you up into spectacular side valleys from Estany de Sant Maurici or Aigüestortes. Espot is 4km east of the park's eastern boundary and 8km away from the huge Estany de Sant Maurici lake.

THE DRIVE

The scenery just keeps getting better as you travel through the mountains. From Espot, go east along the LV5004 to C28, and take this north 37km, passing sleepy villages and ski resorts along the way

04 SALARDÚ

Salardú's nucleus of old houses and narrow streets has largely resisted the temptation to sprawl. In the apse of the village's 12th- and 13th-century Sant Andreu church, you can admire the 13th-century Crist de Salardú crucifixion carving. The 1858 **Refugi Rosta** houses a tiny museum (admission €5 for non-guests) covering the seminal explorers, photographers and map-makers who brought renown to the Pyrenees in the 19th century.

THE DRIVE It's a quick hop (3.5km) west along C28 to Arties, with green peaks looming above you.

05 ARTIES

This village on the southern side of the highway sits astride the confluence of the Garona and Valarties rivers. Among its cheerful stone houses is the Romanesque **Església de Santa Maria**, with its three-storey belfry and triple apse. Arties has cachet, and is packed with upmarket restaurants and bars. You can also visit the **Banys d'Arties** for a soak in a small open-air thermal pool a short walk from the village.

THE DRIVE Begin this 70-minute drive by going west towards Vielha along C28. From there drive 38km south along N230, which skirts the boundary between Aragon and Catalonia. About 17km after passing the mountain-fringed Baserca Reservoir, you'll turn onto the L500 and follow signs to La Vall de Boí.

06 ERILL LA VALL

The sublime Vall de Boí is dotted with some of Catalonia's loveliest little Romanesque churches – unadorned stone structures sitting in the crisp alpine air, constructed between the 11th and 14th centuries – which together were declared a Unesco World Heritage site in 2000. Start off in the **Centre del Romànic de la Vall de Boí** (*centreromanic.com*). Here you'll find a small Romanesque art collection; it's also where you can organise guided tours of the churches.

THE DRIVE It's a short (5.5km) but scenic drive, past pine forests and the tiny village of Boí, to Taüll. Take L500 1km north and turn onto the L501 heading south. After about 3.5km you'll see Sant Climent de Taüll on the left.

07 TAÜLL

Continue the journey back in time at **Sant Climent de Taüll** (*centreromanic.com*). Located at the entrance to Taüll, this church, with its slender six-storey bell tower, is a gem, not only for its elegant, simple lines but also for the art that once graced its interior. The central apse contains a copy of a famous 1123 mural that now resides in Barcelona's Museu Nacional d'Art de Catalunya; at its centre is a Pantocrator, whose rich Mozarabic-influenced colours and expressive but superhuman features have become an emblem of Catalan Romanesque art. It's worth timing your visit for the outstanding audiovisual projection (five times daily) that casts the original art onto the church walls. In the old village centre of Taüll you can see the **Santa Maria de Taüll** (*centreromanic.com*) church, with its striking five-storey tower. The central fresco, a reproduction, is here (again, the original is preserved in Barcelona).

THE DRIVE Start this 70-minute drive by heading back to the L500 and going south. After 15km, you'll merge onto the N230, which later runs alongside the Escales Reservoir. Turn left onto

Photo opportunity

Mountain-fringed Lake Sant Maurici in Parc Nacional d'Aigüestortes i Estany de Sant Maurici.

HIKING IN THE VALL DE BOÍ

There are some spectacular hikes in the Parc Nacional d'Aigüestortes i Estany de Sant Maurici, but one long-time favourite is the **Marmot Trail** – a round trip of 3½ hours – which begins next to the impressive Cavallers dam and passes a series of waterfalls. The hike ends at **Estany Negré** (Black Lake), close to this trail's first *refugi* (mountain shelter), **Ventosa i Calvell**; you spend a half-day among the beautiful mountains with breathtaking views of the Vall de Boí. There is also a nice three-hour trail from Taüll that takes in the entire valley and passes through the four villages along the way – Boí, Durro, Barruerra, Boí again, and back to Taüll.

You can also plan longer multiday hikes and spend the night in a *refugi*. Keep in mind that these can get quite crowded in July and August. Things are much more comfortable in May, June, September and October.

Many people wonder when is the best season to visit the park. In spring the valley is at its greenest, and the rivers are running the fastest from the snowmelt; in autumn the colours are at their best, and both spring and autumn are great times for hiking as there are not too many visitors.

the C1311 towards Tremp, and look for the turn-off to the right onto the narrow road signed for Reserva del Congost de Mont-rebei.

08 CONGOST DE MONT-REBEI

Hidden along the western fringes of Catalonia, on the border of Aragón, the spectacular river gorge of Mont-rebei offers a dazzling vision of Catalan wilderness. Carved by the sinewy Rio Noguera Ribagorçana through the pre-Pyrenean mountain range of Montsec, the narrow gorge has walls reaching some 500m with a width of just 20m in some places. A small path cut into the cliff face follows along the gorge, offering dramatic views (and sometimes precipitous descents) along the way. Allow around four hours to cover the 9.2km return hike. Parking is limited. On weekends and from mid-June to mid-September, it's wise to reserve a parking space (€5) through the website *fundaciocatalunya-lapedrera.com.* At other times, arrive early to beat the crowds.

FOOD MATTERS

Quality dining options are limited in this sparsely inhabited corner of Catalonia, so stock up on picnic fare before hitting the road. A good place to start is the expansive green market that takes over the streets of La Seu d'Urgell's historic centre on Tuesdays and Saturdays. You'll find over 70 vendors, selling a mix of seasonal fruits and vegetables, farm-fresh cheeses, olives, breads, preserves and other temptations.

Erill la Vall

18

BARCELONA & EASTERN SPAIN

The Pyrenees

BEST FOR OUTDOORS

Hiking through breathtaking mountain scenery near Núria.

DURATION	DISTANCE	GREAT FOR
5-7 days	1040km / 646 miles	Wine, history, nature

BEST TIME TO GO	From May to October for warm weather and outdoor activities.

San Sebastián

The rolling, mist-covered hills and snow-plastered mountains that make up the Pyrenees are a playground for outdoor enthusiasts. Aside from offering hiking, skiing and the most incredible view, the Pyrenees are home to old-fashioned villages that are rich in history. Foodies will delight in the abundant Basque, Aragonese and Catalan produce – not to mention two world-class dining cities (San Sebastián and Barcelona) bookending the drive.

Link your trip

07 Northern Spain Pilgrimage

At Roncesvalles, join pilgrims on the Camino de Santiago for a drive through stunning scenery and history-rich villages.

17 Peaks & Valleys in Northwest Catalonia

You can add on to this trip by connecting in Vielha (just west of Arties) with a scenic drive around northwest Catalonia.

01 SAN SEBASTIÁN

San Sebastián (Basque: Donostia) is a stunning city that loves to indulge. With Michelin stars apparently falling from the heavens onto its restaurants and a *pintxos* culture almost unmatched anywhere else in Spain, San Sebastián frequently tops lists of the world's best places to eat. But just as good as the food is the summer fun in the sun. For its setting, form and attitude, Playa de la Concha is the equal of any city beach in Europe. Then there's Playa de Gros (also known as Playa de la Zurriola), with its surfers and sultry beachgoers.

About 700m from Playa de la Concha, the Isla de Santa Clara is accessible by boats that run every half-hour from the fishing port. At low tide the island gains its own tiny beach and you can climb its forested paths to a small lighthouse. For great views over the city, head up to **Monte Igueldo**, just west of town. The best way to get there is via the old-world **funicular railway** (*monteigueldo.es*) to the Parque de Atracciones.

THE DRIVE
Start this 50km journey by taking the GI20 east and continuing onto the AP8. Just before hitting France, take N121 south, then switch to the peaceful country road NA4410 near Bera. As it crosses into France, the road becomes D406. Cut back south and into Spain, before reaching Sare.

02 ZUGARRAMURDI

Just before the French border is the pretty village of Zugarramurdi, home to the decidedly less pretty Cuevas de Las Brujas. These caves were once, according to the Inquisition, the scene of evil debauchery. Having established this, the perverse masters of the Inquisition promptly tortured and burned scores of alleged witches. Playing on the flying-broomstick theme is the **Museo de las Brujas** (*turismozugarramurdi.com*), a fascinating dip into the mysterious cauldron of witchcraft in the Pyrenees.

THE DRIVE
Drive east of town then take the N121B south. After 18km or so, take windy NA2600 east. The 52km drive takes about 75 minutes, and passes through stunning mountain scenery with great views lurking around every turn.

03 PUERTO DE IZPEGUI

The road here meanders dreamily amid picturesque farms, villages and hills before climbing sharply to the French border pass of Puerto de Izpegui, where the world becomes a spectacular collision of crags, peaks and valleys. At the pass, you can stop for a short, sharp hike up to the top of Mt Izpegui. You'll find a good number of *casas rurales* (village or farmstead accommodation) throughout the area.

THE DRIVE
To avoid lengthy backtracking, continue into France towards the pretty town of Saint-Jean Pied de Port. From there take the D933, which turns into the N135 as it crosses south back into Spain. The 48km drive takes a little over an hour.

04 RONCESVALLES

Roncesvalles (known in Basque as Orreaga) has a fascinating history. Legend has it that it was here that the armies of Charlemagne were defeated and Roland, commander of Charlemagne's rearguard, was killed by Basque tribes in 778. In addition to violence and bloodshed, though, Roncesvalles is also a pivotal stop on the road to Santiago de Compostela, where Camino pilgrims visit the famous monastery before continuing the eastward journey. Don't miss the Real Colegiata de Santa María, an atmospheric monastery with an iconic statue of the Virgin Mary.

THE DRIVE
It's a scenic 70km drive to the next stop. Head south out of Roncesvalles to get on to the NA140 east. Follow this to the NA137 south, which takes you into Roncal.

05 RONCAL

Navarra's most spectacular mountain area is around Roncal, a charming village of cobblestone alleyways that twist and turn between dark stone houses and meander down to a river full of trout. Roncal is renowned for its Queso de Roncal, a sheep's-milk cheese that's sold in the village.

Roncal

THE DRIVE
Start this 70km drive by taking NA137 south, then turn onto A21 west, which offers fine views of the Yesa reservoir (the shoreline-hugging NA2420 is even more scenic). At Liédena, take NA127 south, which turns into A127.

SOS DEL REY CATÓLICO

Sos del Rey Católico is one of Aragón's most beautiful villages. The old medieval town is a glorious maze of twisting, cobbled lanes that wriggle between dark stone houses with deeply overhung eaves. Fernando II of Aragón is said to have been born in the **Casa Palacio de Seda** in 1452. It's an impressive noble mansion, which now contains an interpretative centre, with fine exhibits on the history of Sos and the life of the king. The Gothic **Iglesia de San Esteban**, with a weathered Romanesque portal, has a deliciously gloomy crypt decorated with medieval frescoes. Above the central Plaza de la Villa, the Renaissance-era town hall is one of the grandest public buildings in Sos. Duck inside to admire the magnificent central courtyard.

Photo opportunity

A mouthwatering plate of *pintxos* (tapas) at a San Sebastián eatery.

THE DRIVE
Retrace the drive back to N240 and continue east. At Puente de la Reina de Jaca, take the A176 north. Plan on 75 minutes or so to complete the 90km drive.

HECHO

The verdant Hecho valley is mountain magic at its best, beginning with gentle climbs through the valley and the accumulating charms of old stone villages punctuating slopes of dense mixed woods of beech, pine, rowan, elm and hazel. As the valleys narrow to the north, 2000m-plus peaks rise triumphantly at their heads. Lovely Hecho (Echo), the largest village in the valley, is an attractive warren of solid stone houses with steep roofs and flower-decked balconies. It's also endowed with a large collection of contemporary sculpture, with over 40 pieces, mostly in stone, scattered around the village.

THE DRIVE
Take A176 back south, cross the bridge at Puente de la Reina de Jaca, and continue east along the N240. It takes about 40 minutes to do the drive, which takes in rolling green hillsides and wide open fields.

08 JACA

A gateway to the western valleys of the Aragonese Pyrenees, Jaca has a compact and attractive old town dotted with remnants of its past as the capital of the nascent 11th-century Aragón kingdom. These include an unusual fortress and a sturdy cathedral, while the town also has some great places to eat. Jaca's 11th-century **Catedral de San Pedro** is a formidable building, its imposing facade typical of the sturdy stone architecture of northern Aragón. There are some lovely old buildings in the streets of the *casco historico* (old town) that fans out south of the cathedral, including the 15th-century **Torre del Reloj** and the charming little **Ermita de Sarsa**. The star-shaped, 16th-century **Ciudadela** (*ciudadeladejaca.es*) is Spain's only extant pentagonal fortress. Inside, you can explore the bastions, casemates, powder magazines and chapel as well as the broad central Patio de Armas.

THE DRIVE
Take the E7 east. At Sabiñánigo, take the N260 north. Keep following the N260 as it loops east around Biescas and continues towards Torla, with winding roads offering spectacular panoramas. The 60km drive takes a little over an hour.

WHAT'S COOKING IN ARAGÓN

The kitchens and tables of Aragón are dominated by meat. The region's cold harsh winds create the ideal conditions for curing *jamón* (ham), a top tapa here; some of the best can be found in no-frills bars. Likewise, another meaty favourite, *jarretes* (hock of ham or shanks), is available in simple village restaurants like Torla's **La Brecha** (*lucienbriet.com*), while heartier ternasco (suckling lamb) is generally served as a steak or ribs with potatoes – try it at **Bodegón de Mallacán** in Aínsa.

Other popular dishes include *conejo a la montañesa* (rabbit mountain-style) served with gusto (and sometimes with snails) at Hecho's **Restaurante Gaby** (*casablasquico.es*), while (phew!) vegetarians can seek out tasty *pochas viudas* (white-bean stew with peppers, tomatoes and onion), a popular starter at restaurants like **La Cocina del Principal** (*lacocinadelprincipal.es*) in Sos del Rey Católico.

09 TORLA

This is where the Spanish Pyrenees really take your breath away. At the heart of it all is a dragon's back of limestone peaks skirting the French border. Torla is gateway to spectacular walking in the **Parque Nacional de Ordesa y Monte Perdido**, located 3km northeast. This lovely Alpine-style village has stone houses with slate roofs, and a delightful setting above Río Ara under a backdrop of the national park's mountains. In your ramblings around town, make for the 13th-century **Iglesia de San Salvador**; there are fine views from the small park on the church's northern side.

THE DRIVE
It's a 45km drive to Aínsa along the N260. You'll pass sunlit streams with forested conical peaks on either side of you on this straightforward trip.

10 AÍNSA

The beautiful hilltop village of medieval Aínsa, which stands above the modern town of the same name, is one of Aragón's gems, a stunning village hewn from uneven stone. From its perch, you'll have commanding panoramic views of the mountains. The **Castillo** and fortifications off the western end of the Plaza de San Salvador contain a fascinating ecomuseum on Pyrenean fauna and an exhibition space covering the region's geology.

THE DRIVE
Take N260 east. Around Castarnés, switch to the N230 north. Allow about 1¾ hours to cover the 105km drive.

11 VIELHA

Vielha is Aran's junction capital, a sprawl of holiday housing and apartments straggled along the valley and creeping up the sides, crowded with skiers in winter. The tiny centre retains some charm in the form of the **Església de Sant Miquèu**, which houses some notable medieval artwork, namely the 12th-century *Crist de Mijaran*.

THE DRIVE
This 214km drive takes about four hours, owing to curving mountain roads. From Vielha take C28 down to Sort, continue east on N260 to Ribes de Freser.

DETOUR:
Andorra

START: 11 VIELHA

If you're on the lookout for great hiking or skiing, or just want to say you've been in a different country, then don't miss the curious nation of Andorra, just 10km north of La Seu d'Urgell – and a little over halfway along the drive from Vielha to Ribes de Freser. At only 468 sq km, it's one of Europe's smallest countries and, though it has a democratic parliament, the nominal heads of state are two co-princes: the bishop of Urgell in Spain and the president of France. Catalan is the official tongue, though Spanish, French and, due to a large immigrant workforce, Portuguese are widely spoken. Make sure you fuel up in Andorra, as it's significantly cheaper. There's rarely any passport control, though you may be stopped by customs on the way back into Spain, so don't go over the duty-free limit.

12 RIBES DE FRESER

Sheltered within the Vall de Ribes is small, well-equipped Ribes de Freser, a stone village that makes a great base for exploring the pine forests, plummeting dales and spectacular rugged hills of the Vall de Núria. From Ribes de Freser, you can hop aboard a narrow-gauge rack-and-pinion railway (*cremallera*) that ascends some 1000m on its 12km journey to mountain-ringed Núria, which is equal parts pilgrimage site and ski resort. Once there, you'll find some fabulous marked trails throughout the valley and up nearby peaks; one of the best is the Camí Vell, an 8km walk down through the gorge from Núria to Queralbs (which is also a stop on the railway).

THE DRIVE
Take N260 south to Ripoll and east to Olot. The 50km drive, which passes over forested hillsides and offers fine views, takes about an hour.

13 OLOT

Olot is the spread-out capital of La Garrotxa region, with wide, tree-lined walkways (with the exception of its serpentine medieval heart) and plenty of options for rambling in the surrounding countryside. This area has been shaped by the ancient activity of now-dormant volcanoes. Four hills of volcanic origin stand sentry on the fringes of **Olot**. You can follow a 2km (45-minute) trail up the Volcà del Montsacopa, north of the centre.

THE DRIVE
It's a quick drive to the next stop, which is 22km east along the fast-moving A26. Take exit 67 to reach Besalú.

ANA LARROSA/SHUTTERSTOCK ©

Torla

14 BESALÚ

The tall, crooked 11th-century Pont Fortificat (Fortified Bridge) over Río Fluvià in medieval Besalú, with its two tower gates and heavy portcullis, is an arresting sight, leading you into the coiled maze of cobbled narrow streets that make up the core of this delightfully well-preserved town. Besalú's thriving Jewish community fled the town in 1436 after relentless Christian persecution, leaving behind a **miqvé** – a 12th-century ritual bath – the only survivor of its kind in Spain. Access to the miqvé is by guided tour with the **tourist office** (*besalu.cat*), but you can see the square and ruin exterior independently.

THE DRIVE

The journey to Barcelona ends with a 130km drive (1¾ hours) from the mountains down to the sea. Take C66 south. At Montegut, take the AP7 and follow signs to Barcelona.

15 BARCELONA

After rolling through remote mountain villages, the buzzing metropolis of Barcelona may come as a shock. But don't delay, dive in. One way into the city's heart is through its celebrated food scene. Start the culinary journey at the **Mercat de Sant Antoni** (*mercatdesantantoni.com*), a glorious 19th-century market with some fine tapas bars. Afterwards, stop by the nearby **MACBA** (Museu d'Art Contemporani de Barcelona; *macba.cat*) for a look at some of the city's best contemporary exhibitions. The building, designed by Richard Meier, is a work of art in itself. Barcelona is justly famous for its Modernista architecture. You can wander through a Gaudí-designed fairy tale in spacious **Park Güell** (*parkguell.barcelona*), which is located north of downtown. End the day with a meal in one of the atmospheric restaurants in El Born.

Park Güell

19

BARCELONA & EASTERN SPAIN

Barcelona to Valencia

BEST FOR CULTURE

Exploring the fascinating Islamic-era Aljafería in Zaragoza.

DURATION	DISTANCE	GREAT FOR
5–7 days	767km / 477 miles	Wine, history, nature

BEST TIME TO GO	Any time, but March to May and October to November to beat the summer crowds.

Plaça Reial

Some of Spain's great unsung wonders are on display on this looping drive between coast and mountain. You'll find architectural and culinary treasures courtesy of Valencia and Barcelona, Unesco World Heritage gardens, Spain's largest lake (a birdwatcher's delight) and adrenaline-fuelled canyon adventures near Alquézar. There are also fascinating relics from the past, from Roman ruins and an Islamic-era palace to Gothic and Modernista masterpieces.

Link your trip

15 Artistic Inspiration on the Costa Brava

From Barcelona, go 90km up the coast for a drive past sunny beaches, rugged coves and Dalí theatrics.

05 Mediterranean Meander

Once you hit Valencia, keep going! Follow this sea-lover's drive all the way to Málaga.

01 BARCELONA

Home to historical treasures, brilliantly inventive architecture, and a boundless dining and drinking scene, Barcelona is one of Europe's most enchanting cities. Start off with a visit to the Barri Gòtic, the old medieval quarter of Barcelona, which is packed with quaint squares, cobblestone lanes with old shops and looming churches. Delve into the past at the **Museu d'Història de Barcelona** (*ajuntament.barcelona.cat/museuhistoria*). This fascinating museum takes you back through the centuries to the very foundations of Roman Barcino. Afterwards, stop in the palm-filled **Plaça Reial**, where

you'll find eateries and bars with outdoor tables on the square. You can't leave Barcelona without touring at least one building designed by Antoni Gaudí. A good starting point is Casa Batlló.

THE DRIVE
In Barcelona take the waterfront Passeig de Colom southwest and get onto the B10. After 7km continue onto the A2. Stay on this for 165km then take exit 474 for Lleida. It's about two hours' drive total from Barcelona to Lleida.

02 LLEIDA

The mighty fortress-church on top of the hill in the town centre – Lleida's major historical landmark – is one of the most spectacular in Spain and is in itself reason enough to visit. Enclosed within a fortress complex, Lleida's 'old cathedral', **La Seu Vella** (*turoseuvella.cat*), towers above the city. The cathedral is a masterpiece with beautiful cloisters, the windows of which are laced with exceptional Gothic tracery. Lleida has several intriguing museums, including the **Museu de Lleida** (*museudelleida.cat*). This expansive collection encompasses artefacts reaching back to the Stone Age, Roman remains, Visigothic relics, medieval art and works by 19th-century Catalan artists.

THE DRIVE
Take Av Alcalde Rovira Roure (just north of Plaça Cervantes) to the N240, which merges into the A22. Stay on this for 50km then take exit 51 onto the N240. From here you'll pass through the winemaking centre of Somontano. Around Barbastro (the epicentre of this winery region), follow signs to A1232 and follow this to Alquézar.

03 ALQUÉZAR

Picturesque Alquézar is a handsome village that's famed for its canyoning (*descenso de barrancos*), which involves following canyons downstream by whatever means available – walking, abseiling, swimming, even diving. There are many local outfitters that lead tours, including **Vertientes** (*vertientes aventura.com*). Alquézar is crowned by the large castle-monastery of the **Colegiata de Santa María**. Originally built as an *alcázar* (fortress) by the Arabs in the 9th century, it was subsequently conquered and replaced by an Augustinian monastery in 1099.

THE DRIVE
It's a short drive (50 minutes or so) to Huesca. From Alquézar take the A1233, then switch to the A1229 around Adahuesca. After 11km get onto the A22 towards Huesca.

04 HUESCA

Huesca is a provincial capital in more than name, a town that shutters down during the afternoon hours and stirs back into life in the evenings. That said, its old centre retains considerable appeal. The Gothic **Catedral de Santa María** (*museo.diocesisdehuesca.org*) is one of Aragón's great surprises.

The richly carved main portal dates from 1300, the attached Museo Diocesano contains some extraordinary frescoes, and you can round off your visit by climbing the 180 steps of the bell tower for 360-degree views.

THE DRIVE
Zaragoza is about an hour's drive (75km). From Huesca, take Av Martínez de Velasco west. Hop onto the E7 heading southwest. Stay on this for 59km, then take exit 298 onto N330 toward Zaragoza.

05 ZARAGOZA

Zaragoza (Saragossa) is a vibrant, elegant and fascinating city. Located on the banks of the mighty Río Ebro, the residents comprise over half of Aragón's population and enjoy a lifestyle that revolves around some of the best tapas bars in the province, as well as superb shopping and a vigorous nightlife. The restoration of the riverbank has created footpaths on either side of the Río Ebro, resulting in an 8km circular route. It's superb birdwatching territory, with herons, kingfishers and many other species. Brace yourself for the great baroque cavern of Catholicism known as the **Basílica de Nuestra Señora del Pilar** (*basilicadelpilar.es*). The faithful believe that it was here on 2 January 40 CE that Santiago saw the Virgin Mary descend atop a marble *pilar* (pillar). A lift whisks you most of the way up the north tower from where you climb to a superb viewpoint over the city. The 11th-century **Aljafería** (*cortesaragon.es*) is Spain's finest Islamic-era edifice outside Andalucía.

THE DRIVE
From Zaragoza take Avenida de Valencia west. Turn right onto Avenida Séptimo Arte and follow this as it merges onto the A23. Follow the A23 for 68km and take exit 210 near Romanos onto the A1506. From here follow signs into

BARBARA_C/SHUTTERSTOCK ©

Basílica de Nuestra Señora del Pilar

Daroca. The 87km drive takes just over an hour.

06 DAROCA

Daroca, a sleepy medieval town, was a one-time Islamic stronghold and, later, a Christian fortress town in the early medieval wars against Castilla. Its well-preserved old quarter is laden with historic references and the crumbling old city walls encircle the hilltops; the walls once boasted 114 military towers. The pretty **Plaza de España**, at the top of the village, is dominated by an ornate Romanesque Mudéjar Renaissance-style church, which boasts a lavish interior and organ.

THE DRIVE

From Daroca, take Avenida de Madrid southwest and merge onto the A211. Follow this 23km then follow signs to Gallocanta, another 1km south of the A211.

07 LAGUNA DE GALLOCANTA

This is Spain's largest natural lake, with an area of about 15 sq km (though it can almost dry up in summer). It's a winter home for tens of thousands of cranes, as well as many other waterfowl – more than 260 bird species have been recorded here. The cranes arrive in mid-October and leave for the return flight to their breeding grounds in Scandinavia in March. Unpaved roads of over 30km encircle the lake, passing a series of hides and observation points, and can be driven in normal vehicles except after heavy rain. The **Centro de Interpretación Laguna de Gallocanta** (*facebook.com/oficinaturismo.gallocanta*), at the lake's northeast corner, has binoculars and picture windows for lake viewing.

THE DRIVE

Take the A1507 east. Around Calamocha, get on the N234, then merge onto the A23. Stay on this for 53km, before taking exit 131 onto A2515. Around Cella switch to the TEV 9011 and follow signs towards Albarracín. The drive takes about 90 minutes.

08 ALBARRACÍN

Built on a steep, rocky outcrop and surrounded by a deep valley carved out by the Río Guadalaviar, Albarracín is one of Spain's most beautiful villages. It's famous for its half-timbered houses with dusky-pink facades, reminiscent of southern Italy. Crowning the old town is a castle that dates from the 9th century when Albarracín was an important Islamic military post. Visits are by hour-long Spanish-language tours starting at the **Museo de Albarracín**. Albarracín's highest point, the **Torre del Andador**, has enviable views over town. Reach it by heading uphill alongside the imposing *murallas* (walls) that once protected the village.

THE DRIVE

From Albarracín get back on the A1512, and follow it for 37km to Teruel. It's a scenic 40-minute drive that takes in forest and rocky foothills, before descending into the wide open plains outside Teruel.

09 TERUEL

Lovely, compact Teruel is an open-air museum of ornate Mudéjar monuments. But this is very much a living museum where the streets are filled with life – a reflection of a city with serious cultural attitude. Teruel's **Catedral de Santa María de Mediavilla** is a rich example of the Mudéjar imagination at work with its kaleidoscopic brickwork and colourful ceramic tiles. The curious **Fundación Amantes** (*amantesdeteruel.es*) pulls out the stops on the city's famous legend of Isabel and Juan Diego. Here, the 13th-century couple lie beneath modern alabaster effigies, their hands almost (but not quite) touching.

THE LOVERS OF TERUEL

In the early 13th century, Juan Diego de Marcilla and Isabel de Segura fell in love, but, in the manner of other star-crossed historical lovers, there was a catch: Isabel was the only daughter of a wealthy family, while poor old Juan Diego was, well, poor. Juan Diego convinced Isabel's reluctant father to postpone plans for Isabel's marriage to someone more appropriate for five years, during which time Juan Diego would seek his fortune. Not waiting a second longer than the five years, Isabel's father married off his daughter in 1217, only for Juan Diego to return, triumphant, immediately after the wedding. He begged Isabel for a kiss, which she refused, condemning Juan Diego to die of a broken heart. A final twist saw Isabel attend the funeral in mourning, whereupon she gave Juan Diego the kiss he had craved in life. Isabel promptly died and the two lovers were buried together. You can see their tombs at the **Fundación Amantes**.

The most impressive of Teruel's Mudéjar towers is the **Torre de El Salvador** (*teruelmudejar.com*), an early-14th-century extravaganza of brick and ceramics built around an older Islamic minaret. Climb up the narrow stairways for Teruel's best views.

THE DRIVE
It's 120km southeast to Sagunto, though just a 70-minute drive on the A23. From Teruel, take Avenida de Sagunto south. Just beyond the centre, you'll pass by Dinópolis, a dinosaur theme park that's a hit with families. From here, continue onto the N234 and the A23.

10 SAGUNTO

The port town of Sagunto offers spectacular panoramas of the coast, Balearics and sea of orange groves from its hilltop castle complex. Sagunto was once a thriving Iberian community (called – infelicitously, with hindsight – Arse) that traded with Greeks and Phoenicians. A highlight here is the restored Roman theatre. Above it, the stone walls of the castle complex girdle the hilltop for almost 1km.

Photo opportunity

A flock of cranes flying over the Laguna de Gallocanta.

THE DRIVE
It's about a 30-minute drive to Valencia. From Sagunto, take the N340 south, and merge onto the V23. Around Puçol, merge onto the V21, and enjoy the view along the coast as you near the city.

11 VALENCIA

The vibrant city of Valencia has much going for it, from stunning architecture and scenic parks to an embarrassing wealth of restaurants. Bright and spacious, the **Museo de Bellas Artes** (*museobellasartesvalencia.gva.es*) ranks among Spain's best. Highlights include the grandiose Roman Mosaic of the Nine Muses, a collection of magnificent late-medieval altarpieces, and works by El Greco, Goya and Velázquez. For a dose of greenery, stroll the **Jardines del Turia**. Stretching the length of the Río Turia's former course, this 9km-long park is a fabulous mix of playing fields, walking paths, lawns and playgrounds.

Museo de Bellas Artes

Almendralejo
Castuera
Cabeza del Buey
Puertollano
Argamasilla de Calatrava
Valdepeñas
Villanueva de los Infantes
Villanueva de la Fuente
Pozo Cañada
Zafra
Hellín
Peñarroya-Pueblonuevo
Pozoblanco
Llerena
Río Guadiato
Parque Natural Sierra de Andújar
Río Segura
Beas de Segura
Monesterio
Río Benamor
Villaviciosa de Córdoba
Cardeña
Bailén
Parque Natural Sierra Norte de Sevilla
Montoro
Andújar
Villacarrillo
Constantina
Córdoba
Baeza
Úbeda
Parque Natural Sierras de Cazorla, Segura y las Villas
Puebla de Don Fadrique
Caravaca de la Cruz
Porcuna
Palma del Río
Mancha Real
Jódar
Cazorla
Huéscar
Lora del Río
Castro del Río
Torredonjimeno
Jaén
Río Genil
La Carlota
Parque Natural Sierra de María-Los Vélez
Río Guadalquivir
Pozo Alcón
Bollullos Par del Condado
Baena
Alcaudete
Lorca
Écija
Montilla
Carmona
Zuheros
Guadahortuna
Seville
Aguilar de la Frontera
Vélez Rubio
Puerto Lumbreras
Alcalá de Guadaira
Río Corbones
Lucena
Parque Natural Sierras Subbéticas
Baza
Almonte
Estepa
Montefrío
Huércal-Overa
Los Palacios y Villafranca
Osuna
Pinos Puente
Parque Natural Sierra de Baza
Arahal
Guadix
Utrera
Río Almanzora
Barcelona (690km)
Morón de la Frontera
Loja
Vera
Parque Nacional de Doñana
Santa Fé
Granada
Lebrija
Antequera
Parque Nacional Sierra Nevada
Mojácar
Olvera
Alhama de Granada
Sanlúcar de Barrameda
Algodonales
Capileira
Parque Natural Sierras de Tejeda, Almijara y Alhama
Níjar
Villamartín
Ronda
Almería
Parque Natural de Cabo de Gata-Níjar
Jerez de la Frontera
Arcos de la Frontera
Cártama
Motril
Ubrique
Coín
Málaga
Nerja
Almuñécar
Golfo de Almería
San José
Cádiz
Mijas
Adra
Torre del Mar
Torremolinos
San Fernando
Jimena de la Frontera
Marbella
Almerimar
Chiclana de la Frontera
Medina Sidonia
Casares
Fuengirola
Estepona
Parque Natural Los Alcornocales
Barbate
La Línea de la Concepción
Mediterranean Sea
Los Caños de Meca
Algeciras
Gibraltar (UK)
Bolonia
Tarifa
Strait of Gibraltar
ATLANTIC OCEAN
MOROCCO
Tangier
0
100 km
0
50 miles
A66
A4
A431
N432
A407
A92
A384
A393
AP4
A381
N340
AP7
A7
A45
A44
A32
A92N
20
21
22
23
24
25

GEORGIOS TSICHLIS/SHUTTERSTOCK ©

Real Alcázar, Seville (p158)

Andalucía & Southern Spain

Explore

Andalucía & Southern Spain

Andalucía is Spain as you always imagined it, and yet it's also so much more than you ever imagined. The region seems custom-made for a road trip, whether it's along the country's fascinating stretches of Mediterranean shore or inland though Spain's highest mountains, pretty valleys and enchanted hilltop villages all dressed in white. Any drive through the region will also take you within striking distance of Seville, Córdoba and Granada, each a magical collection of famous architecture, fabulous food and joyous Spanish-style street life. Even though this is one of Spain's most heavily touristed areas, it's possible to escape the crowds.

Seville

Seville is the very essence of Andalucía, a whitewashed fantasy of cobbled laneways punctuated by bright bougainvillea and strewn with intimate little squares. Elsewhere you'll find towering monuments to the region's fabled past, and a tapas and culinary culture without peer in Spain's south. And so much of what happens in this busy, beautiful city does so to the accompaniment of a flamenco soundtrack and often the kind of celebration or festival that could only happen in Andalucía.

Granada

Granada has gravitas, and not just because of La Alhambra, the gilded pleasure palace of exquisite design and lavish ornamental gardens that could be argued to be the pinnacle of Islamic architecture on Spanish soil. Glorious public buildings, an enchanting old quarter called the Albaicín, a backdrop of the snow-dusted Sierra Nevada and one of southern Spain's most underrated tapas scenes – no wonder Granada very often ends up being many visitors' favourite Spanish city.

Córdoba

Everyone loves Córdoba. With its compact centre and excellent transport connections, the city would make a convenient stopover even if it didn't have so many wonderful attractions to detain you longer. The jewel in Córdoba's crown is the Mezquita, the city's 8th-century mosque, which is known for its delicate horseshoe arches. Rounding

WHEN TO GO

Although Andalucía's coastline is one of Europe's most popular summer destinations (especially in July and August), and summer is also a good season for high-altitude hiking, the region's interior bakes at this time. Most areas are good to visit during the rest of the year, although the Sierra Nevada in winter usually appeals just to skiers.

out the appeal are a Roman-era bridge, evocative flower-strewn laneways and the delights of a fun and varied restaurant scene.

Málaga

Once viewed as the gateway to the Costa del Sol, Málaga has gone and got sophisticated. A fine fortress guards the city, a slew of world-class museums (including one devoted to Pablo Picasso, who was born here) call to culture lovers, and the place is quietly acquiring a reputation for culinary innovation. But some things don't change: Málaga boasts one of Europe's best climates, and its rail and air links to the rest of Spain and Europe are second to none in the region.

Arcos de la Frontera

Clinging to the clifftops, Arcos de la Frontera is the archetypal hill town – spectacularly sited, dazzlingly white and as magnificent from afar as it is intimate from within. There are other hill towns nearby, and each has its own charm, but if you could only visit one, Arcos de la Frontera would have to be it. And then there are the views from the summit…

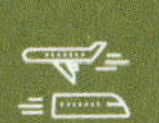

TRANSPORT

Motorways crisscross the region, connecting most areas with each other and the rest of Spain. The same is true of rail links, with high-speed services reaching Seville, Córdoba, Cádiz, Granada and Málaga from Madrid and elsewhere. It's slower going in mountain areas, and delightfully slow and quiet back roads wind among the region's hilltop villages.

WHAT'S ON

Semana Santa

Solemn processions of hooded penitents in Holy Week (Easter); at its best in Seville, Málaga and Granada.

Feria de Abril

In late April, Seville's is the biggest of Andalucía's fairs.

Fiesta de los Patios de Córdoba

Beautiful private courtyards in Córdoba open to the public in May.

Festival de la Guitarra de Córdoba

Córdoba's July international guitar festival ranges from flamenco and classical to rock, blues and beyond.

WHERE TO STAY

You'll never be far from somewhere special to stay throughout southern Spain, but book as early as you can in summer, especially in coastal areas. Cities such as Seville, Córdoba and Granada are always busy thanks to a wide and varied accommodation scene; the best places (even budget ones) occupy historic palaces or other notable buildings. Check out the Parador Hotels (parador.es) network for some gorgeous choices. Options are more limited in the region's many villages, which is another reason to reserve early. The region has lots of *casas rurales* (rural homestays) and *hostales* (guesthouses) to complement the hotels.

Resources

Andalucía (*andalucia.org*) Your online gateway to Andalucía in all its glory.

Alhambra de Granada (*alhambradegranada.org*) Whet your appetite (and book your visit) for Andalucía's most remarkable architectural experience.

Lonely Planet (*lonelyplanet.com/spain/andalucia*) Destination information, hotel bookings, traveller forum and more.

Piccavey (*piccavey.com*) Excellent Andalucía coverage by a Granada-based blogger.

20

BEST FOR OUTDOORS

Parque Natural de Cabo de Gata-Nijar.

ANDALUCÍA & SOUTHERN SPAIN

Mediterranean Meander

DURATION	DISTANCE	GREAT FOR
7 days	1107km/ 688 miles	History, nature

BEST TIME TO GO	March to June is sunny, but not too hot, and there are plenty of festivals, including Las Fallas.

Alcazaba

From the Costa Daurada to the Costa del Sol, from Catalan pride to Andalucian passion, from Roman ruins in Tarragona to Barcelona's flamboyant Modernisme buildings: this drive provides technicolour proof that not all southern Spain is a beach bucket of cheesy tourist clichés. The full 1107km trajectory passes through four regions, two languages, Spain's second-, third- and sixth-largest cities, and beaches too numerous to count.

Link your trip

15 Artistic Inspiration on the Costa Brava

You can extend this trip at its Catalan nexus, heading north out of Barcelona along the Costa Brava.

21 Costa del Sol Beyond the Beaches

Can't get enough of the Mediterranean? Jump on this trip in Málaga and hug the coast all the way to Gibraltar.

01 MÁLAGA

The Costa del Sol can seem a pretty soulless place until you hit Málaga, the Andalucian city everyone is talking about. For decades the city was overlooked by the millions of tourists who crowded the Costa's seaside resorts but in recent years it has transformed itself into a hip, stylish metropolis brimming with youthful vigour. It boasts 30-odd museums and an edgy urban art scene as well as contemporary restaurants, boutique hotels and stylish shopping. Art-lovers are spoiled for choice at museums such as the **Museo Ruso de Málaga** (*coleccionmuseoruso.es*) and **Centre**

Pompidou Málaga (*centre pompidou.es*), while the **Museo de Málaga** (*museosdeandalucia.es/museodemalaga*) houses an extensive archaeology collection. The city's premier museum is the unmissable **Museo Picasso Málaga** (*museopicassomalaga.org*), dedicated to the Málaga-born artist. For an edgier, urban scene, head to the Soho neighbourhood near the port where you'll find giant murals, arty cafes, ethnic restaurants and street markets.

THE DRIVE
Head east out of Málaga on the A7. This is southern Spain's main coastal road (also known as the E15) and will be your companion for much of this trip. The coast gets ever more precipitous as you move east into Granada province. After 68km turn south on the N340 and follow for 8km into Almuñécar.

02 ALMUÑÉCAR

There's a hint of Italy's Amalfi Coast about the Costa Tropical, Granada province's 80km coastline. Named for its subtropical microclimate, it's often dramatically beautiful, with dun-brown mountains and whitewashed villages huddled into coves and bays. The area's main resort is the popular summer destination of Almuñécar. Summer action is focused on Almuñécar's long seafront whose two beaches are divided by a rocky outcrop, the **Peñón del Santo**. To the west of this stretches the pebbly **Playa de San Cristóbal**, while to the east the grey-sanded **Playa Puerta del Mar** fronts the old town. Up in the *casco antiguo*, the small **Museo Arqueológico Cueva de Siete Palacios** displays ancient finds in a series of underground stone cellars. Tickets also include entry to the hilltop **Castillo de San Miguel**.

THE DRIVE
Continue eastwards on the A7, skirting around Motril and passing increasing numbers of unsightly plastic greenhouses as the landscape becomes ever more arid. Almería beckons. All told, it's about 130km to Almería.

03 ALMERÍA

Don't overlook Almería, a waterfront city with an illustrious past. Once the main port for the 10th-century Córdoba caliphate, the sun-baked city has a handsome centre, punctuated by palm-fringed plazas and old churches, as well as several museums and plenty of fantastic tapas bars. Its main draw is its spectacular **Alcazaba**, once one of the most powerful Moorish fortresses in Spain. At the foot of the hilltop fort sprawls the maze-like **Almedina**, the old Moorish quarter. Continue through this to the city's six-towered **catedral** (*catedralalmeria.com*), another formidable structure with an impressive Gothic interior. Nearby, the **Museo de la Guitarra** charts Almeria's role in the development of the iconic instrument. Round off your sightseeing with a soak at the **Hammam Aire de Almería** (*beaire.com*), a modern-day version of an Arabic bathhouse.

THE DRIVE
Head east out of Almería on the N340a to join up with the AL12 airport road and its continuation the N344. Continue on this, following signs to San José through a series of small roundabouts near Retamar. Eventually you should emerge onto the AL3108, which runs through low hills to Cabo de Gata (total distance 40km).

04 CABO DE GATA

Covering Spain's south-eastern tip, the **Parque Natural de Cabo de Gata-Níjar** boasts some of Andalucía's most flawless and least crowded beaches. These glorious *playas* lie strung along the area's dramatic cliff-bound coastline while inland remote white villages dot the stark, semi-desert hinterland. On the park's east coast, the low-key resort of **San José** makes an ideal base. It's well set up with hotels and restaurants and the surrounding coastline hides several sublime beaches. The most beautiful, including **Playa de los Genoveses** and **Playa de Mónsul,** are accessible by a dirt road signposted 'Playas' and/or 'Genoveses/Mónsul'. For more active pursuits, you can walk the park's coastal paths or organise diving, kayaking, bike hire and guided tours at agencies across town – try **MedialunAventura** (*medialunaventura.com*).

THE DRIVE
Follow the AL3108 inland from San José until you hit the A7 just shy of Nijar. Head northeast towards Valencia for 43km to exit 520. Come off here and follow signs to Mojácar along the A370 and AL6111.

05 MOJÁCAR

Tucked away in an isolated corner of Almería province, Mojácar is both a seaside resort and a charming hill town. Mojácar Pueblo, a picturesque jumble of white-cube houses, sits atop a hillside 3km inland from Mojácar Playa, a modern low-rise resort fronting 7km of sandy beach. Exploring Mojácar Pueblo is mainly a matter of wandering its maze-like streets, stopping off at craft shops, galleries and boutiques. You can see how life in the town once was at the **Casa La Canana**, and admire sweeping views from the lofty Mirador del Castillo (Plaza Mirador del Castillo, Mojácar Pueblo). Down at Mojácar Playa, you'll find the best sands at the southern end of town, which also has a pleasant seafront promenade.

THE DRIVE
Retrace your steps from Mojácar back onto the northbound A7. After 10km merge onto the toll-charging AP7 near Vera and continue to the exit for Cartagena Oeste. Take this and follow the signposted route along the N332

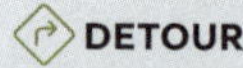

DETOUR:

Orihuela

START: 06 CARTAGENA

Beside the Río Segura and flush with the base of a barren mountain of rock, Orihuela harbours some superb Gothic, Renaissance and baroque buildings. Its old town, once the second city of the kingdom of Valencia, is strung out between the river and the castle-capped mountain.

Standout sights include the 14th-century **Catalan Gothic Catedral de San Salvador**, which features three finely carved portals and an exquisite two-level cloister. Nearby, the **Museo Diocesano de Arte Sacro** has a fine display of religious art, culminating in Velázquez' *Temptation of St Thomas*. Also worth searching out is the **Colegio de Santo Domingo** (*colegio.cdsantodomingo.com*), a 16th-century convent with two fine Renaissance cloisters. To reach Orihuela, branch west off the AP7 around 60km north of Cartagena and continue on the CV945 and CV95.

THE PICASSO TRAIL

Málaga and Barcelona are linked by more than Mediterranean beaches – both cities have a strong connection with Pablo Ruiz Picasso (1881–1973). The great painter was born in Málaga and spent the first 10 years of his life there. In 1891 he and his family moved to A Coruña and then, in 1895, he transferred to Barcelona where he lived on and off during the early 1900s.

In Málaga you can get an intimate insight into the painter's childhood at the **Casa Natal de Picasso** (*fundacionpicasso.malaga.eu*), the house where he was born in 1881. Nearby, the Museo Picasso Málaga (p145) displays more than 200 of his works. The collection at the Museu Picasso (p150) in Barcelona is even larger, comprising around 3500 works, many from his formative years. On a more modest scale, Alicante's Museo de Arte Contemporáneo (p148) displays his *Portrait d'Arthur Rimbaud* (1960), while the Museu del Cau Ferrat(p150) is housed in the Sitges home of his friend, the late artist Santiago Rusiñol.

into the city. Mojácar to Cartagena is 134km.

CARTAGENA

Cartagena's fabulous natural harbour has been used for thousands of years. Stand on the battlements of the castle that overlooks the city and you can literally see layer upon layer of history spread below you, from the wharf where Phoenician traders docked their ships to the streets where Roman legionaries once marched, from the factories of the industrial age to the contemporary warships of what is still an important naval base. As archaeologists continue to unearth the city's ancient roots, it is finally starting to get the recognition it deserves. Highlights include the **Museo Nacional de Arqueología Subacuática**, an excellent museum dedicated to underwater archaeology and maritime history, and the **Museo del Teatro Romano** (*teatroromano cartagena.org*), centred on a 1st-century-BCE Roman theatre.

THE DRIVE
Double back to the AP7 and head north towards Alicante. After 75km the *autopista* rejoins the A7. Follow this for 32km before taking exit 17A signposted for Alicante.

ALICANTE

Of all mainland Spain's provincial capitals, Alicante is the most tourist-driven. Nevertheless, it's a dynamic, attractive city with a castle, old quarter and long waterfront. The eating scene is exciting and the nightlife is legendary. There are

TOP TIP:

Toll Roads

The AP7 (also known as E15), is a toll-charging *autopista* (motorway) that parallels much of Spain's southern and eastern coastlines. You will have to stop periodically to pay a toll at staffed booths. However, as of 1 January 2020, tolls were scrapped on the AP7 between Tarragona and Alicante. The confusingly named A7 follows a similar route to the AP7, but is entirely toll-free. The N340 is a third road paralleling Spain's southern coast, although much of it has merged with the A7. Some of the N340 follows the route of the Roman Vía Augustus.

UNAI HUIZI PHOTOGRAPHY/SHUTTERSTOCK ©

Playa de Mónsul

FESTIVALS

If you're undertaking this trip in February, March or August, look out for the following festivals. **Feria de Malaga** (*feria.malaga.eu*) Málaga's nine-day feria (fair), launched by a huge fireworks display, is the most ebullient of Andalucía's summer ferias. Head for the city centre to be in the thick of it. At night, festivities switch to large fairgrounds and nightly rock and flamenco shows at Cortijo de Torres, 3km southwest of the city centre. **Las Fallas de San José** (*fallas.com*) The exuberant, anarchic swirl of Las Fallas de San José – fireworks, music, festive bonfires and all-night partying – is a must if you're visiting Valencia in mid-March. The *fallas* themselves are huge papier mâché sculptures satirising celebrities, current affairs and local customs. After midnight on the final day, each *falla* goes up in flames. **Sitges Carnaval** (*visitsitges.com*) Carnaval in Sitges is a sparkly weeklong booze-soaked riot, complete with masked balls and capped by extravagant gay parades on the Sunday and Tuesday, featuring flamboyantly dressed drag queens, giant sound systems and a wild all-night party.

sweeping views over the city from the large 16th-century **Castillo de Santa Bárbara** (*castillodesantabarbara.com*), which also houses a museum recounting the history of Alicante. Further historical artefacts await in the **Museo Arqueológico de Alicante** (*marqalicante.com*), which has a strong collection of ceramics and Iberian art. For a more contemporary outlook, the free **Museo de Arte Contemporáneo de Alicante** (*maca-alicante.es*) impresses with its displays of works by the likes of Dalí, Miró, Picasso and others.

THE DRIVE
Leave Alicante on the A77 signposted, Valencia, and continue on to the A7. The *autovia* proceeds north, passing through a couple of tunnels and heading progressively downhill as it forges inland towards Valencia. After almost 90km, exit on the CV645 signposted Xàtiva. From here it's about 5km to the town.

Photo opportunity

The chameleonic Sagrada Familia, which changes every time you visit.

ROMANSLAVIK.COM/SHUTTERSTOCK ©

Castillo de Santa Bárbara

08 XÀTIVA

Xàtiva (Spanish: Játiva) is often visited on a day trip from Valencia or, as in this case, as a stop on the way north from Alicante. It has an intriguing historic quarter and a mighty castle strung along the crest of the Serra Vernissa, with the town snuggled at its base.The Muslims established Europe's first paper-manufacturing plant in Xàtiva, which is also famous as the birthplace of the Borgia Popes Calixtus III and Alexander VI. The town's glory days ended in 1707 when Felipe V's troops torched most of the town. **Xàtiva's castle** (*xativa turismo.com*), which clasps the summit of a double-peaked hill overlooking the old town, is one of the most evocative in the Valencia region. Behind its crumbling battlements you'll find flower gardens (bring a picnic), tumbledown turrets, towers and other buildings. The walk up to the castle is a long one (2km), but the views are sensational.

THE DRIVE
Use the N340 to rejoin the A7 and head north to Valencia. Just outside the city, where the A7 merges with the AP7, take the V31, Valencia's main southern access road for the final push into the city centre. All told, the 63km journey should take around 50 minutes.

09 VALENCIA

Valencia, Spain's third-largest city, exudes confidence. Content for Madrid and Barcelona to grab the headlines, it quietly gets on with being a wonderfully liveable spot, hosting thriving cultural, eating and nightlife scenes. Its star attraction is the strikingly futuristic **Ciudad de las Artes y las Ciencias** (*cac.es*) on the old Turia riverbed. Counting an opera house, science museum, 3D cinema and aquarium, the complex was largely the work of local-born starchitect Santiago Calatrava. Other brilliant contemporary buildings grace the city, which also has a fistful of fabulous Modernista buildings, great museums, a long stretch of beach and a large, characterful old quarter. Look out for **La Lonja** (*valencia.es*), Valencia's late 15th-century silk and commodity exchange, and the **Mercado Central** (*mercadocentralvalencia.es*), the vast Modernista market. The city also enjoys prime foodie credentials as the home of paella but its buzzing dining scene offers plenty more besides.

THE DRIVE
Leave Valencia on the V21 signposted Puçol. After 23km or so you'll rejoin your old friend, the AP7, which will whisk you 200km up the coast into Catalonia. Come off at exit 38 and continue on the A7 for the final 35km into Tarragona. Reckon on 257km for the entire leg.

WHY I LOVE THIS TRIP

Duncan Garwood, writer

What makes this epic coastal drive so special is the sheer variety it provides. There's history and culture galore with Roman ruins in Tarragona, Picasso paintings in Málaga and modern architecture in Barcelona and Valencia. Boisterous beach resorts offer hedonism and hard partying while peace-lovers will enjoy the unsullied coastal beauty of Cabo de Gata, one of Andalucía's great natural highlights.

DETOUR:

Delta de l'Ebre

START: 09 VALENCIA

Near Catalonia's southern border, the Delta de l'Ebre is a remote, exposed place of reed-fringed lagoons, dune-backed beaches and mirror-smooth marshes. Some 78 sq km are protected in the **Parc Natural del Delta de l'Ebre**, northern Spain's most important waterbird habitat. Migration season (October and November) sees bird populations peak, but birds are also numerous in winter and spring.

Even if you're not a twitcher, the park is worth a visit. The landscape, with its whitewashed farmhouses and electric-green rice paddies, is hauntingly beautiful and the flat waterside trails are ideal for cyclists and ramblers.

Scruffy **Deltebre** sits at the centre of the delta but smaller villages like **Riumar** or **Poblenou del Delta** are more appealing. To reach Deltebre, branch off the AP7 at exit 41, 180km north of Valencia. Take the N340 to connect with the TV3454, which leads to the town some 13km to the east.

10 TARRAGONA

In the effervescent port city of Tarragona, Roman history collides with beaches, bars and a food scene that perfumes the air with freshly grilled seafood. The main drawcard is the city's collection of ancient ruins, including a mosaic-packed museum and a seaside amphitheatre where gladiators once faced each other (or wild animals) in mortal combat. The Unesco-listed Roman sites are scattered around town but you can get a combined ticket at the **Museu d'Historia de Tarragona** (*tarragona.cat/patrimoni/museu-historia*). A roll-call of fantastic places to eat and drink is a good reason to linger in the attractive medieval centre. This maze of cobbled lanes is encircled by steep walls and crowned by a towering **catedral** (*catedraldetarragona.com*) with Romanesque and Gothic flourishes.

THE DRIVE
From Tarragona use the N240 to get back on the AP7 and head east towards Barcelona. After about 11km take exit 31 onto the C32. Follow this for just over 30km, crossing one viaduct and burrowing through two tunnels, to Sitges.

11 SITGES

Just 40km shy of Barcelona, Sitges has been a favourite beach resort since the 19th century. The former fishing village, which was a key location for the Modernisme art movement and is now one of Spain's premier gay destinations, is renowned for its party beach life, riotous carnival celebrations and hedonistic nightlife – at its most bacchanalian in July and August. Despite this, it remains a classy destination with a good array of galleries and museums and plenty of restaurants in its boutique-laden historic centre. Sunseekers will enjoy its long sandy beach, which is flanked by the seafront **Passeig Maritim**. The cultural highlight is the **Museu del Cau Ferrat** (*museusdesitges.cat*), built in the 1890s as a house-studio by artist Santiago Rusiñol – a pioneer of the Modernisme movement. The whitewashed mansion is full of his own art and that of his contemporaries, including his friend Picasso.

THE DRIVE
It's only 40km to Barcelona. Get back onto the toll-charging C32 and fly through a multitude of tunnels. After about 30km, exit at junction 16B and follow signs for Barcelona, Gran Via and Centre Ciutat.

12 BARCELONA

Barcelona is a guidebook in itself and a cultural colossus to rival Paris or Rome. The city's ever-evolving symbol is Gaudí's **Sagrada Familia** (*sagradafamilia.org*), which rises like an unfinished symphony over L'Eixample district. The surrounding neighbourhood is renowned for its Modernisme architecture, which appears in buildings such as **La Pedrera** (*lapedrera.com*), a madcap Unesco-listed masterpiece with a rippling grey-stone facade and chimney pots resembling medieval knights. For more conventional, historical sights head to the Barri Gótic, home to the city's vast Gothic **La Catedral** (*catedralbcn.org*), and the medieval La Ribera quarter where you'll find the excellent **Museu Picasso** (*museupicasso.bcn.cat*). A good orientation point in this complex city is **La Rambla** – its tree-lined pedestrian promenade was made with the evening *paseo* (stroll) in mind. La Rambla divides the Barri Gòtic and La Ribera from the bohemian, multicultural El Raval neighbourhood. To the northeast lies the Modernisme-inspired L'Eixample quarter; to the south are the steep parks and gardens of Montjuic, site of the 1992 Olympics.

LEGACY OF THE ROMANS

What did the Romans ever do for us? Well, quite a lot actually, as you'll discover as you drive up Spain's Mediterranean coast.

The Roman colonies in Hispania (their name for the Iberian Peninsula) lasted from around 400 BCE to 200 BCE, and reminders of their existence lie dotted along the coast, from Andalucía to Catalonia.

In **Málaga** you can admire an amphitheatre, dating from the 1st century CE when the settlement was called Malaca. An adjacent interpretive centre outlines its history and displays a few artefacts unearthed on the site.

Cartagena (Carthago Nova to the Romans) boasts several Roman sites, including the Museo del Teatro Romano (p147), centred on a 1st-century-BCE Roman theatre.

Further north, **Tarragona** (Tarraco) was once capital of Rome's Spanish provinces and has ruins to prove it, including an amphitheatre, a forum, street foundations and the two-tiered **Aqüeducte de les Ferreres**. Ocean-themed mosaics can be seen in the nearby **Museu Nacional Arqueològic de Tarragona** (*mnat.cat*).

La Sagrada Familia

IESUS NAZARENUS

21

BEST FOR FAMILIES

Beaches, theme parks, and the Andalucian love for kids.

ANDALUCÍA & SOUTHERN SPAIN

Costa del Sol Beyond the Beaches

DURATION	DISTANCE	GREAT FOR
3-4 days	208km / 129 miles	Wine

BEST TIME TO GO	March to June or September to November when temperatures are cooler and traffic less.

Cueva de Nerja

This drive from Nerja in the east to Gibraltar in the west leads through a constantly shifting landscape, taking you from orchards of subtropical fruit trees to shimmering white resorts, from a culture-loving metropolis to the cobbled backstreets of a former fishing village. Be prepared for a trip that challenges any preconceived ideas you may have about this, Spain's most famous, tourist-driven coastline.

Link your trip

20 Mediterranean Meander

Málaga is the start of this east-coast adventure that takes in several of Spain's most stunning cities, including its final destination: Barcelona.

22 Golden Triangle

Nerja is a speedy hour's drive from Granada, home of the monumental Alhambra; this winning drive also takes in Seville and Córdoba, two of Andalucía's most celebrated cities.

01 NERJA

Sitting in a charmed spot at the base of the Sierra Almijara mountains, this former fishing village has retained its low-rise village charm, despite the proliferation of souvenir shops and the large number of visitors it sees. At its heart is the Balcón de Europa, a seafront balcony built over the site of a Moorish castle. Grab a coffee at one of the terraced cafes before heading north of town to the extraordinary **Cueva de Nerja** (*cuevadenerja.es*). This 4km-long cave complex, which dates back a cool five million years, is a wonderland of extraordinary rock formations, subtle shifting colours, stalactites and stalagmites.

THE DRIVE

The quickest route to Málaga is via the main A7 (E15). More scenic, if slower, is the N340 which meanders along the coast, traversing pretty agricultural land and bypassing centuries-old watchtowers. At Rincón de la Victoria, join the A7 for the last few kilometres into Málaga. It's a total drive of 58km (1¼ hours).

MÁLAGA

Book a night or two to get the best out of Málaga. The city crackles with energy, hosting a buzzing bar life and vibrant restaurant scene. It also boasts genuine cultural credentials and its art museums are seriously impressive – check out the **Museo Carmen Thyssen** (*carmenthyssenmalaga.org*), the Museo Ruso (p144) and the unmissable Museo Picasso Málaga (p145), dedicated to the city's most famous son. A short walk away, the 16th-century **Catedral de Málaga** (*malagacatedral.com*) offers fabulous rooftop views and an interior bedecked with gorgeous retables and 18th-century religious art. Travel further back in time at the Roman Amphitheatre (p150) and adjacent **Alcazaba** (*alcazabaygibralfaro.malaga.eu*), a fascinating 11th-century Moorish palace-fortress.

THE DRIVE

Leaving Málaga, take the A7 in the direction of Algecíras, Torremolinos and Cádiz, then follow the MA20 signposted to Torremolinos. This is a busy stretch of *autovia* that passes the airport. It's a drive of about 18km (25 minutes).

TORREMOLINOS

Torremolinos, once the poster child of industrial-scale package tourism, now attracts a wide cross-section of people, including trendy clubbers, beach-loving families, gay visitors and, yes, even some Spanish tourists. The centre of town revolves around the pedestrian shopping street **Calle San Miguel**, from

DETOUR:

Frigiliana

START: 01 NERJA

After the cavernous gloom of the Cueva de Nerja, consider heading inland to Frigiliana, a *pueblo blanco* (white village) once voted Andalucía's prettiest by the Spanish tourism authority. It's an enchanting place with a tangible Moroccan feel and a steeply banked old town of pretty, whitewashed houses. Wander its quaint streets and pick up some of its famous sweet wine and honey in the small village shops. It's a straightforward 7km drive from Nerja: take the M5105 inland, passing groves of mango and avocado trees, and follow signs to the casco historico and car park.

where steps lead down to the main beach at **Playamar**. To the southwest, round a small rocky outcrop (La Punta), **La Carihuela** is a former fishing *barrio* which is now, fittingly, home to some hugely popular seafood restaurants such as **Casa Juan** (*losmellizos.net*). The beachfront *paseo* continues to Benalmádena, Torre's western twin, where you'll find a large marina designed as a kind of homage to Gaudí and a giant **Buddhist stupa** (*stupa benalmadena.org*).

THE DRIVE
It's a straightforward 17km drive to Fuengirola on the N340, which hugs the coast and passes through the busy coastal resort of Benalmádena Costa. Note that there's a 50km speed limit on this scenic stretch.

04 FUENGIROLA

Fuengirola's appeal, apart from its 7km of beaches, lies in the fact that it is a genuine Spanish working town, as well as a popular resort. It has a large population of foreign residents, many of whom arrived in the

Mijas

'60s and stayed long after their ponytails had gone grey. Stop by **Plaza de la Constitucíon**, a pretty square overlooked by the baroque-style facade of Fuengirola's main church, then explore the surrounding streets lined with idiosyncratic shops and tapas bars. A five-minute walk away, the **Bioparc** (*bioparcfuengirola.es*) is the Costa's best zoo, with spacious enclosures, and conservation and breeding programmes.

THE DRIVE
From Fuengirola, take Avenida Alcalde Clemente Díaz Ruiz then the Carretera de Mijas to join the A387. This crosses the A7 and continues up to Mijas about 9km (20 minutes) away. In Mijas follow signs to the underground car park (€1 for 24 hours).

05 MIJAS

The *pueblo blanco* (white village) of Mijas has retained its sugar-cube cuteness despite being on the coach-tour circuit. Art buffs should check out the **Centro de Arte Contemporáneo de Mijas** (*cacmijas.info*), a contemporary art museum that houses the world's second-largest collection of Picasso ceramics. Otherwise the village is all about strolling the narrow cobbled streets, dipping into tapas bars and shopping for souvenirs. Be sure to walk up to the **Plaza de Toros**, an unusual square-shaped bullring at the top of the village, surrounded by lush ornamental gardens with spectacular coastal views. For more exercise, there are numerous trails leading out from the village, including a tough, well-marked route up to **Pico Mijas** (1151m) – allow about five hours to get there and back.

Photo opportunity

A flock of cranes flying over the Laguna de Gallocanta.

THE DRIVE
Return to the A7 *autovia*. This dual carriageway traverses the most densely built-up stretch of the Costa, passing through resorts like Calahonda and Miraflores that were developed during the Costa's 1980s boom period. Continue west along the A7 until you reach the exit for Marbella; a total drive of 33km (25 minutes).

06 MARBELLA

Marbella is the Costa del Sol's most high-profile resort town and a good choice for an overnight stop. Well known for its star-studded clubs, shiny restaurants and expensive hotels, it also has other, less ostentatious charms: a magnificent natural setting, sheltered by the beautiful Sierra Blanca mountains, and a gorgeous old town replete with pristine white houses, narrow traffic-free lanes and well-tended flower boxes. At its heart is picturesque **Plaza de los Naranjos**, dating back to 1485 with tropical plants, palms and orange trees. From here you can walk down to the seafront via the lush **Parque de la Alameda** gardens. Follow along the so-called **Golden Mile** (actually, it's about 6km) and you'll eventually reach the luxurious marina of Puerto Banús. En route, take time to check out the **Museo Ralli** (*museoralli.es*), a wonderful private museum displaying works by primarily Latin American and European artists in bright, well-lit galleries.

THE DRIVE
Continue west on the A7 *autovia*, following signs to Algeciras and Cádiz. This stretch of highway is less built up and passes by San Pedro de Alcántara, as well as five golf courses (they don't nickname this the Costa del Golf for nothing!). It's a snappy 20 minutes (24km) to your next stop: Estepona.

DETOUR:
Comares

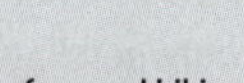

START: 02 MÁLAGA

Heading northeast from Málaga brings you to La Axarquía, an area of rugged hiking country stippled with pretty, unspoiled *pueblos* (villages). A highlight, quite literally, is Comares, which sits like a snowdrift on a lofty mountain (739m), commanding spectacular views over the surrounding mountains. Stroll its steep winding lanes and don't miss the remarkable summit cemetery. There are also several walking trails that start here, as well as a 436m-long zip line, the **Tirolina de Comares**, which provides a 50-second ride over to the opposite slopes. This is generally open on an appointment-only basis so it's best to book a ride through an activity company like **Vive Aventura** (*viveaventura.es*). To get to Comares from Málaga, take the A45 towards Granada, Córdoba and Seville, then exit for Casabermeja and continue onto Comares via the A356 (through Riogordo) and MA3107. The journey is about 60km and should take about 70 minutes.

WHY I LOVE THIS TRIP

Duncan Garwood, writer

Loud, brash and always fun, Spain's most famous *costa* makes for a wonderfully entertaining trip. Our route reveals the sunshine coast in all its gaudy glory, taking in Malaga's cultural hits, a giant Buddhist stupa in party-loving Torremolinos, and Marbella's star-studded seafront. Providing the grand finale is Gibraltar, the legendary Rock that guards the gateway to the Mediterranean.

07 ESTEPONA

Estepona was one of the first resorts to attract tourists almost 50 years ago and, despite the surrounding development, it retains a charming historic centre of narrow cobbled streets, simple *pueblo* houses and well-tended pots of geraniums. Make a beeline for Plaza de las Flores with its fountain centrepoint, orange trees and handy **tourist office** (*estepona.es*). A 10-minute walk from here, Estepona's fabulous **Orchidarium** (*orchidariumestepona.com*) houses 1500 species of orchid – the largest collection in Europe – as well as 5000 subtropical plants, flowers and trees, and a 17m-high artificial waterfall. To the southwest of the town centre, Puerto Deportivo is the focal point of the town's nightlife, especially at weekends, and is also excellent for water sports.

THE DRIVE

For the final leg consider taking the AP7 toll road for the first 20km (€3.35 in peak summer months) as the N340 here is very slow, with numerous roundabouts. At Guadiaro the AP7 merges with the A7 for the rest of the 49km journey. Consider a refreshment stop at swanky Sotogrande harbour, home to Spain's leading golf course, the Real Club Valderrama.

08 GIBRALTAR

Red pillar boxes, fish-and-chip shops and creaky 1970s seaside hotels – there's no getting away from Gibraltar's Britishness. Poised strategically at the jaws of Europe and Africa, Gibraltar, with its Palladian architecture and camera-hogging Barbary apes, makes an interesting finale to your trip. The Rock is one of the most dramatic landforms in southern Europe and most of its upper sections (but not the main lookouts) fall within the **Upper Rock Nature Reserve**. Entry to this includes admission to **St Michael's Cave**, the Apes' Den, the **Great Siege Tunnels**, the **Military Heritage Centre** and **Nelson's Anchorage**. The Rock's most famous residents are the 160 or so tailless Barbary macaques that hang around the top cable-car station and Apes' Den. Most Gibraltar visits start in Grand Casemates Sq, once the sight of public executions but now a jolly square surrounded by bars and restaurants. Learn more about the Rock's history at the fine **Gibraltar Museum** (*gibmuseum.gi*), which displays exhibits ranging from prehistoric and Phoenician Gibraltar to the infamous Great Siege (1779–83).

TOP TIP:

Toll Roads

If you're travelling in July and August, consider taking the AP7 toll road, at least between Fuengirola and Marbella, as the A7 can become horribly congested. This particular A7 stretch (formerly part of the N340) used to be notorious for accidents; however, the situation has improved since the introduction of a 80km/h speed limit in former trouble spots.

The Rock, Gibraltar

22

ANDALUCÍA & SOUTHERN SPAIN

Golden Triangle

BEST FOR TAPAS

Seville is renowned for its traditional and modern tapas.

Real Alcázar

DURATION	DISTANCE	GREAT FOR
5-7 days	576km / 358 miles	History, wine

BEST TIME TO GO	
	April to June is good for multiple spring festivals; September and October to avoid the ferocious summer heat.

The three cities of Seville, Córdoba and Granada have taken it in turns to dominate cultural and political life in Andalucía for the past 1000 years, and between them they guard a truly golden legacy. This triangular drive links all three cities while also revealing snippets of small-town beauty and quiet rural life.

Link your trip

23 The Great Outdoors

This vastly different take on Andalucía intersects with the Golden Triangle at both Antequera and Osuna.

24 Andalucía's White Villages

After finishing this trip in Seville, retrace 35km to Carmona and join this spectacular mountain drive through Cádiz and Málaga provinces.

01 SEVILLE

Shaped by half a dozen civilisations and reborn in numerous incarnations during its 2000-year history, Seville is a city of flamboyant beauty and contrasting seasonal moods. Historic monuments and romantic plazas adorn its energetic streets, which are drenched in spirit-enriching sunshine for much of the year. Navigate through the former Jewish quarter of **Santa Cruz** and see the city's main sights, including obligatory visits to the Real Alcázar and Catedral. Try to take in a flamenco show and experience enjoying a tapas meal in one of

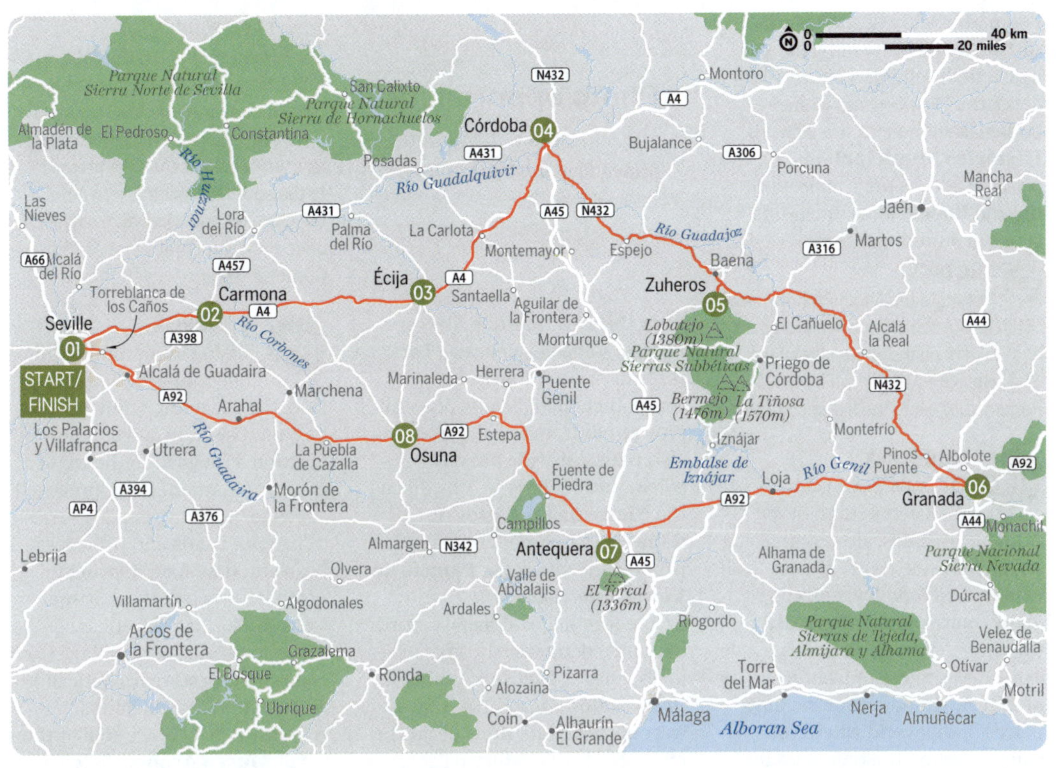

the centre's many teeming bars. With more time, check out **Plaza de España** in the **Parque de María Luisa** and the **Metropol Parasol** (*setasdesevilla.com*). Overnighters can get a taste of the city's kicking nightlife on the Alameda de Hércules.

THE DRIVE
Leave Seville on the eastbound A4 (also known as the E5). Pass Seville airport on your right and follow signs towards Carmona on the fast-moving four-lane carriageway. Take the first exit for Carmona after 33km.

02 CARMONA

Set atop a ridge overlooking golden, sun-baked plains, Carmona is like a mini-Seville that never grew up. Its centre is packed with stately palaces, Mudéjar churches and two Moorish forts while, nearby, a haunting **Necrópolis Romana** (*museosdeandalucia.es*) tells of the town's ancient origins. The town's signature sight is the **Alcázar de la Puerta de Sevilla**, a golden fort built by the Muslim Almohads over an earlier Roman structure. At the other end of the historic centre, the ruined **Alcázar de Arriba** provides a stirring backdrop to Carmona's panoramic **parador** (*parador.es/en/paradores/parador-de-carmona*).

THE DRIVE
Double back to the A4 and follow it 53km east to Écija. The agricultural landscapes around the Genil and Guadalquivir river valleys act as a heat trap in summer earning Écija its nickname, 'El sartén de Andalucía' (the frying pan of Andalucía).

03 ÉCIJA

A city of baroque church towers, suffocating summer heat, and an unpronounceable name, Écija (eth-ee-ha) is a hardworking provincial town where tourism is an afterthought and history reverberates around its compact centre. Of the town's famous spires, most of which date to an 18th-century building boom, the belfry of the **Iglesia de San Juan** is the only one you can actually climb. A short walk away, the 18th-century Palacio de Benamejí houses the **Museo Histórico Municipal** (*museo.ecija.es*) and its prize collection of local Roman finds, including a series of stunning mosaics.

THE DRIVE
Return to the A4 and follow it for 55km to Córdoba. Once in the city, it's best to park on the south side of the Guadalquivir River and walk across the Roman bridge into the historic centre.

Photo opportunity

The Alhambra with the Sierra Nevada in the background.

04 CÓRDOBA

Córdoba has easier road access than other Andalucian cities, although its labyrinthine centre is best explored on foot. Its centrepiece is the multi-arched **Mezquita** (*mezquita-catedraldecordoba.es*), a masterpiece of Islamic architecture and one of the only places in the world where you can celebrate Christian mass in a mosque. The narrow streets of the old **Judería** (Jewish quarter) and Muslim quarter stretch out from the great mosque like capillaries, some clogged with bars, restaurants and tourist bric-a-brac, others delightfully peaceful. Flower boxes and cool, geranium-clad patios provide bursts of colour, particularly in May during the **Fiesta de los Patios de Córdoba** (*patios.cordoba.es*). Another prime patio site is the **Palacio de Viana** (*palaciodeviana.com*). Before leaving Córdoba, it's worth making a detour to the archaeological site of **Medina Azahara** (*museosdeandalucia.es*), 8km west of town. The ruins of this remarkable 10th-century palace-city testify to Córdoba's past as one of medieval Europe's greatest cities.

THE DRIVE
Head south from Córdoba on the N432. Soon after bypassing Baena, branch west onto the A318 (Autovía del Olivar). Zuheros will soon appear as a white splash amid the green crags to the south. To reach it, turn onto the CO6209 and wind your way up to the town. Total distance from Córdoba: 77km.

05 ZUHEROS

Rising above undulating emerald-green countryside, the charming white village of Zuheros sits in a dramatic location, crouched in the lee of a craggy mountain. It's approached via a steep road through a series of hairpin bends and provides a beautiful base for exploring the northern reaches of the Parque Natural Sierras Subbéticas.
The main sight in the village itself is its small **castle**, dramatically grafted onto a rocky pinnacle. Admission tickets are sold at the small **Museo Arqueológico** just across the square.

THE DRIVE
Retrace your tracks via the CO6209 and A318 back to the arterial N432 and head 100km southeast towards the Sierra Nevada mountains and Granada nestled beneath them.

06 GRANADA

The last bastion of the Moors in Europe, Granada is a gritty, tempestuous city where Andalucía's complex history is laid out in ornate detail. Its great headline act is the **Alhambra** (*alhambra-patronato.es*), the Nasrid emir's opulent palace complex. Below it sprawls the city where bohemian bars and shadowy *teterías* (teahouses) go hand in hand with monumental churches, whitewashed *cármenes*

LEGACY OF THE ROMANS

One of Andalucía's least visited parks, the **Parque Natural Sierras Subbéticas** is crisscrossed by numerous walking and cycling trails, many of which start near Zuheros. The park's easiest and best-marked path is the Vía Verde de la Subbética, which runs along a disused railway for 58km across southern Córdoba province from Camporreal near Puente Genil to the Río Guadajoz on the Jaén border.

There are no fierce gradients as it passes through tunnels and over old bridges and viaducts, and with plenty of informative map-boards, it's impossible to get lost. You can fuel up at cafes and hire bikes at outlets in old station buildings along the route.

The **Centro Cicloturista Subbética** (*subbeticabikesfriends.com*) at Doña Mencía station, 4km downhill from Zuheros, rents a range of different bikes, and can provide local tourist information as well as showers and other services for cyclists.

(mansions with walled gardens), and counterculture graffiti art. If this is your first time in Granada, prioritise the Alhambra, for if ever a monument lived up to the hype, this is it. However, to enjoy the experience, make sure to pre-purchase tickets – you can buy them from two hours to three months in advance, either online or by phone. When you've visited the Alhambra, take time to explore the steeply stacked **Albayzin** (old Moorish quarter) and admire the street art in the **Realejo** district. More traditional artistic offerings await in the **catedral** (*catedraldegranada.com*) and **Capilla Real** (*capillarealgranada.com*), the last resting place of Spain's *Reyes Católicos* (Catholic Monarchs).

SEVILLE'S FLAMENCO CLUBS

Casa de la Memoria (*casadelamemoria.es*) Cultural centre that stages passionate shows often touted as the best in Seville.

Museo del Baile Flamenco (*museoflamenco.com*) Better known as a museum, this place holds nightly flamenco performances with aficionados yelling encouragement.

Tablao Los Gallos (*tablaolosgallos.com*) Seville's oldest *tablao* (venue for choreographed flamenco) puts on two nightly shows featuring top-notch dancers, singers and guitarists.

THE DRIVE

Head west out of Granada on the main Seville road, the A92. After 95km you'll cross the A45, the main north–south *autovia* between Málaga and Córdoba. A couple of kilometres further on, turn south on the A7281 to Antequera, which sits beneath the rocky moonscapes of the uplands.

07 ANTEQUERA

Antequera is a fascinating town, both architecturally and historically, yet few visitors linger long. The town has a rich tapestry of architectural and archaeological gems, ranging from two Bronze Age burial sites to a grand Moorish **Alcazaba**, whose

VALERY BARETA/SHUTTERSTOCK ©

Mezquita, Córdoba

substantial remains are within easy (if uphill) walking distance of the town centre. However, the undoubted highlight here is the lavish Spanish baroque architecture that gives the town its character.

THE DRIVE
Get back on the A92 and strike northwest towards Seville. The *autopista* bypasses the towns of La Roda de Andalucía and Estepa before the small but grandiose baroque town of Osuna comes into sight after about 76km.

08 OSUNA

Osuna is a small provincial town with a legacy that far outweighs its size. Many of its artistic and architectural treasures were commissioned by the rich dukes of Osuna between the 16th and 18th centuries. Striking heirlooms include a series of baroque mansions and the **Colegiata de Santa María de la Asunción**, a landmark Renaissance monastery filled with baroque art. This formidable ensemble provided a suitably fantastical location for the *Game of Thrones* whose fifth season was partly filmed here – check out the **Museo de Osuna** for more on the town's GoT role. Among the most ornate of Osuna's 18th-century mansions is the Palacio del Marqués de La Gomera, now a princely four-star hotel.

TAIGA/SHUTTERSTOCK ©

The Alhambra (p160)

23

ANDALUCÍA & SOUTHERN SPAIN

The Great Outdoors

BEST FOR WILDLIFE

Huelva's majestic World Heritage-listed Parque Nacional de Doñana.

DURATION	DISTANCE	GREAT FOR
7 days	783km / 486 miles	Nature, history, families

BEST TIME TO GO	From April to June and September to October for ideal weather.

Mulhacén

Starting high in the Sierra Nevada, this outdoors itinerary swings west and south through a mesmerising patchwork of contrasting landscapes. The long, winding road leads from the dramatic mountain gorges of Las Alpujarras through the dry, billowing plains of the Sevillan Campiña to Doñana national park and on to Tarifa's white-sand surfer beaches. En route, you'll come across historical monuments, archaeological treasures and culinary delights as richly varied as the ever-changing natural backdrop.

Link your trip

21 Costa del Sol Beyond the Beaches

Pick up the N340 at Tarifa and push northeast on the A7 for the 44km drive to Gibraltar, the endpoint of this whistle-stop tour of the Costa del Sol.

24 Andalucía's White Villages

From Osuna, head 61km northwest to Carmona to pick up this trip through Andalucía's classic white villages.

01 CAPILEIRA

Kick things off in pretty Capileira in Las Alpujarras, the 70km stretch of valleys that runs along the southern flank of the Sierra Nevada. At 1436m, the whitewashed village is the highest, largest and prettiest of the three in the Barranco de Poqueira (Poqueira Gorge), sitting high above Pampaneira and Bubión. Despite its dramatic location it's just an hour's drive from the A44 via the A348, A4132 and A4129. Two nights here allow you to enjoy a full day of walking, mountain cooking and shopping for leather work at **J Brown**

(*tallerbrown@gmail.com*). There's superb walking in the surrounding mountains, with many trails doable in a day. The area's most dramatic hike is to the summit of **Mulhacén** (3479m), mainland Spain's highest peak. To tackle this, catch the summer shuttle bus to the Mirador de Trevélez (2710m), from where it's a three-hour walk to the summit (5.1km, 800m ascent). The best hiking months are April to mid-June and then mid-September to October; July to early September is best for the high peaks.

THE DRIVE
From Capileira, wind 36km downhill past Bubión, Pampaneira, Órgiva and Lanjarón (A4129, A4132 and A348). Take the northbound A44 for 50km, bypassing Granada to join the A92. Continue west for 92km, exiting at turn-off 149 to reach Antequera. Skirt around town to pick up the A343 and then the A7075 to the Paraje Natural Torcal de Antequera. As you climb, the Mediterranean sparkles just south

02 PARAJE NATURAL TORCAL DE ANTEQUERA

The bizarre and beautiful rock formations of the Paraje Natural Torcal de Antequera are a magnificent sight. The 12-sq-km park, declared a Unesco World Heritage site in 2016, is a rugged, almost otherworldly area of gnarled, serrated and pillared limestone that formed as a seabed 150 million years ago but now rises to a height of 1336m (El Torcal). Leave your car at the park's excellent **Centro de Visitantes** (*torcaldeantequera.com*) and continue on foot along one of three walking trails: the 1.5km Ruta Verde (Green Route), the 3km Ruta Amarilla (Yellow Route), or the 3.6km Ruta Naranja (Orange Route).

THE DRIVE
Drive back into Antequera, where there's convenient underground parking on Calle Diego Ponce north of Plaza de San Sebastián.

03 ANTEQUERA

Despite its impressive collection of archaeological riches and Spanish-baroque sights, Antequera gets refreshingly little tourist traffic. Looming over the historic centre are the imposing hilltop remains of a 14th-century Moorish Alcazaba (p00). Down in the heart of town, the **Museo de la Ciudad**) has an impressive array of Roman artefacts, including a 1.4m bronze statue, Efebe, that's considered one of the finest examples of Roman sculpture ever unearthed in Spain. Travel further back in time at Antequera's **dolmens**, some 1km out of the centre. Built by Bronze Age people in around 2500 BCE, the **Dolmen de Veira** and **Dolmen de Menga** are two of Europe's oldest burial chambers. The **Dolmen del Romeral**, another 3km to the northeast, dates to 1800 BCE.

Photo opportunity

Tarifa, beaches and kitesurfers backed by Morocco, from Punta Paloma dune.

THE DRIVE
Continue 16km northwest on the A92 to the signposted Laguna de Fuente de Piedra turn-off. 'Laguna' signs lead you through Fuente de Piedra village to the lagoon's visitor centre (2km).

04 LAGUNA DE FUENTE DE PIEDRA

When it's not dried up, Laguna de Fuente de Piedra is Andalucía's largest natural lake and one of Europe's two main breeding grounds for the greater flamingo (the other is in the Camargue region of southwestern France). After a wet winter as many as 20,000 pairs of flamingos will breed here. The birds arrive in January or February, and the chicks hatch in April and May. The flamingos stay until about August, when the lake, which they share with about 170 other bird species, no longer contains enough water to support them. For maps, binoculars and bird-spotting tips, swing by the lakeside **visitor centre** (*visitas fuentepiedra.es*).

THE DRIVE
From Fuente de Piedra, it's a 54km spin west on the A92 to Osuna. As you go you'll pass low-lying hills, endless olive groves and the hillside town of Estepa.

05 OSUNA

Unassuming Osuna harbours a cache of architectural and artistic treasures courtesy of the fabulously wealthy dukes of Osuna. A steep climb from Plaza Mayor leads to the magnificent Renaissance Colegiata de Santa María de la Asunción (p162) – actually two superposed churches set above the 16th-century crypt of the Duques de Osuna. Its impressive art collection includes paintings by José de Ribera (El Españoleto) and a fine sculpture by Juan de Mesa. Stroll the streets northwest of Plaza Mayor to uncover Osuna's other stars: a string of ornately decorated baroque mansions, including the late-18th-century **Palacio de los Cepeda**.

THE DRIVE
Head west on the A92 across the flat Campiña region (82km). Follow 'Huelva' signs to bypass Seville and link up with the A49 to Portugal. Drive 49km west, then exit onto the A483 for the last 27km south to El Rocío. Please heed lynx warning signs in the Doñana area.

THE IBERIAN LYNX

For wildlife-watchers, the Iberian lynx is Doñana's most sought-after prize. Along with the Sierra Morena, Parque Nacional de Doñana and Parque Natural de Doñana are the main habitats for this elusive feline, one of the world's most endangered cats.

Over the years, the park's lynxes have had to battle a disastrous slump in Doñana's population of rabbits (the lynx's main prey), as well as threats from hunters, developers, habitat loss, and even tourism. Some resident lynxes have also been run over around Doñana – in 2019, 29 lynxes were killed in road accidents in the park and elsewhere in Spain.

However, recent years have seen an increase in numbers and there are now believed to be between 70 and 100 individuals in the Doñana area – the official figure in 2018 was 94, up significantly from the 41 recorded in 2002. Factors contributing to this include the recent release of 10,000 rabbits into the area and an increasingly successful captive breeding program – in 2020, 26 breeding pairs were expected to produce between 37 and 45 kittens.

Catch live videos of lynxes at Doñana's breeding centre at the **Centro de Visitantes El Acebuche.**

06 PARQUE NACIONAL DE DOÑANA

Welcome to Spain's most celebrated national park, a hauntingly beautiful 601-sq-km expanse of wetlands, beaches, dunes and woodlands. Its protected habitats provide refuge for a huge variety of flora and fauna, including 360 bird species and the endangered Iberian lynx, one of 37 types of mammal. Much of the park's perimeter is bordered by the separate **Parque Natural de Doñana**. The obvious base for the park is El Rocío, a dusky, sand-blown town that bursts into life every Penetecost weekend for the **Romería del Rocío**, Spain's largest religious pilgrimage. Two nights here gives you a full day for Doñana. El Rocío's gleaming wetlands offer some of Doñana's finest bird- and wildlife-watching. Look out for spoonbills, pink flamingos, horses and deer from the waterfront promenade and the **Francisco Bernis Birdwatching Centre** (*facebook.com/centroFranciscoBernis*). You can't enter the national park in your own car, though you can drive to the four visitor centres, including the Centro de Visitantes El Acebuche (p166), 12km south of El Rocío. To access the park, you'll need to go on a guided trip with a licensed operator such as **Doñana Nature** (*donana-nature.com*), **Cooperativa Marismas del Rocío** (*donanavisitas.es*) or **Doñana Reservas** (*donanareservas.com*). These offer four-hour trips in all-terrain vehicles. Book as far ahead as possible, especially in spring and summer.

TOP TIP:

Sierra Nevada Hiking Maps

Get maps and hiking advice at **Nevadensis** (*nevadensis.com*) in Pampaneira. Many local hotels also provide their own maps with walk descriptions. The best maps for Las Alpujarras are Editorial Alpina's *Sierra Nevada, La Alpujarra* (1:40,000) and Editorial Penibética's *Sierra Nevada* (1:40,000).

Flamingos, Parque Natural de Doñana

TOP TIP:

Surfing El Palmar

Cádiz' Costa de la Luz boasts brilliant windsurfing and kitesurfing. El Palmar beach, about 7km northwest of Los Caños, has Andalucía's best board-surfing waves from October to May. For classes and boards, contact **Escuela de Surf 9 Pies** (*escueladesurf9pies.com*).

THE DRIVE

Rev up for a 245km drive. Backtrack to the A49 from El Rocío and head east. Follow the signs for A4 Cádiz signs to circumnavigate Seville onto the AP4 and whizz 85km south. Continue south on the A4 and A48 for 48km, then turn onto the A2232 to Conil. From here it's 15km on the A2233 to Los Caños de Meca.

07 LOS CAÑOS DE MECA

Los Caños de Meca sprawls along a series of stunning white-sand beaches on the wind-battered Costa de la Luz. Once a hippie hangout, it still attracts beach-lovers of all stripes with its bohemian summer scene, nudist beaches and excellent water sports – kitesurfing, windsurfing and board-surfing are all big here. Follow a tiny side road (often covered in sand) at the western end of town to a lighthouse, the **Cabo de Trafalgar**, off which the Spanish navy was defeated by Nelson's British fleet in 1805. Nearby, stop off at the ultimate relaxation spot, **Las Dunas** (*barlasdunas.es*), for Bob Marley tunes, great *bocadillos* (filled rolls), and a chilled, beach-shack vibe. For a good walk, head to the eastern end of Caños. Here you can pick up the 7.2km **Sendero del Acantilado**, a spectacular clifftop path that runs to Barbate through the protected pine forests

El Palmar

and marshlands of the 50-sq-km **Parque Natural de la Breña y Marismas del Barbate** (*juntadeandalucia.es*). Then retrace your steps or jump on a bus back to Caños (Monday to Friday).

THE DRIVE
This is classic Costa de la Luz driving. From Caños, head 10km east to Barbate, then take the A2231 for 10km to Zahara de los Atunes. Turn inland here and continue past towering wind turbines to the N340. Join this and push southeast for 15km to the signposted CA8202 Bolonia turn-off, from where it's a lovely, hilly 7km drive to Bolonia.

08 BOLONIA

With its gorgeous white-sand dune, broad beach and wind-bashed *chiringuitos* (beach bars) nestled beneath rolling green hills, sleepy Bolonia makes a wonderfully low-key stop on your trip down the Costa de la Luz. Sands aside, the main draw here is the ruined Roman settlement of **Baelo Claudia** (*museosdeandalucia.es*), one of Andalucía's most important archaeological sites. The town, which flourished during the reign of Claudius (41–54 CE), was known across the Roman world for its garum (a spicy seasoning made from leftover fish parts). Nowadays, its magnificent seaside ruins – with views across to Morocco – include the substantial remains of thermal baths, workshops, a theatre, a paved forum and a basilica. There's also a good museum.

THE DRIVE
Backtrack to the N340 for the 15km drive southeast to Tarifa. Parking in Tarifa can be tricky, but there's metered space on Avenida de la Constitución beside the Alameda.

09 TARIFA

Wrap up this epic drive in Tarifa, on Spain's southernmost tip where the Mediterranean meets the Atlantic. The town, which gives off a tangible North African feel, is a haven of sporting fun with a laid-back, surf-inspired buzz, long history and international-focused culinary scene. Duck under the Mudéjar **Puerta de Jerez** to enter the old town, whose narrow, whitewashed streets are mostly of Islamic origin. The main sight here is the 10th-century **Castillo de Guzmán El Bueno**, where Reconquista hero Guzmán El Bueno legendarily sacrificed his own son in 1294 to save Tarifa from Moroccan attackers. A short hop away, the **Miramar** commands spectacular views across to Africa just 14km away. For a change of scene, check out the surf-style boutiques on Calle Batalla del Salado. Then hit the bleach-blond sands that stretch 10km northwest to **Playa de Valdevaqueros** and **Punta Paloma**, one of Andalucía's most fabulous beaches. Tarifa's waters provide some of Europe's finest kitesurfing and windsurfing, particularly in May, June and September. Link up with operators like **ION Club Hurricane** (*ion-club.net*) for equipment rental and classes. **Aventura Ecuestre** (*aventuraecuestre.com*) runs fabulous horse rides.The **tourist office** (*turismodetarifa.com*) can provide details of other activities including hiking, diving, biking and whale-watching.

WHY I LOVE THIS TRIP

Duncan Garwood, writer

This trip is the perfect showcase for Andalucía's diverse landscapes, leading from mainland Spain's highest mountains to wild, windswept beaches and eerie wetlands. One day you'll be be inching up steep valley roads in the Sierra Nevada, the next you'll be spying on flocks of pink flamingos in the otherworldly Parque Nacional de Doñana. It's a thrilling ride.

DETOUR:

Parque Natural Los Alcornocales

START: 09 TARIFA

The Parque Natural Los Alcornocales, a gorgeous 1736-sq-km reserve of crinkled, medium-height hills and extensive *alcornocales* (cork-oak woodlands), sits about 75km inland from the Strait of Gibraltar. Rich in archaeological, historical and natural interest, it's particularly rewarding to explore with your own wheels.

The best base is bucolic sun-bleached **Jimena de la Frontera**, about an hour's drive (64km) northeast of Tarifa. The town's 13th-century **Nasrid castle** commands mesmerising views of Gibraltar and Africa, while trails offer excellent hiking.

One of the park's best trails is the 3.3km **Sendero Subida al Picacho,** which leads up through cork-oak forest to the park's second-highest peak, El Picacho (882m). To do this walk, and a number of other local hikes, you'll need a (free) permit – you must request this at least three days in advance from the **Oficina del Parque Natural Los Alcornocales** (*juntadeandalucia.es*).

24

ANDALUCÍA & SOUTHERN SPAIN

Andalucía's White Villages

BEST FOR OUTDOORS

Beautiful Sierra de Grazalema mountain walks.

DURATION	DISTANCE	GREAT FOR
4 days	239km/ 148 miles	History, nature

BEST TIME TO GO	May, June, September and October for perfect temperatures.

Arcos de la Frontera

Crumbling, aeons-old fortifications soar over whitewashed terracotta-tiled homes huddled together in a rocky, green landscape: a visual spectacle that threads through this tour of Andalucía's prettiest *pueblos blancos*. This trip showcases the historical allure of the region's quintessential white towns while also paving the way for some fantastic hiking and exhilarating driving over spine-tingling mountain roads. Kick off with Roman tombs in Carmona; end with mountain magic in Ronda.

Link your trip

20 Mediterranean Meander

Make for Málaga, 103km southeast of Ronda, to hook up with this coastal cruise to Barcelona.

23 The Great Outdoors

From Carmona head 61km southeast to Osuna to join this epic outdoors adventure.

01 CARMONA

Crowning a low-rise hill 35km east of Seville, Carmona provides a living snapshot of Andalucian history. The town's tumultuous past is writ large on its maze-like old town whose narrow streets are crammed with Mudéjar and Christian churches, aristocratic mansions, centuries-old monuments, and buzzy tapas bars. Dig back to Paleolithic times at the **Museo de la Ciudad** (*museociudad.carmona.org*) before stopping off at the splendidly over-the-top **Prioral de Santa María de la Asunción** (*santamariacarmona.org*) with its gorgeous Patio de los Naranjos. A short walk away, the **Puerta de Córdoba** provides great

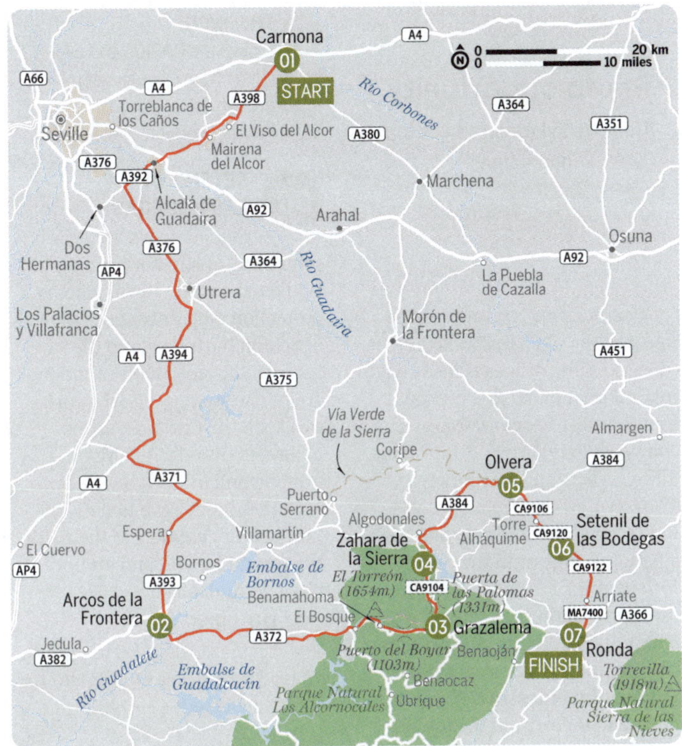

photo opportunities. On Carmona's southwestern fringe stands the eerily fascinating 1st- and 2nd-century **Necrópolis Romana** (*museosdeandalucia.es*).

THE DRIVE
Take the A398 southwest, then continue on the A392 and A376 to Utrera (50km). Here pick up the A394 and continue down this and the NIV towards Jerez de la Frontera. Turn off the NIV onto the A371, signposted to Villamartín, and after 4km or so, turn right towards Espera. Arcos is about 14km beyond Espera on the A393.

02 ARCOS DE LA FRONTERA

If there's one white town in Cádiz province that outshines them all, it's Arcos de la Frontera. Thrillingly sited atop a dramatic sheer-sided crag, it charms with its whitewashed arches, twisting alleyways and air of historical mystery. The main attraction is **Plaza del Cabildo**, which commands spectacular vistas over the Río Guadalete from its vertiginous mirador. The real knockout view, though, is the dramatic clifftop panorama from the adjacent **parador** (*parador.es*). Bordering the plaza's northern edge is the Gothic-baroque **Basílica Menor de Santa María de la Asunción**, an intriguing church whose gold-leaf altarpiece is a miniature of the one in Seville's cathedral.

THE DRIVE
It's a tame 30km eastbound drive on the A372 to El Bosque, then suddenly you find yourself on a thrilling, winding 20km climb to Grazalema. Stop at the signposted Puerto del Boyar (1103m) for glorious mountainscapes.

03 GRAZALEMA

Craving some physical activity? Clinging to verdant rocky slopes, rust-roofed Grazalema is an idyllic white mountain town as well as an ideal base for exploring the rugged, 534-sq-km Parque Natural Sierra de Grazalema. It's also reputed to be the rainiest spot in Spain (yes, really). Stretch your legs on the **El Calvario-Corazón de Jesús** trail to a ruined chapel, or choose from numerous paths starting near Grazalema. **Horizon** (*horizonaventura.com*) organises all kinds of adventure activities: hiking, kayaking, canyoning and paragliding. In town, you can hang out on **Plaza de España** and learn about Grazalema's traditional wool production at the **Museo de Artesanía Textil** (*mantasdegrazalema.com*).

THE DRIVE
What a fantastic 17km. Full of sharp switchbacks, the steep CA9104 snakes north from Grazalema over the 1331m Puerto de las Palomas to Zahara de la Sierra. The views are fabulous: Zahara's reservoir twinkles turquoise as jagged mountains melt into the distance.

04 ZAHARA DE LA SIERRA

Laced around a vertiginous castle-topped crag at the foot of the Grazalema mountains, Zahara de la Sierra is a vision of classic white-town beauty. A Moorish stronghold in the 14th and 15th centuries, it's now a popular base for hiking the Garganta Verde. To reach the 12th-century **castillo**, it's a steep-ish 10- to 15-minute climb up a path starting opposite Hotel Arco de la Villa. The castle's recapture from the Christians by Abu al-Hasan of Granada in 1481 triggered the last phase of the Reconquista, culminating in the 1492 fall of Granada.

THE DRIVE
Exit Zahara northbound and work your way down to the A2300, which skirts Zahara's reservoir for around 6km to the A384. Whizz along this for about 22km to Olvera, which you'll spot from miles away across the sun-drenched, olive-cloaked countryside. The road passes the Peñón de Zaframagón, an important griffon vulture refuge.

05 OLVERA

Gutsier than its neighbours, Olvera is as known for its olive oil as for the wonderful 36km **Vía Verde de la Sierra** (*viasverdes.com*), considered the finest of Andalucía's 23 *vías verdes* (disused railway lines transformed into hiking/cycling greenways). Rent bikes at **Sesca** (*sesca.es*) and spin west to Puerto Serrano along four viaducts and 30 tunnels. The town, which probably dates to Roman times and was used as a bandit refuge until the mid-19th century, is also well worth exploring. Main sights include the 630m-high, late-12th-century **Castillo Árabe**, neoclassical **Iglesia Parroquial Nuestra Señora de la Encarnación** and the town's history museum inside **La Cilla**.

Photo opportunity

Arcos de la Frontera's clifftop panoramas.

SIERRA DE GRAZALEMA WALKS

Lovely marked walking trails fan out across the Sierra de Grazalema. Pick up maps and info at the **Centro de Visitantes El Bosque** (*juntadeandalucia.es*), **Punto de Información Zahara de la Sierra** or Grazalema's **Oficina de Turismo** (*grazalema.es*).

The following walks all require free pre-booked permits from the Centro de Visitantes El Bosque.

Garganta Verde Starting 3.5km south of Zahara de la Sierra (off the CA9104), this 2.5km (one hour) path meanders into the precipitous Garganta Verde (Green Throat), a lushly vegetated gorge over 100m deep. It's one of the Sierra's most spectacular walks.

El Torreón Cádiz province's highest peak (1648m) and, on clear days, you can see Gibraltar, the Sierra Nevada and Morocco's Rif mountains from the summit. The challenging 3km trail (2½ hours) begins 8km west of Grazalema on the A372.

El Pinsapar This 12km (six-hour) walk winds past rare dark-green *pinsapos* (Spanish firs) to Benamahoma. It starts 2km from Grazalema off the CA9104.

THE DRIVE
Follow the CA9106 and CA9120 southwards from Olvera past rolling hills, through Torre Alháquime, to Setenil de las Bodegas, 15km away.

06 SETENIL DE LAS BODEGAS

Setenil de las Bodegas is something of a historic anomaly. While most white towns sought protection atop lofty crags, the folk of Setenil burrowed into the caves beneath the steep cliffs of the Río Trejo. The strategy clearly worked as it took the Christian armies 15 days to dislodge the Moors from Setenil in 1484. Swing by to explore original cave-houses, the 12th-century **castle** and the rustic bar-restaurants on and around Plaza de Andalucía.

THE DRIVE
Zip 17km south into Málaga province to Ronda via the CA9127, MA7403, and from Arriate, the MA7400.

07 RONDA

End your trip on a high at rugged Ronda. Spectacularly straddling the 100m-wide Tajo gorge, Ronda is the largest and busiest of Andalucía's white towns and the (alleged) birthplace of modern bullfighting. The town's most recognisable sight is the 18th-century **Puente Nuevo**, which spans the gorge separating the old and new towns. The old town (aka La Ciudad) is a walled tangle of streets, peppered with Renaissance mansions and intriguing museums such as the **Museo de Ronda**. In the new town, **Plaza de España** was the scene of events in the Civil War that inspired a grisly episode in Hemingway's *For Whom the Bell Tolls*. Nearby, the 200-year-old **Plaza de Toros** is one of Spain's oldest and most celebrated bullrings.

Ronda

RESTAURANTE

25

BEST FOR AESTHETES

The architecture of Úbeda's Plaza Vázquez de Molina.

ANDALUCÍA & SOUTHERN SPAIN

Olive Oil & the Renaissance in Jaén

DURATION	DISTANCE	GREAT FOR
3-4 days	115km/ 71 miles	History, wine

BEST TIME TO GO	From April to June, and September and October for perfect weather.

Catedral de la Asunción

The 16th-century grandees of this rural region beautified their towns just as classically inspired Renaissance architecture was sweeping into Spain from Italy. The resulting buildings dazzle to this day, particularly in World Heritage–listed Úbeda and Baeza. Beyond these towns, the landscape is a never-ending carpet of silvery-green olive trees, an almost hypnotic spectacle that will whet the appetite of olive oil aficionados.

Link your trip

22 Golden Triangle

From Jaén, zip 90km down the A44 to Granada to link with this tour of Andalucía's most splendid cities.

23 The Great Outdoors

Continue past Granada to the Sierra Nevada to start this adventurous exploration of Andalucía's wild, unspoiled spaces.

01 JAÉN

Everything in the charming, if mildly dilapidated, historic centre of this provincial capital is dwarfed by the **Catedral de la Asunción** (*catedraldejaen.org*), designed by Andrés de Vandelvira, the master Renaissance architect whose work you'll see more of in Úbeda and Baeza. The cathedral's huge, round arches, clustered Corinthian columns, beautifully carved stone ceilings and great circular dome are all part and parcel of its Renaissance aesthetic. Avoid the aggravation of Jaén's traffic system by taking a taxi or walking (about 40 minutes) up to the **Cerro de Santa Catalina**, the wooded hill towering above the

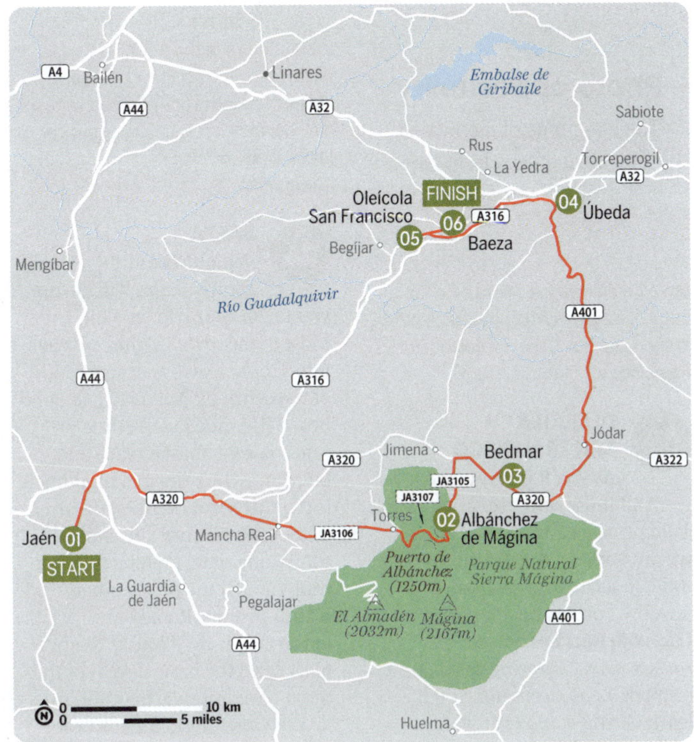

city. The views from the large cross at the end of the castle ridge are magnificent. The castle itself, the **Castillo de Santa Catalina**, was built by the conquering Christians to replace the Muslim fortress they captured in 1246. What exists today is only about one-third of the original castle – the rest was demolished to make way for a luxury hotel, the **Parador Castillo de Santa Catalina** 0, in the 1960s. If you're not staying at the *parador*, drop in for a drink to see the extraordinary vaulted ceilings in the main salon and restaurant. Back down in the centre, get a taste of Jaén's atmosphere with an evening tour of the ancient and atmospheric tapas bars clustered in the wafer-thin streets north of the cathedral.

THE DRIVE
The quickest route to Albánchez de Mágina is along the A31w6, then the A320 via Mancha Real and Jimena, and finally the JA3105. For a more scenic drive, head to the pretty village of Torres from Mancha Real. Then, from Torres take the dramatic JA3107, which winds over the 1250m-high Puerto de Albánchez pass and down to Albánchez de Mágina. Either way, it's about 46km.

02 ALBÁNCHEZ DE MÁGINA

This classic white village nestled beneath a towering cliff is home to one of Jaén province's most dramatic apparitions: the **Castillo de Albánchez**. The castle's 14th-century leaning tower is spectacularly perched atop a sheer cliff rising directly above the village. You can, amazingly enough, walk up to it in about 20 steep minutes – ask for directions in the central Plaza de la Constitución. Make the effort and you're rewarded with stunning bird's-eye views over the whitewashed village and surrounding mountains. Back in the village, there are several cafes and bars if you'd like refreshments.

THE DRIVE
From Albánchez, head north down the JA3105 and turn right along the A320 as you enter Jimena. It's 8km to Bedmar.

03 BEDMAR

Stop at this sizeable white village, with a backdrop of rugged crags, to wander its winding streets up to the picturesque remains of a 15th-century castle set on a panoramic rocky outcrop at the top of the village.

THE DRIVE
Continue along the A320 to the A401 where you should turn left towards Jódar and Úbeda. Parking in Úbeda's old town is free but often difficult to find – the best bet is the 24-hour free car park on Redonda de Miradores.

04 ÚBEDA

Beautiful Renaissance buildings grace almost every street and plaza in Úbeda's charming *casco antiguo* (old quarter). The World Heritage–listed town also offers top-class restaurants and tapas bars, making a stopover a real delight. Start your exploring in **Plaza Vázquez de Molina**, Úbeda's elegant showpiece square bedecked with orange and cypress trees and framed by grand Renaissance buildings. At its east end stands the **Sacra Capilla de El Salvador** (*fundacion medinaceli.org*), built between 1536 and 1559 by Andrés de Vandelvira for local aristocrat Francisco de los Cobos y Molina. Its ornately sculpted facade is a superb example of the early Renaissance style known as plateresque. On the plaza's northern flank, the **Palacio de Vázquez de Molina** is Úbeda's strikingly beautiful *ayuntamiento* (town hall). This perfectly proportioned Italianate mansion was built by Vandelvira in about 1562 for Juan Vázquez de Molina, whose coat of arms surmounts the doorway. Other standout sights include the medieval **Sinagoga del Agua** (*sinagogadelagua.com*), a sensitive re-creation of a centuries-old synagogue and rabbi's house, and the **Casa Museo Andalusí** (*vandelviraturismo.com*), a private museum in a 16th-century house with a huge collection of antiques. Informal guided tours led by the owner's art-historian daughter make it all come alive.

THE DRIVE
Head west out of Úbeda onto the A316. Then exit onto the A6109 at the Baeza Oeste turn-off and continue on to Begíjar via the JA4107. On the edge of Begíjar, turn right after a petrol station and you'll reach Oleícola San Francisco after about 200m.

Photo opportunity
The panorama of mountains and olive groves from the Castillo de Albánchez.

05 OLEÍCOLA SAN FRANCISCO

As you'll have guessed from all those olive trees out there, Jaén province produces a lot of olive oil – up to a fifth of the world's total, in fact. For a first-hand lowdown on the business, the **Oleícola San Francisco** (*oleo turismojaen.com*) runs fascinating tours of its modern mill. You'll learn all you could ever want to know about the process of turning olives into oil, how the best oil is made and what distinguishes extra virgin from the rest. At the end you'll get the chance to taste a few varieties and buy a bottle or two. Reserve ahead and specify your preferred language.

THE DRIVE
Return to the A6109 and head east, following signs into Baeza. Street parking is fairly limited in town so your best bet is to leave your car at the underground car park on Calle Compañía.

06 BAEZA

With its beautiful historic centre, Baeza will ensure you finish your trip on a high. Most of the town's sights are clustered in the narrow streets south of the central Plaza de España and broad Paseo de la Constitución (once Baeza's marketplace and bullring). The principal monument is the **Catedral de Baeza**. Dating to the 13th century, the church is something of an architectural hybrid, though the predominant style is 16th-century Renaissance, visible in the facade on Plaza de Santa María and the basic design of the three-nave interior (by Andrés de Vandelvira). Climb the tower for great views over the town and countryside. Other architectural gems include **Plaza del Pópulo**, a handsome square surrounded by elegant 16th-century buildings, and **Palacio de Jabalquinto**, with a flamboyant Gothic facade featuring a bizarre array of naked humans clambering along the moulding over the doorway.

For a post-sightseeing breather, stroll along the **Paseo de las Murallas** for superb views over to the distant mountains of the Sierra Mágina (south) and Sierra de Cazorla (east). For more energetic entertainment, catch a gig at the **Café Teatro Central** (*facebook.com/cafeteatrocentral*).

JAÉN'S RENAISSANCE MASTERMIND

Most of the finest buildings you'll see in Úbeda, Baeza and Jaén are the creations of one man: Andrés de Vandelvira, born in Alcaraz, Castilla-La Mancha, in 1509. Under the patronage of Úbeda's powerful Cobos and Molina families, Vandelvira almost single-handedly brought the Renaissance to Jaén province. Little is known about his life, but his oeuvre is a jewel of Spanish culture, spanning all the main phases of Spanish Renaissance architecture, as shown by three exemplary buildings in Úbeda – the ornamental early phase called plateresque, on the **Sacra Capilla de El Salvador**; the purer lines and classical proportions of the later **Palacio de Vázquez de Molina**; and the sober late-Renaissance style of the **Hospital de Santiago**, completed the year he died, in 1575.

Sacra Capilla de El Salvador

100 km
50 miles
SPAIN
Valença do Minho
Puebla de Sanabria
Verín
Viana do Castelo
Ponte de Lima
Parque Nacional da Peneda-Gerês
Chaves
Parque Natural de Montesinho
Bragança
Esposende
Braga
Vila Pouca de Aguiar
Guimarães
Miranda do Douro
Villa do Conde
Vila Nova de Famalicão
Mirandela
Porto
Vila Real
Rio Douro
Peso da Régua
Vila Nova de Foz Côa
Parque Natural do Douro Internacional
Aveiro
Viseu
Trancoso
Pinhel
Tondela
Vilar Formosa
Guarda
Ciudad Rodrigo
Parque Natural da Serra da Estrela
Rio Mondego
Coimbra
Figueira da Foz
Covilhã
Conímbriga
ATLANTIC OCEAN
Rio Zêzere
Plasencia
Castelo Branco
Leiria
Caldas da Rainha
Tomar
Parque Natural do Tejo Internacional
Rio Tejo
Peniche
Parque Natural das Serrasde Aire e Candeeiros
Constância
Cáceres
Parque Natural da Serra de São Mamede
Santarem
Portalegre
Torres Vedras
PORTUGAL
Sintra
LISBON
Elvas
Badajoz
Cascais
Estremoz
Mérida
Montemor-o-Novo
Setúbal
Évora
Reguengos de Monsaraz
SPAIN
Alcácer do Sal
Zafra
Grândola
Sines
Moura
Beja
Parque Natural Sierra de Aracena y Picos de Aroche
Parque Natural Sierra Norte de Sevilla
Vila Nova de Milfontes
Parque Natural do Vale do Guadiana
Parque Natural do Sudoeste Alentejano e Costa Vicentina
Castro Verde
Mértola
Vila Real de Santo António
Seville
Portimão
Cacela Velha
Huelva
Sagres
Lagos
Albufeira
Tavira
Faro
Golfo de Cádiz
Parque Nacional de Doñana

Porto (p188)

Portugal

Explore

Portugal

Down along Europe's sultry southwestern shore, Portugal is a wonderful world unto itself, and because it's so compact it's the perfect place for a road trip. Historic towns and villages, astonishing beaches and dramatic landscapes all cram into this remarkable terrain. The beaches and iconic towns have a deserved place on your itinerary, but they've also been on the tourist trail for many years. Travel beyond them, though, and there are still so many places that'll feel as though they're yours to discover. All you need to do is get behind the wheel and drive into one of the continent's most beautiful corners.

Lisbon

There's nowhere quite like Lisbon. It's impossible to overstate the decadent charm of this magnificent old city on Europe's outer rim. Extraordinary food, unique architecture and a sensibility like that of nowhere else on the continent all combine to offer a magical experience. Arrayed around steep hills and with superb lookouts at every turn, it's the kind of place that calls you to return many times over.

Porto

Porto has in recent years acquired a reputation for being one of Europe's favourite short getaways. Perhaps it's the atmospheric waterfront district with its excellent places to eat and drink. Or maybe its appeal is best seen in the hilly backstreets of Miragaia, Ribeira and Massarelos, the intoxicating mix of street-art-adorned architecture that spans the ages or the ornate gardens down by the Douro. Whatever makes the place for you, you'll quickly see that the reputation is well deserved.

Coimbra

Coimbra may be the most delightful Portuguese city beyond the coast. Rising scenically from the Rio Mondego, it's an animated place that was Portugal's medieval capital for more than a century, and it's home to the country's oldest and most prestigious university. Coimbra's steeply stacked historic centre dates to Islamic times and is wonderfully atmospheric, with dark cobbled lanes thronging with tourists and ringing with the haunting sounds of Portuguese guitar and the full, deep voices of fado singers.

WHEN TO GO

All Europe seems to converge on Portugal's coast and its cities in summer (especially July to August), and with good reason – this is as close as Europe comes to the tropics. If you can come at another time, such as autumn (September to November) or spring (March to May), you'll be rewarded by fewer visitors and weather that's still glorious.

Faro

The Algarve's capital has a more distinctly Portuguese feel than most resort towns. Its convenient location and excellent transport connections to the rest of Portugal and Europe mean that many visitors only pass through this underrated city. That's a shame, as it makes for an enjoyable stopover. It has an attractive marina, well-maintained parks and plazas, and a picturesque *cidade velha* (old town) ringed by medieval walls. The old town's winding, cobbled pedestrian streets, squares and buildings provide the backdrop for plenty of alfresco cafes.

Braga

Portugal's third-largest city is an important regional hub and provincial centre for Portugal's inner north. An elegant town, it's laced with ancient narrow lanes closed to vehicles, and strewn with plazas and a splendid array of baroque churches. Braga's upscale old centre is packed with lively cafes, trim boutiques, and excellent restaurants and low-key bars catering to students from the Universidade do Minho. Just east of the city, don't miss the hillside church and sanctuary of Bom Jesus do Monte, one of Portugal's most iconic tourist attractions.

TRANSPORT

Portugal has an excellent road network: motorways connect the major cities and also link Portugal to neighbouring Spain. The same applies to rail services. Where the topography starts to climb, expect smaller, quieter roads and for bus services to replace trains. In such areas, you'll take longer to get from A to B, but you'll have more time to enjoy the view.

WHAT'S ON

Carnaval

Portugal's Carnaval features much merrymaking. Loulé boasts the best parades, but Lisbon, Nazaré and Viana do Castelo all throw a respectable bash.

Semana Santa

Easter Portuguese style is at its best in Braga, whose elaborately staged Holy Week celebrations are famous throughout the country.

Fado no Castelo

Lisbon's love affair with fado reaches a high point at the cinematic Castelo de São Jorge over three evenings in June.

WHERE TO STAY

In all of the major towns and cities you'll be spoiled for accommodation choice. As well as modern hotels, hostels, homestays, beach resorts and summer camping areas, Portugal specialises in what are known as *pousadas*. Each *pousada* is a unique sleeping experience offering accommodation inside former castles, monasteries and estates. You'll find nearly three dozen *pousadas* spread across the country, and they fill up fast, so book ahead. The same applies to anywhere along the coast during any Friday or Saturday night in cities such as Lisbon and Porto that have become popular weekend escapes for northern Europeans.

Resources

Lonely Planet (*lonelyplanet.com/portugal*) Destination information, hotel bookings, traveller forum and more.

Portugal Tourism (*visitportugal.com*) Portugal's official tourism site is the perfect online space for planning your visit.

Wines of Portugal (*winesofportugal.info*) Fine overview of Portugal's favourite beverage, covering wine regions, grape varieties and wine routes.

26

PORTUGAL

Atlantic Coast Surf Trip

DURATION	DISTANCE	GREAT FOR
5-7 days	225km / 140 miles	Nature, wine

BEST TIME TO GO	From spring to early autumn for the best surf and sunshine.

If endless crashing surf sounds like your idea of heaven, you've come to the right country. Surfers and kitesurfers of all levels are in their element on Portugal's sparkling Atlantic coast, which is thrashed by some of Europe's biggest rollers. First-rate (and inexpensive) surf camps, gleaming white towns with authentic seafood restaurants, golden beaches fringed by dunes and pines, and memorable sunsets wrap up this little road trip nicely.

Link your trip

31 Tasting the Dão

Wine after the waves? Detour inland 120km from Praia do Pedrógão to Santa Comba Dão for tastings and cellar tours in a deliciously rural setting.

32 Highlands & History in the Central Interior

Why not tag on a road trip of Portugal's culture-loaded interior? The soulful university town of Coimbra is just a 77km drive northeast of Praia do Pedrógão.

01 PRAIA DO GUINCHO

Just half an hour's drive west of Lisbon, Praia do Guincho is hammered by some terrific Atlantic waves. The site of previous World Surfing Championships, this wild, dune-backed beach holds plenty of pulling power for surfers, windsurfers and kitesurfers with its massive crashing rollers. Beware of the strong undertow, which can be dangerous for swimmers and novice surfers. If you're keen to ride the waves, check out the course available at the highly rated **Moana Surf School** (*moanasurfschool.com*), which arranges private lessons and group courses for all levels. It also rents out boards and wetsuits.

WIRESTOCK CREATORS/SHUTTERSTOCK ©

BEST TWO DAYS

The 129km between Peniche and Nazaré pack the biggest surfing punch.

Praia do Guincho

THE DRIVE
From Guincho, the scenic N247 swings north through the rippling, forest-cloaked mountains of the Parque Natural de Sintra-Cascais, at its most atmospheric when veiled in early-morning mist. Roll down the window and breathe in that fresh air as you cruise north on the hour-long (51km) drive to Ericeira.

02 ERICEIRA

Picturesquely draped across sandstone cliffs with grandstand Atlantic views, sunny, whitewashed Ericeira has a string of golden beaches that have surfers itching to grab their boards and jump in. This is one of just four World Surfing Reserves, starring alongside Malibu and Santa Cruz in California and Manly Beach in Australia. The swells are reliable and the mightiest waves roll in to cliff-backed Praia da Ribeira d'Ilhas. A World Qualifying Series (WQS) site and frequent host to Portuguese national surfing championships, the beach is famous for having one of the best reef breaks in Europe. The other biggie is Coxos, a right-hand point break producing incredible barrels. Most amateurs will find the waves at the nearby Praia de São Sebastião challenging enough. Standing out among the surf camps in Ericeira, **Rapture** (*rapturecamps.com*) offers nicely chilled digs right on the beach and lessons with proficient instructors. For a post-surf beer or cocktail, stop by **Sunset Bamboo**.

THE DRIVE
From Ericeira, the N247 veers north close to the contours of the coast, taking you through gently rolling farmland and past sun-bleached *aldeas* (hamlets), orchards and pinewoods. After a pleasant hour (40km) behind the wheel, you emerge in Lourinhã.

03 LOURINHÃ

Lourinhã is less known than other west-coast surfing hot spots, yet it deserves more than just a cursory glance. In the peaceful shoulder seasons, you'll practically have its waves all to yourself on dune-fringed Praia Areal and Praia da Areia Branca. The former hosts national surfing events, while the latter is perfect for beginners and bodyboarders.

THE DRIVE
It's an easy 20km drive north on the countrified N247 and N114 to Peniche. The road takes you through softly undulating farmland, past bone-white hamlets and the odd ruin and windmill. To the west, you can often glimpse the hazy blue outline of the Atlantic.

DETOUR:

Berlenga Grande

START: 04 NERJA

Sitting about 10km offshore from Peniche, Berlenga Grande is a spectacular, rocky and remote island, with twisting, shocked-rock formations and gaping caverns. It's the only island of the Berlenga archipelago you can visit – the group consists of three tiny islands surrounded by clear, calm, dark-blue waters full of shipwrecks that are great for snorkelling and diving; try **AcuaSubOeste** (*acuasuboeste.com*). From June to September, **Viamar** (*viamar-berlenga.com*) makes the 45-minute boat trip twice daily. In the 16th century Berlenga Grande was home to a monastery, but now the most famous inhabitants are thousands of nesting seabirds, especially guillemots. The birds take priority over visitors and development has been confined to housing for a small fishing community and a lighthouse.

04 PENICHE

Ask a local to rattle off Portugal's top surfing spots and Peniche invariably makes the grade. Straddling a headland with the sea on all sides, it is popular for its long, fabulous town beach and nearby surf strands, with the added charm of a pretty walled historic centre and a 16th-century fortress. But it's the waves you are here for – and what epic waves they are! Long a favourite of clued-up surfers, Peniche shot to celebrity status when Supertubos beach, south of town, was selected as a stop on the ASP World Tour. Supertubos has some of Europe's best beach and reef breaks. Conditions are great year-round. Kitesurfing is also big. On the far side of high dunes about 500m east of the old town, **Peniche Kite & Surf Center** (*penichesurfcenter.com*) offers surfing and kitesurfing lessons.

THE DRIVE
About 5km to the northeast of Peniche is the scenic island-village of Baleal, connected to the mainland village of Casais do Baleal by a causeway.

CULTURE FIX

If you can tear yourself away from the surf for a minute, factor in a detour to some of the hinterland's cultural treasures. Here are three worth the drive.

Óbidos A 25km drive east of Peniche, this fortified wonder conceals a historic centre that is a maze of cobbled streets and flower-bedecked, whitewashed houses livened up with dashes of vivid yellow and blue paint. A hill lifts a medieval castle high above town.

Batalha A detour off the road between Nazaré and São Pedro de Moel, Batalha's crowning glory is its Manueline monastery, a riot of flying buttresses and pinnacles, with gold stone carved into forms as delicate as snowflakes and as pliable as twisted rope.

Alcobaça A 17km drive east of Nazaré, Alcobaça conceals a charming centre that is dwarfed by the magnificence of the 12th-century Mosteiro de Santa Maria de Alcobaça, one of Portugal's most memorable Unesco World Heritage sites.

05 BALEAL

A fine swoop of pale golden sand protected by dunes, Baleal is a paradise of challenging but, above all, consistent waves that make it an ideal learners' beach. Depending on the season, surf camps here charge between €250 and €650 for a week of classes, including equipment and lodging (with both dorms and private apartments available). Well-established picks include **Baleal Surfcamp** (*balealsurfcamp.com*) and **Peniche Surfcamp** (*penichesurfcamp.com*). You can also rent boards and wetsuits.

THE DRIVE
From Baleal, connect up with the N114, taking you onto the A8 north, before veering west onto the N360. The road makes a sweeping arc, leading through pine forest and past farmland and low-rise hills. It skirts the impressive fortified city of Óbidos, where you might want to factor in a pitstop. It's around a 38km drive.

06 FOZ DO ARELHO

With a vast, gorgeous tract of sandy beach backed by a river-mouth estuary ideal for windsurfing, Foz do Arelho remains remarkably undeveloped.

It makes a fine place to laze in the sun, and outside July and August it'll often be just you and the local fishermen. The beach has a row of relaxed bars and restaurants. **Escola de Vela da Lagoa** (*escoladeveladalagou.com*) hires out sailboats, SUP, kayaks, windsurf boards and catamarans. The school also provides windsurfing and sailing lessons and kayak lessons. From Foz do Arelho village, it's a 3.5km drive: turn left on the road that follows the lagoon's inland edge past the curious rock called Penedo Furado and continue.

THE DRIVE
A minor road, the Estrada Atlântica, hugs the coastline as it threads north to Santo Martinho do Porto, a drive of around 15km.

Photo opportunity

Snap the surf rolling in at sunset anywhere on the Atlantic coast.

07 SANTO MARTINHO DO PORTO

Fancy some time to hang out on the beach? Unlike nearby Nazaré, Santo Martinho do Porto is no party town, but it's a cheery place with a broad arc of a half-moon bay, perfect for swimming and just slowing the pace a notch or two.

THE DRIVE
Back behind the wheel, you'll be edging your way north on the N242 through pine woods and farmland before crossing the Río Alcobaça and arriving in Nazaré, 14.5km away.

08 NAZARÉ

With a warren of narrow, cobbled lanes running down to a wide, cliff-backed beach, Nazaré is Estremadura's most scenic coastal resort. The sands are packed with multicoloured umbrellas in July and August, and the town centre is jammed with seafood restaurants and bars with a party vibe. Nazaré generates some of the world's biggest waves. Rodrigo Koxa set a world record when he surfed a 23.77m giant in 2017. Smaller and less intimidating are the waves on the main beach in town, which is less exposed. To get an entirely different perspective of Nazaré, take the funicular

TRABANTOS/SHUTTERSTOCK ©

Berlenga Grande

up to **Promontório do Sítio**, where picture-postcard coastal views unfold from the 110m-high cliffs, gazing down to the thrashing waves on one side and the village on the other. It's nice to walk back down, escaping the crowds of trinket sellers.

THE DRIVE
From Nazaré, the small, coast-hugging Estrada Atlântica heads 21km north through pockets of pine forest and past high sand dunes, affording the occasional tantalising glimpse of ocean. Wind down those windows for delicious breezes.

09 SÃO PEDRO DE MOEL

For a more offbeat experience than Nazaré, turn your gaze north to São Pedro de Moel, which sees some pretty good waves (both lefts and rights) but receives just a trickle of surfers by comparison. The surf here is fairly consistent year-round, though bear the rocks in mind. The village itself is a pretty whitewashed number, with a low-key vibe and some knockout sunsets. Spreading immediately north of São Pedro de Moel is the **Pinhal de Leiria**. First planted by a forward-looking monarch some 700 years ago, this vast forest of towering pines backs one of the loveliest stretches of Portugal's Atlantic coast. Monarch Dom Dinis (1261–1325) expanded it significantly as a barrier against encroaching dunes and also as a source of timber for the maritime industry – a great boon during the Age of Discovery.

THE DRIVE
Continue north on the pretty Estrada Atlântica for the 15km drive to Praia da Vieira. The narrow road cuts through the sun-dappled pinewoods of Pinhal de Leiria and scrubby dunes, with the occasional glimpse of ocean.

10 PRAIA DA VIEIRA

Backed by the sun-dappled Pinhal de Leiria, Praia da Vieira entices with broad golden sands and consistent surf with beach breaks. Come during the week rather than at the weekend to experience it at its tranquil best.

THE DRIVE
From Praia da Vieira, it's a cruisy 5km drive north to Praia do Pedrógão, taking you once again through lush green coastal pinewoods.

11 PRAIA DO PEDRÓGÃO

Your final stop on this road trip is Pedrógão, which has lovely broad, dune-backed sands, few surfers and some pretty impressive beach breaks (both to the left and right). After all those big waves, you might want to take the chance just to kick back and watch in wonder as the Atlantic rolls in before you.

THE INSIDE SCOOP ON SURFING

Read on for the lowdown on when to surf, what to take, surf tuition and rentals.

WHEN TO SURF

Spring and autumn tend to be the best for surfing action. Waves at this time range from 2m to 4.5m high. This is also the low season, meaning you'll pay less for accommodation, and the beaches will be less crowded. Even during the summer, however, the coast gets good waves (1m to 1.5m on average) and, despite the crowds, it's fairly easy to head off and find your own spots (you can often be on your own by driving a few minutes up the road).

WHAT TO TAKE

The water temperature here is colder than it is in most other southern European countries, and even in the summer you'll probably want a wetsuit. Board and wetsuit hire are widely available at surf shops and camps: you can usually score a discount if you rent long-term, otherwise, you'll be paying around €20 to €35 per day for a board and wetsuit.

TUITION

There are dozens of schools that run lessons and courses for surfers of all levels. Surf camps mostly offer weekly packages including simple accommodation (dorms, bungalows or camping), meals and transport to the beach.

SURF SITES

magicseaweed.com International site with English-language surf reports for many Portuguese beaches.

wannasurf.com Global site with the lowdown on surfing hot spots along Portugal's coast. Navigate by interactive map.

surfingportugal.com Official site of the Portuguese Surfing Federation.

surftotal.com Portuguese-language site with news about the national surf scene and webcams showing conditions at a dozen popular beaches.

Nazaré

27

PORTUGAL

Douro Valley Vineyard Trails

BEST FOR FOODIES

Chef Rui Paula keeps it seasonal and regional at DOC, with sublime vineyard and river views from its terrace.

DURATION	DISTANCE	GREAT FOR
5-7 days	381km / 237 miles	Wine, nature

BEST TIME TO GO	Spring for wildflowers, early autumn for the grape harvest.

Vineyards, Douro Valley

You're in for a treat. This Unesco World Heritage region is hands-down one of Portugal's most evocative landscapes, with mile after swoon-worthy mile of vineyards spooling along the contours of its namesake river and marching up terraced hillsides. Go for the food, the fabulous wines, the palatial quintas (estates), the medieval stone villages and the postcard views around almost every bend.

Link your trip

30 The Minho's Lyrical Landscapes

Porto is a 55km drive from castle-crowned Guimarães, birthplace of Portugal and a fine starting point for this Minho meander.

32 Highlands & History in the Central Interior

Dip south of Porto 120km to Coimbra for a foray into Portugal's history-crammed interior and the inspiring Serra da Estrela mountains.

01 PORTO

Before kick-starting your road trip, devote a day or two to Porto, snuggled on banks of the Río Douro, where life is played out in the mazy lanes of the medieval Ribeira district. From here, the double-decker bridge **Ponte de Dom Luís I**, built by an apprentice of Gustav Eiffel in 1877, takes the river in its stride. Cross it to reach Vila Nova de Gaia, where grand 17th-century port lodges march up the hillside. Many open their barrel-lined cellars for guided tours and tastings – usually of three different ports – that will soon help you tell your tawny

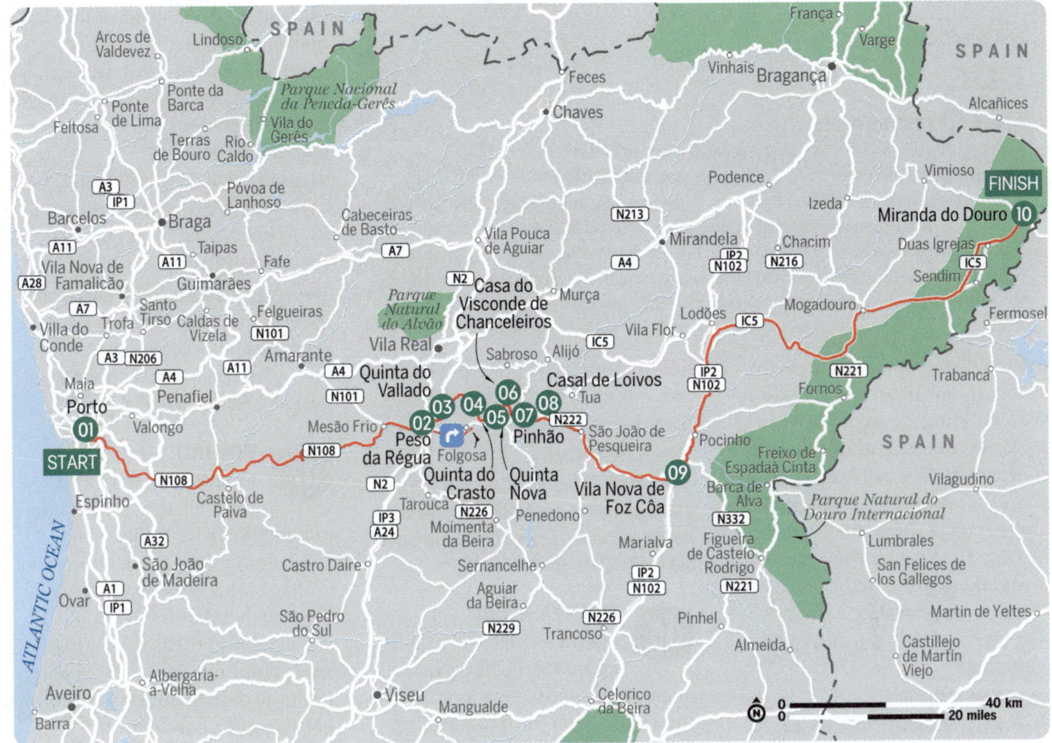

from your late-bottled vintage. Top billing goes to British-run **Taylor's** (*taylor.pt*) and its the immense 100,000L barrel, Graham's (*grahams-port.com*) and Calém (*calem.pt*).

THE DRIVE

There are quicker ways of getting from A to B, but for immersion in Douro wine country, you can't beat the three-hour (137km) drive east on the N108. The serpentine road shadows the Río Douro, with views of hillsides combed with vines, little chapels and woodlands.

02 PESO DA RÉGUA

Terraced hills scaled with vines like a dragon's backbone rise around riverside Peso da Régua. The sun-bleached town is the region's largest, abutting the Río Douro at the western end of the demarcated port-wine area. It grew into a major port-wine entrepôt in the 18th century. While not as charming as its setting, the town is worth visiting for its **Museu do Douro** (*museudodouro.pt*). Housed in a beautifully converted riverside warehouse, the museum whisks you through the entire wine spectrum, from impressionist landscapes to the remains of an old flat-bottomed port hauler. Down at the pier, you'll find frequent 50-minute boat trips to Pinhão, offered by **Tomaz do Douro** (*tomazdodouro.pt*), for instance.

THE DRIVE

Take the first exit onto the N2 at the roundabout at the end of Rua Dr Manuel de Arriaga, then the third exit at the next roundabout to join the N313. Turn right onto the N313-1 when you see the yellow sign to Quinta do Vallado. It's around a 5km drive.

03 QUINTA DO VALLADO

Ah, what views! The vineyards spread picturesquely before you from **Quinta do Vallado** (*quintadovallado.com*), a glorious 70-hectare winery. It brings together five rooms

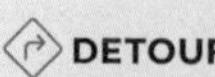

DOC

START: 02 PESO DA RÉGUA

Architect Miguel Saraiva's ode to clean-lined, glass-walled minimalism, **DOC** (*docrestaurante.pt*) is headed by Portuguese star chef Rui Paula. Its terrace peering out across the river is a stunning backdrop. Dishes give a pinch of imagination to seasonal, regional flavours, from fish *açordas* (stews) to game and wild mushrooms – all of which are paired with carefully selected wines from the cellar. It's in Folgosa, midway between Peso da Régua and Pinhão, on the south side of the river. Take the N2 south of Peso da Régua, then hook onto the N222 heading east.

in an old stone manor and eight swank rooms in an ultra-modern slate building, decked out with chestnut and teak wood, each complete with a balcony. They all share a gorgeous pool. Guests get a free tour of the winery, with a tasting. Have a fine wine-paired meal and stay the night. The staff can also help arrange activities like cycling, hiking, fishing and canoeing.

THE DRIVE
From Quinta do Vallado, the N313-2, CM1258 and N322-2 take you on a 29km drive east through the curvaceous wine terraces of the Alto Douro, past immaculate rows of vines and chalk-white hamlets, with tantalising glimpses of the river below. After Gouvinhas, the wiggling road takes you south to Quinta do Crasto.

04 QUINTA DO CRASTO

Perched like an eyrie on a promontory above the Río Douro and a spectacular ripple of terraced vine-yards, **Quinta do Crasto** (*quintadocrasto.pt*) quite literally takes your breath away. The winery is set amid the lyrical landscapes of the Alto Douro, a Unesco World Heritage site. Stop by for a tour and tasting or lunch. It produces some of the country's best wines. Designed by Portuguese starchitect Eduardo Souto Moura, the plunge pool here appears to nosedive directly into the valley below.

THE DRIVE
From Quinta do Crasto it's an easy 4km drive east along the mellow banks of the Río Douro to Quinta Nova via the N322-2 and CM1268.

05 QUINTA NOVA

Set on a ridge, surrounded by 120 hectares of ancient vineyards, overlooking the Douro river with mountains layered in the distance, **Quinta Nova** (*quintanova.com*) is simply stunning. Besides plush lodgings in a beautifully restored 19th-century manor, it offers romantic grounds, a pool gazing out across rolling vineyards, a restaurant, wine tours, tastings and some of the region's top walking trails (the longest of which is three hours).

THE DRIVE
It's a 10km drive east from Quinta Nova to Casa do Visconde de Chanceleiros on the CM1268, tracing the contours of the emerald-green vines unfurling around you.

06 CASA DO VISCONDE DE CHANCELEIROS

Fancy staying the night up in the hills of the sublime Alto Douro? **Casa do Visconde de Chanceleiros** (*chanceleiros.com*) is a gorgeous 250-year-old manor house, with spacious rooms featuring classic decor and patios. The expansive views of the valley and lush gardens steal the show, but so does the outdoor pool, tennis court, Jacuzzi, and sauna in a wine barrel. Delicious dinners (€38) are served on request.

THE DRIVE
A gentle 7.5km drive east along the M590, with spirit-lifting views across the terraced vineyards, the deep-green Douro and family-run *quintas*, brings you to Pinhão.

07 PINHÃO

Encircled by terraced hillsides that yield some of the world's best port – and some damn good table wines, too – little Pinhão sits on a particularly lovely bend of the Río Douro. Wineries and their competing signs dominate the scene and even the delightful train station has *azulejos* (hand-painted tiles) depicting the grape harvest. The town, though cute, holds little of interest, but makes a fine base for exploring the surrounding vineyards. From here, you can also cruise upriver into the heart of the Alto Douro aboard a traditional flat-bottomed port boat with **Douro-a-Vela** (*douroavela.pt*). Catch the boat from the Folgosa do Douro pier. Or enjoy sublime views over two rivers while wine tasting at **Quinta do Tedo** (*quintadotedo.com*).

THE DRIVE
Veer slightly west of Pinhão on the N323 and turn right onto the M585, following the sign for Casal de Loivos, 4.5km away. The country road weaving up through the vines, with the river below, later becomes the cobbled Rua da Calçada, passing *socalcos* (stone-walled terraced vineyards).

08 CASAL DE LOIVOS

It's a tough call, but Casal de Loivos has one of the most staggeringly beautiful views in the region. From the *miradouro* (viewpoint), the uplifting vista reduces the Douro to postcard format, taking in the full sweep of its stone-walled terraced vineyards, stitched into the hillsides and fringing the sweeping contours of the valley, and the river scything through them. To maximise these dreamy views, stay the night at **Casa de Casal de Loivros** (*casadecasaldeloivos.com*). The elegant house has been in this winemaking family for nearly 350 years. The halls are enlivened by museum-level displays of folkloric dresses, and the perch is spectacular. Swim laps in the pool while peering down across the vines spreading in all directions.

THE DRIVE

Backtrack on the N323, then pick up the N222 south of the river for the 64km drive southeast to Vila Nova de Foz Côa. The winding road takes you through some picture-book scenery, with whitewashed hamlets and *quintas* punctuating vines, orchards and olive groves.

09 VILA NOVA DE FOZ CÔA

Welcome to the heart of the Douro's *terra quente* (hot land). This once-remote, whitewashed town has been on the map since the 1990s, when researchers, during a proposed project for a dam, stumbled across an astounding stash of Paleolithic

WHY I LOVE THIS TRIP

Regis St Louis, writer

The meandering journey along the Río Douro takes in some of Portugal's most breathtaking scenery. Hilltop vineyards and sleepy riverside villages encourage you to take your time, sample the great wine (and food) on offer, overnight at guesthouses among the vines and get off the beaten path. The region also has plenty of surprises, including an astonishing collection of Paleolithic rock art and a forest- and cliff-filled wilderness reserve.

***Azulejos* (hand-painted tiles), Pinhão**

art. Thousands of these mysterious rock engravings speckle the Río Côa valley. Come to see its world-famous gallery of rock art at the **Parque Arqueológico do Vale do Côa** (*arte-coa.pt*). The three sites open to the public include Canada do Inferno, with departures at around 9.30am from the park museum in Vila Nova de Foz Côa, which is the ideal place to understand just how close these aeons-old drawings came to disappearing.

THE DRIVE
Wrap up your road trip by driving 120km northeast to Miranda do Douro via the N102, IP2 and IC5. Closer to the Spanish border you'll notice the shift in scenery, with lushness giving way to more arid, rugged terrain, speckled with vineyards and olive groves.

10 MIRANDA DO DOURO

A fortified frontier town hunkering down on the precipice of the Río Douro canyon, Miranda do Douro was long a bulwark of Portugal's 'wild east'. While its crumbling castle and handsomely severe 16th-century cathedral still lend an air of medieval charm, modern-day Miranda now receives weekend Spanish tourists. For an insight into the region's border culture, including ancient rites such as the 'stick dancing' of the *pauliteiros*, visit the **Museu da Terra de Miranda**. If you'd rather get a taste of the rugged nature on Miranda's doorstep, **Europarques** (*europarques.com*) runs one- and two-hour river boat trips along a dramatic gorge. Boats leave from beside the dam on the Portuguese side. Stop by the **Parque Natural do Douro Internacional Office** (*natural.pt*) for the inside scoop on hiking among the woods and towering granite cliffs of the 832-sq-km park. It's home to bird species including black storks, peregrine falcons and golden eagles.

LONE WOLF//SHUTTERSTOCK ©

Río Douro, near Miranda do Douro

WINES OF THE DOURO

The Douro has been world-famous for port wines for centuries, but only recently has the region carved out a reputation for its equally outstanding table wines. The region's steep, terraced slopes, schist soils (with good drainage), blisteringly hot summers and cold winters, and old, established vines are a winning combination.

Dozens of grape varieties – nearly all of which are red and uniquely Portuguese – are grown in the region. Alone or as a blend, these grapes produce well-structured, tannic and powerful wines, with finesse, length and ripe-fruit flavours. The more expensive ones kept for ageing are usually labelled 'Reserva' or 'Grande Reserva' and these are big, gutsy wines – complex, oaky and full of jammy dark-fruit flavours.

White grapes account for a tiny proportion of wine production, but they have also come on in leaps and bounds. Grapes such as malvasia, viosinho, gouveio and rabigato produce pale whites that are crisp-edged, minerally, fresh and fruity. Those kept for ageing are gold-hued and more complex, with oaky, nutty flavours.

Photo opportunity

The staggering view of the Douro vineyards from Casal de Loivos *miradouro*.

28

PORTUGAL

Alentejo & Algarve Beaches

BEST FOR WILDLIFE

The Sagres area offers great birdwatching and boat trips to view dolphins and perhaps whales.

DURATION	DISTANCE	GREAT FOR
4-6 days	360km / 224 miles	Wine, nature, families

BEST TIME TO GO	
	Good all year, but crowded in July and August.

Odeceixe

Portugal's southern coasts offer a Mediterranean ideal, with fragrances of pine, rosemary, wine and grilling fish drifting over some absolutely stunning beaches. Only this isn't the Med, it's the Atlantic, so add serious surfable waves, important maritime history and great wildlife-watching opportunities to the mix. This drive takes in some of the fi nest beaches in the region, and explores the intriguing towns, which conserve their tight-knit Moorish street plans.

Link your trip

24 Andalucía's White Villages

From the end of this trip, it's an easy 192km on the A22 and A49 motorways, skirting Seville, to Carmona, the starting point of this route.

29 Medieval Jewels in the Southern Interior

From the end of this trip, head 75km north to Mértola, the finishing point of this route, and do it in reverse.

01 VILA NOVA DE MILFONTES

One of the loveliest towns along this stretch of the coast, Vila Nova de Milfontes has an attractive, whitewashed centre, sparkling beaches nearby and a laid-back population who couldn't imagine living anywhere else. Milfontes remains much more low-key than most resort towns, except in August when it's packed to the hilt with surfers and sun-seekers. It's located in the middle of the beautiful Parque Natural do Sudoeste Alentejano e Costa Vicentina and is still a port (Hannibal is said to have sheltered here) alongside a lovely, sand-

edged limb of estuary. Milfonte's narrow lanes, tiny plazas and beach harbour offer varied eating and drinking options. The town beach is sheltered but can get busy; the best strand in the vicinity is fantastic **Praia do Malhão**, backed by rocky dunes and covered in fragrant scrub, around 7km to the north.

THE DRIVE
It's a 26km drive through protected parkland on the N393 south to Zambujeira do Mar.

02 ZAMBUJEIRA DO MAR

Enchantingly wild beaches backed by rugged cliffs form the setting of this sleepy seaside village. The main street terminates at the cliff; paths lead to the attractive sands below. Quieter than Vila Nova, Zambujeira attracts a backpacker, surfy crowd, though in August the town is a party place and hosts the massive music fest **Festa do Sudoeste**. The high-season crowds obscure Zambujeira's out-of-season charms: fresh fish in family-run restaurants, blustering clifftop walks and a dramatic, empty coast.

THE DRIVE
Cutting back to the main road, you then head south on the N120. It's about 25km to Odeceixe through beautiful coastal woodland.

03 ODECEIXE

Located just as you cross into the Algarve from the Alentejo, Odeceixe is an endearing whitewashed village cascading down a hill below a picture-perfect windmill on the southern side of the Riberia de Seixe valley. It's a sleepy town, except in summer, when it fills with people keen on its nearby beach. This tongue of sand is winningly set at a rivermouth and flanked by imposing schist cliffs (try saying that with a mouthful of porridge...). It's a particularly good option for families, as smaller children can paddle on the peaceful river side of the strand while older kids tackle the waves on the ocean side. The beach is 3.5km from Odeceixe itself along a charming country road. At the beach, a small village has eating and surfing options. The **Rota Vicentina**, a long-distance walking path that leads right to the south-western tip of Portugal, passes through Odeceixe, and there are great day walks in the vicinity.

THE DRIVE
It's an easy 15km down the N120 to Aljezur, through woodland and open shrubland patched with heather and gorse.

ALJEZUR

The old part of Aljezur is an attractive village with a Moorish feel. A collection of cottages winds down the hill below a ruined 10th-century hilltop **castle** (Rua dom Paio Pires Correìa). Aljezur is close to some fantastic beaches, edged by black rocks that reach into the white-tipped, bracing sea – surfing hot spots.

Photo opportunity

The rock formations at Praia da Marinha.

The handsomest beach in the Aljezur area, on the north side of the picturesque rivermouth and backed by wild dunes, is **Praia da Amoreira**. It's 9km by road from Aljezur, signposted off the main road north of town.

THE DRIVE
A couple of kilometres south of Aljezur, the beaches of Monte Clérigo and Arrifana are signposted off to the right. At the top of the hill, head right (towards Monte Clérigo) for the full coastal panorama before winding your way south to Arrifana.

PRAIA DA ARRIFANA

Arrifana is a seductive fingernail-shaped cove

Lagos

TOP TIP:

The Sagres Eat Scene

A closely packed string of surfer-oriented places on Rua Comandante Matoso offer a bit of everything, whether it's a coffee or a *caipirinha* you're after. They are cafes by day, restaurants serving international favourites by night, whatever time hunger drags you away from the beach and lively bars. Further down the same street, near the port, is a cluster of more traditional Portuguese restaurants.

embraced by cliffs. Just to add to the picturesqueness, it also sports an offshore pinnacle and a petite traditional fishing harbour. The beach is wildly popular with surfers of all abilities and there are several surf schools in the area. The beach break is reliable, but there's also a right-hand reef break that can offer some of the Algarve's best surfing when there's a big swell. There's a small, very popular beachside restaurant, and clifftop eateries near the ruined fortress up above, which offer breathtaking vistas. Good diving is also possible here.

THE DRIVE
Praia de Vale Figueira is reached by a rough, partly paved road that runs some 5km from the main road at a point 10km south of Aljezur. Before reaching the turn-off, you must turn right off the N120 on to the N268.

06 PRAIA DE VALE FIGUEIRA

One of the remoter west coast beaches, this is a long, wide and magnificent stretch of whitish sand with an ethereal beauty, backed by stratified cliffs hazy in the ocean spray. It's reached by a rough, partly paved road and there are no facilities. The beach faces due west and has pretty reliable surf, especially when a southeaster is blowing. It's one of those lonely, romantic beaches that's great to stroll, even when the weather's nasty.

THE DRIVE
Head back to the main road (N268) and turn right on to it. It's about 10km from here to Carrapateira.

07 CARRAPATEIRA

Surf-central Carrapateira is a tranquil, pretty, spread-out village offering two fabulous beaches with spectacular settings and turquoise seas. Bordeira is a mammoth swath of sand merging into dunes 2km from the north side of town. Amado, with even better surf, is at the southern end. The circuit of both from Carrapateira (9km) is a visually stunning hike (or drive), with lookouts over the beaches and rocky coves and cliffs between them. In town, the **Museu do Mar e da Terra da Carrapateira** (*cm-aljezur.pt*) is an intriguing place to visit, with great views.

THE DRIVE
The N268 barrels on right down to Portugal's tip at Sagres (22km), via the regional centre of Vila do Bispo.

08 SAGRES

The small, elongated village of Sagres, with a rich nautical history, has an appealingly out-of-the-way feel. It sits on a remote peninsula amid picturesque seaside scenery with a sculpted coastline and stern **fortress** (*monumentosdoalgarve.pt*) leading to a stunning clifftop walk. It also appeals for its access to fine beaches and water-based activities; it's especially popular with a surfing crowd. Outside town, the striking cliffs of **Cabo de São Vicente** (N258), the southwesternmost point of Europe, make for an enchanting visit, especially at sunset. Make sure you pop into the small **museum** (*faros.pt*) here, which has interesting background information on the Algarve's starring role in the Age of Discovery. From Sagres' harbour, worthwhile excursions head out to observe dolphins and seabirds. **Mar Ilimitado** (*marilimitado.com*) is a recommended operator.

THE DRIVE
Head back to Vila do Bispo and turn right onto the N125 that will take you to Lagos, a total drive of 34km. Promising beach detours include Zavial and Salema.

09 LAGOS

Touristy, likeable Lagos lies on a riverbank, with 16th-century walls enclosing the old town's pretty, cobbled streets and picturesque plazas. A huge range of restaurants and pumping nightlife add to the allure provided by fabulous beaches and numerous watery activities. Aside from the hedonism, there's plenty of history here: start by visiting the lovably higgledy-piggledy **Museu Municipal** (*cm-lagos.com*), which incorporates the fabulous baroque church **Igreja de Santo António**. Heading out on to the water is a must, perhaps cetacean-spotting with **Algarve Water World** (*algarvewaterworld.com*), paddling with **Kayak Adventures** (*kayaktrip.pt*) or learning to surf with **Lagos Surf Center** (*lagossurfcenter.com*). East of town stretch the long, golden sands of Meia Praia, backed by worthwhile beach restaurants.

THE DRIVE
Portimão is really just along the coast from Lagos, but it's a 24km detour inland via the N125 in a car.

10 PORTIMÃO & PRAIA DA ROCHA

The Algarve's second-largest town, Portimão's history dates back to the Phoenicians before it became the region's fishing and canning hub in the 19th century. Though that industry has since declined, it's still an intriguing port with plenty of maritime

DETOUR:
Monchique

START: 10 PORTIMÃO & PRAIA DA ROCHA

High above the coast, in cooler mountainous woodlands, the picturesque little town of Monchique makes a lovely detour, with some excellent options for day hikes, including climbing the Algarve's highest hills, Picota and Fóia, for super views over the coast. Monchique and the surrounding area have some excellent eating choices and nearby Caldas de Monchique is a sweet little spa hamlet in a narrow wooded valley. The N266 heads north from the N124 north of Portimão; it's a 27km drive from Lagos to Monchique, then another 30km on to Silves.

atmosphere. Learn all about the town's fishing heritage in the excellent **Museu de Portimão** (*museudeportimao.pt*), before strolling through the no-frills sardine restaurants of the fishers' quarter of Largo da Barca near the road bridge. At the southern end of Portimão stretches the impressive resort beach of **Praia da Rocha**, backed by numerous restaurants and nightlife options.

THE DRIVE
The N125 leads you east to the junction with the N124-1 that takes you north to Silves. It's a drive of only 20km.

11 SILVES

Silves is one of the Algarve's prettiest towns and replete with history: it was an important trading city in Moorish times and preserves a tightly woven medieval centre. At the top of the town, its sizeable **castle** (*cm-silves.pt*) offers great views from the ramparts. Originally occupied in the Visigothic period, what you see today dates mostly from the Moorish era, though the castle was heavily restored in the 20th century. Below this, the atmospheric **catedral** is the region's best-preserved Gothic church. The **Museu Municipal** (*cm-silves.pt*) gives good background on the city's history and is built around a fascinating Moorish-era well, complete with spiral staircase. The old-town streets are great for strolling.

THE DRIVE
Cruise 14km straight down the N124-1 to the beach at Carvoeiro.

12 CARVOEIRO

Carvoeiro is a cluster of whitewashed buildings rising up from tawny, gold and green cliffs and backed by hills. This diminutive seaside resort is prettier and more laid-back than many of the bigger resorts. The town beach is pretty but small and crowded – there are lots of other excellent options in the area. The most picturesque of all, with stunning rock formations, is **Praia da Marinha**, 8km east of Carvoeira. On foot, it's best reached by the **Percurso dos Sete Vales Suspensos** clifftop walk, beginning at Praia Vale Centianes, 2.3km east of town.

THE DRIVE
Head back to Lagoa to join the N125 eastwards. After 25km, turn right and head towards the coast, emerging atop the long beach. It's a 37km total drive.

TOP TIP:
Toll Roads

This central section of the Algarve coast is great for families, with numerous water parks and other attractions in the area. Two of the most popular are **Slide & Splash** (*slidesplash.com*) and **Aqualand** (*aqualand.pt*).

13 PRAIA DA FALÉSIA

This long, straight strip of sand offers one of the region's most impressive first glimpses of coast as you arrive from above. It's backed by stunning cliffs in white and several shades of ochre, gouged by weather into intriguing shapes and topped by typical pines. The areas near the car parks get packed in summer (especially as high tides cover much of the beach), but as the strip is over 3km long, it's easy enough to walk and find plenty of breathing room. It's a good beach for strolling, as the cliffscape constantly changes colours and shapes, and there's a surprising range of hardy seaside plants in the cracks and crevices.

THE DRIVE
Head back to the N125 and continue eastwards. Just after bypassing the town of Almancil, there's an exit to 'Almancil, São Lourenço, praias'. The church is signposted from here.

14 IGREJA DE SÃO LOURENÇO DE MATOS

It's worth stopping here to visit the marvellous interior of this small **church** (*diocese-algarve.pt*), built over a ruined chapel after local people, while digging a well, had implored the saint for help and then struck water. The resulting baroque masterpiece, built by fraternal master-team Antão and Manuel Borges, is wall-to-wall *azulejos* (painted tiles) inside, with beautiful panels depicting the life of the Roman-era saint, and his death by barbecue. In the 1755 earthquake, only five tiles fell from the roof.

THE DRIVE
Back on the N125, head southeastwards and after 12km you're in Faro.

15 FARO

The capital of the Algarve has a distinctly Portuguese feel and plenty to see. Its evocative waterside old town is very scenic and has several interesting sights, including the excellent **Museu Municipal** (*cm-faro.pt*), set in a former convent. The area is centred around Faro's **catedral** (*paroquiasedefaro.org*), built in the 13th century but heavily damaged in the 1755 earthquake. What you see now is a variety of Renaissance, Gothic and baroque features. Climb the tower for lovely views across the walled town and estuary islands. Part of the Parque Natural da Ria Formosa, these islands can be explored on excellent boat trips run by **Formosamar** (*facebook.com/formosamar*). The cathedral has a small bone chapel, but much spookier is the one at the **Igreja de Nossa Senhora do Carmo** (*diocese-algarve.pt*), built from the mortal remains of over a thousand monks. Faro's impressive modern **market building** (*mercadomunicipaldefaro.pt*) makes a great place to wander, people-watch, buy fresh produce, sit down on a terrace with a coffee, or lunch at one of the several worthwhile eateries.

THE DRIVE
It's 35km east along the N125 to Tavira. Despite the road's proximity to the coast, you won't see much unless you turn off: Fuzeta is a pleasant waterside village to investigate, with boat connections to island beaches.

16 TAVIRA

Set on either side of the meandering Rio Gilão, Tavira is a charming town. The ruins of a hilltop **castle**, now housing a pleasant little botanic garden; the Renaissance **Igreja da Misericórdia** (*diocese-algarve.pt*); and the **Núcleo Islâmico** (*cm-tavira.pt*) museum of Moorish history are among the attractions. It's ideal for wandering; the warren of cobblestone streets hides pretty, historic gardens and shady plazas. Tavira is the launching point for the stunning, unspoilt beaches of the Ilha de Tavira, a sandy island that's another part of the Parque Natural da Ria Formosa.

WHY I LOVE THIS TRIP

Regis St Louis, writer

There's a reason why so many people think of coastline when they imagine southern Portugal: the beaches here are simply spectacular. Among the bounty, you'll find dramatic cliff-backed shorelines, hidden coves nestled beside whitewashed villages, and sun-drenched strands perfect for surfing, kayaking and other aquatic adventures. There are also alluring island sands that can only be reached by boat – in short, a paradise for beach lovers.

THE DRIVE
Cacela Velha is 14km east of Tavira: head along the N125 and you'll see it signposted; it's 1km south of the N125.

17 CACELA VELHA

Enchanting, small and cobbled, Cacela Velha is a huddle of whitewashed cottages edged with bright borders, and has a pocket-sized fort, orange and olive groves, and gardens blazing with colour. It sits above a gorgeous stretch of sea, with a bar, plus other restaurants, a church and heart-lifting views. From nearby Fábrica, you can get a boat across to the splendid Cacela Velha beach, which has a low-key LGBTIQ+ scene in summer.

29

PORTUGAL

Medieval Jewels in the Southern Interior

DURATION	DISTANCE	GREAT FOR
6-9 days	720 km / 448 miles	Nature, wine

BEST TIME TO GO	From March to June and September to October for pleasant weather without extreme heat.

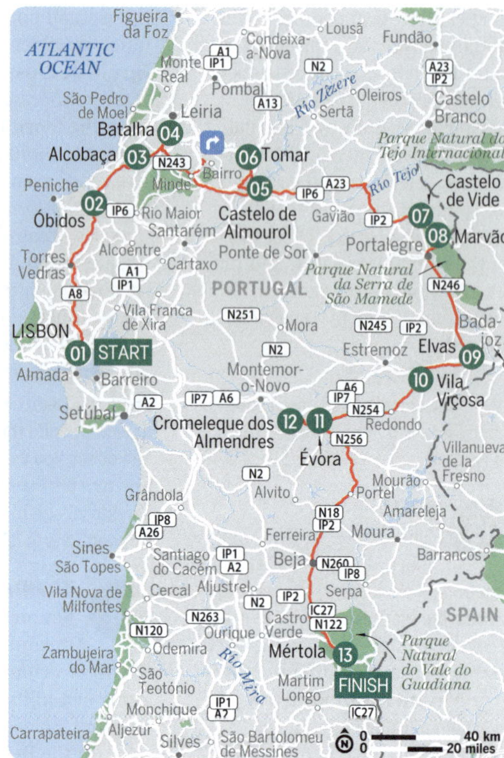

War defined medieval Portugal. Towns were fortified with sturdy walls, castles defended them, and when you won a victory, you built a monastery in thanks to the powers that be. That turbulent history has left a region studded in architectural jewels. This drive takes you from Portugal's romantic capital around a stunning selection of them, through typical hill landscapes softened by cork oaks and pine. Hearty inland cuisine adds to the authentically Portuguese experience.

Link your trip

06 Ancient Extremadura

From Évora, it's a direct 160km northeast on motorways A6 and A5 to Mérida in Spain, starting point for this trip.

28 Alentejo & Algarve Beaches

After all the inland scenery, time to hit the coast! You can do this route in reverse by hitting Cacela Velha, 75km south of Mértola.

01 LISBON

Spread across steep hillsides overlooking the Rio Tejo (Tagus), Portugal's capital offers real enchantment in its narrow cobbled streets, centenarian cafes and local *bairro* (neighbourhood) life. On either side of the low central district, Baixo, rise hills. Bairro Alto is a bohemian district of restaurants and bars, while facing it, Alfama is Lisbon's Moorish time capsule: a medina-like district of tangled alleys, hidden palm-shaded squares and narrow terracotta-roofed houses that tumble down to the glittering Tejo. It is the birthplace of fado, the melancholic Portuguese singing that you can investigate at the excellent

BEST TWO DAYS

From Alcobaça to Tomar, with a dash to Évora if you have time.

Castelo de São Jorge

Museu do Fado (*museu dofado.pt*). Atop the district is the dramatic **Castelo de São Jorge** (*castelodesaojorge.pt*), which still has a residential district within its outer walls. Farther afield, in the district of Belém, the spectacular Manueline **Mosteiro dos Jerónimos** (*patrimoniocultural.gov*) and **Torre de Belém** (*patrimonio cultural.gov.pt*) fortress jutting out onto the river, are World Heritage–listed sights.

THE DRIVE
It's a fairly dull 84km run north up the A8 motorway to Óbidos.

ÓBIDOS

Surrounded by a classic crenellated wall, Óbidos' gorgeous historic centre is a labyrinth of cobblestoned streets and flower-bedecked, whitewashed houses livened up with dashes of vivid yellow and blue paint. The main gate, **Porta da Vila**, leads directly into the main street, Rua Direita, lined with chocolate and cherry-liqueur shops. It's quite touristy, so wind your way away from it and you'll soon capture some of the town's atmosphere in more peace. There are pretty bits outside the walls too. You can walk around the wall for uplifting views over the town and surrounding countryside. The walls date from Moorish times (later restored), but the *castelo* (castle) itself is one of monarch Dom Dinis' 13th-century creations. It's a stern edifice, with lots of towers, battlements and big gates. Converted into a palace in the 16th century (some Manueline touches add levity), it's now a deluxe hotel. The town's elegant main church, **Igreja de Santa Maria**, stands out for its interior, with a wonderful painted ceiling and tiled walls. The aqueduct, southeast of the main gate, dates from the 16th century and is 3km long.

THE DRIVE
It's a quick but unexciting 42km drive north up the IC1/A8. Take exit 22, signposted to Alcobaça among other places.

03 ALCOBAÇA

The little town of Alcobaça has a charming if touristed centre with a little river and bijou bridges. All, however, yields centre stage to the magnificent 12th-century **Mosteiro de Santa Maria de Alcobaça** (*mosteiroalcobaca.gov.pt*). One of Iberia's great monasteries, it utterly dominates the town. Hiding behind the imposing baroque facade lies a high, austere, monkish church (free entry) with a forest of unadorned 12th-century arches. But make sure you visit the rest too: the beautiful cloisters, atmospheric refectory, vast dormitory and other spaces bring back the Cistercian life, which, according to sources, wasn't quite as austere here as it should have been. The monastery was founded in 1153 by Afonso Henriques, first king of Portugal. The monastery estate became one of the richest and most powerful in the country, apparently housing 999 monks, who held Mass nonstop in shifts. In the 18th century, however, it was the monks' growing decadence that became famous. The party ended in 1834 with the dissolution of the religious orders.

THE DRIVE
It's a short drive eastwards on the IC9, then northwards on the IC2 to Batalha, 24km away.

04 BATALHA

The 1385 Battle of Aljubarrota fought here put the Castilians from Spain in their place and set the foundations for Portugal's golden age. An extraordinary abbey, the **Mosteiro de Santa Maria da Vitória** (*mosteirobatalha.gov.pt*), was built to commemorate it. Most of the monument was completed by 1434 in Flamboyant Gothic, but Manueline exuberance steals the show, thanks to additions made in the 15th and 16th centuries. The sublime Claustro Real is a masterpiece, as are the unfinished Capelas Imperfeitas. The battlefield itself is on the southern edge of town. Here, the **Batalha de Aljubarrota Centro de Interpretação** (*fundacao-aljubarrota.pt*) is a museum whose crowning glory is a blood-and-thunder 30-minute film depicting the battle.

THE DRIVE
This picturesque one-hour drive takes you south on the N362 to castle-topped Porto de Mós. The N243 then takes you across the lonely landscapes of the Serra de Aire before the A23 brings you to Constância, near the next stop.

DETOUR:

Monumento Natural das Pegadas dos Dinossáurios

START: 04 NERJA

On your way between stops 4 and 5, turn off onto the N360 at Minde, head north for 7km, then another 5km east. On the N357, 10km south of Fátima in a village called Bairro, the **Monumento Natural das Pegadas dos Dinossáurios** (*pegadasdedinossaurios.org*) is one of the most important locations for sauropod prints in the world. The visit starts with a 20-minute video in Portuguese, then you take a 1.5km walk around the quarry, first seeing the prints from above then walking among them (ask at the admissions counter for info in English). These, the oldest and longest sauropod tracks in the world, record walks in the mud 175 million years ago. As you walk across the slope, you can clearly see the large elliptical prints made by the hind feet and the smaller, half-moon prints made by the forefeet.

05 CASTELO DE ALMOUROL

Like the stuff of legend, 10-towered **Castelo de Almourol** stands tantalisingly close to shore but just out of reach in the Rio Tejo. The castle is 5km from Constância. Boats (€4, five minutes) leave regularly from a riverside landing directly opposite the castle. Once on the island, a short walk leads up to the ramparts, where you're free to linger as long as you like. The island, almost jumping distance from land, was once the site of a Roman fort; the castle was built by Gualdim Pais, Grand Master of the Order of the Knights Templar, in 1171. It's no surprise that Almourol has long caught the imagination of excitable poets longing for the Age of Chivalry.

THE DRIVE
The next stop lies around 30km north, easily accomplished by following the N358 through typical central Portuguese farmland.

06 TOMAR

Tomar is one of central Portugal's most appealing small towns, with a pedestrian-friendly historic centre and pretty riverside park in a charming natural setting adjacent to the lush Mata Nacional dos Sete Montes (Seven Hills National Forest). But to understand what makes Tomar truly extraordinary, cast your gaze skywards. Wrapped in splendour and mystery, the Knights Templar held enormous power in Portugal from the 12th to 16th centuries, and largely bankrolled the Age of Discovery. The **Convento de Cristo** (*conventocristo.pt*), their headquarters, sits on wooded slopes above the town and is enclosed within 12th-century walls. It's a stony expression of magnificence, with chapels, cloisters and choirs in diverging styles, added over the centuries by successive kings and Grand Masters. **The Charola**, an extraordinary 16-sided church, dominates the complex. Its eastern influences give it a very different feel to most Portuguese churches; the interior is otherworldly in its vast heights – an awesome combination of simple forms and rich embellishment. It's said that the circular design enabled knights to attend Mass on horseback.

THE DRIVE
It's time to head into deep Portugal, first south on the A13, then eastwards along the A23. Take exit 15 onto the IP2 towards Portalegre, then slip onto the N246 heading east. It's a total drive of 125km through increasingly wild inland landscapes.

07 CASTELO DE VIDE

High above lush, rolling countryside, Castelo de Vide is one of Portugal's most attractive and underrated villages. Its fine hilltop vantage point, dazzlingly white houses, flower-lined lanes and proud locals are reason alone to visit. Originally inhabitants lived within the walls of the **castle**, which preserves a small inner village. Nearby is a Jewish quarter with a **synagogue** and **museum**. Castelo de Vide is famous for its crystal-clear mineral water, which spouts out of numerous pretty public fountains.

THE DRIVE
Marvão is just 10km east of Castelo de Vide, signposted off the N246.

08 MARVÃO

On a jutting crag high above the surrounding countryside, the narrow lanes of Marvão feel like a retreat far removed from the settlements below. The whitewashed village of picturesque tiled roofs and bright flowers has marvellous views, a splendid **castle** built into the rock at the western end of the village, and a handful of low-key guesthouses and restaurants.

THE DRIVE
Take the N359 to Portalegre, then continue south on the N246 through a typical Alentejan landscape of shrubs and cork-oaks to Elvas, 78km from your starting point.

09 ELVAS

The impressive Unesco-listed fortifications zigzagging around this pleasant little town reflect an extraordinarily sophisticated military technology. Its moats, fort and heavy walls would indicate a certain paranoia if it weren't for Elvas' position, near the Spanish border. Inside the stout, buttressed fortifications, you'll find a lovely town plaza, some quaint museums, narrow medina-like streets and a few excellent eateries. Outside, a magnificently ambitious **aqueduct** brings water from a point 7km west of town.

THE DRIVE
Head west and a little south from Elvas to reach Vila Viçosa, some 40km away via the N4.

10 VILA VIÇOSA

Once home to the Bragança dynasty, this is the most rewarding of several 'marble towns' hereabouts. One of Portugal's largest palaces dominates the centre of town. The **Paço Ducal** (*fcbraganca.pt*), built in the 16th century, is imposingly enormous. The palace's best furniture went to Lisbon after Dom João IV ascended the throne, and some went to Brazil after the royal family fled there in 1807, but there are still some stunning pieces on display. Lots of royal portraits put into context the interesting background on the royal family.

THE DRIVE
The more scenic of the routes to Évora is the N254 running southwest. It's around 60km between stops via the handsome little town of Redondo.

11 ÉVORA

One of Portugal's most beautifully preserved medieval towns, Évora is an enchanting place to delve into the past. Inside the 14th-century walls, Évora's narrow, winding lanes lead to striking architectural works.

TOP TIP:

Combined Monastery Ticket

If you're planning to visit the monasteries at Alcobaça and Batalha, as well as the Convento de Cristo in Tomar, you can get (from any one of them) a combined ticket for €15 (a saving of €3) that will let you in to all three and is valid for a week.

Guarded by a pair of rose granite towers, the fortress-like medieval **catedral** (*evoracathedral.com*) has fabulous cloisters and a museum jam-packed with ecclesiastical treasures. Once part of the Roman Forum, the cinematic columns of the **Templo Romano**, dating from the 2nd or early 3rd century, are a heady slice of drama right in town. The city's main square, **Praça do Giraldo**, has seen some potent moments in Portuguese history, including the 1483 execution of Fernando, Duke of Bragança; the public burning of victims of the Inquisition in the 16th century; and fiery debates on agrarian reform in the 1970s. The narrow lanes to the southwest were once the *judiaria* (Jewish quarter). Aside from its historic and aesthetic virtues, Évora is also a lively university town, and its many attractive restaurants serve up hearty Alentejan cuisine.

THE DRIVE
Head west of Évora on the N114, then after 11km take a left turn signposted to Guadalupe and the Cromeleque dos Almendres. Follow signs to reach the monument, some 17km in total from Évora.

Photo opportunity

Any of the medieval town walls at sunset.

12 CROMELEQUE DOS ALMENDRES

Set within a beautiful landscape of olive and cork trees stands the Cromeleque dos Almendres. This huge, spectacular oval of standing stones is the Iberian Peninsula's most important megalithic group and an extraordinary place to visit. Some 95 rounded granite monoliths – some of which are engraved with symbolic markings – spread down a rough slope. They were erected over different periods, it seems, with basic astronomic orientations, and were probably used for social gatherings or sacred rituals back in the dawn of the Neolithic period. Two and a half kilometres before Cromeleque dos Almendres stands **Menir dos Almendres**, a single stone about 4m high, with some very faint carvings near the top. Look for the sign; to reach the menhir you must walk a few hundred metres from the road.

THE DRIVE
Backtrack through the Évora ring road and onto the N256 southeast. When you hit the IP2, head south across the Alentejan hills and plains, skirting the city of Beja before continuing on the IC27/N122 to Mértola, a total drive of 150km.

13 MÉRTOLA

Spectacularly set on a rocky spur, high above the peaceful Rio Guadiana, the cobbled streets of medieval Mértola are a delightful place to roam. A small but imposing castle stands high, overlooking the jumble of dazzlingly white houses and a picturesque church that was once a mosque. A long bout of economic stagnation at this remote town has left many traces of Islamic occupation intact, so much so that Mértola is considered a *vila museu* (open-air museum). There's a lot to see here, from the parish church, formerly a mosque, to the castle and a group of museums covering various aspects of the town's history.

Cathedral, Évora

30

PORTUGAL

BEST FOR OUTDOORS

Hit the trail in the granite wilds of Parque Nacional da Peneda-Gerês.

The Minho's Lyrical Landscapes

DURATION	DISTANCE	GREAT FOR
2-4 days	208km/ 129 miles	History, nature

BEST TIME TO GO	Year-round in the cities; spring to autumn on the coast.

Escadaria do Bom Jesus

Sidling up to Spain on Portugal's northwestern tip, the Minho is the birthplace of the Portuguese kingdom and the home of its emblematic cockerel – and you feel it. The region has a pinch of everything that makes this country special – fortified villages and vineyards, gorgeous dune-backed beaches and lush river valleys, high meadows patrolled by shepherds, granite peaks, and cities with both medieval looks and personality.

Link your trip

27 Douro Valley Vineyard Trails

From Guimarães, it's just a 55km drive to Porto, from where you can easily dip into the terraced vineyards and outstanding wineries of the Unesco World Heritage Douro.

13 Coast of Galicia

Head just across the border to A Guarda, for a drive along Galicia's wild, storm-buffeted coast, past quaint fishing villages and coves steeped in legend.

01 GUIMARÃES

The cradle of the Portuguese nation, Guimarães is the birthplace of Alfonso Henriques, who became Portugal's first king in 1139. Guimarães hides one of the most exquisitely preserved medieval centres in the country – a warren of cafe-filled plazas and labyrinthine lanes. Unesco duly noted this and made its alley-woven heart a World Heritage site. It is crowned by a 1000-year-old bird's nest of a **castle** (*pacodosduques.gov.pt*), which commands sweeping views over town to a ripple of hills beyond. Looming over the city on Guimarães' hilltop, with its crenulated towers

and cylindrical brick chimneys, **Paço dos Duques de Bragança** (*pacodosduques.gov.pt*) was first built in 1401 and later pompously restored as a presidential residence for Salazar. Its rooms now house Flemish tapestries, medieval weapons and a chapel with glittering stained-glass windows. Some 7km southeast of Guimarães up a twisting, cobbled road is Penha (617m), whose cool woods make it a wonderful escape from the summer heat. If you'd rather leave the car in town, hitch a ride on the Teleférico da Penha, 600m east of Guimarães' old centre.

THE DRIVE
Head on the N101 northwest of Guimarães, then the M583 (direction Prazins), which leads through gentle countryside and takes you onto the N309 to Citânia de Briteiros. It's a 16km drive.

02 CITÂNIA DE BRITEIROS

Factor in at least an hour or so for a ramble around one of Portugal's most evocative archaeological sites, **Citânia de Briteiros**. This is the largest of a liberal scattering of northern Celtic hill settlements, or *citânias* (fortified villages), which date back at least 2500 years. It's likely that this sprawling 3.8-hectare site, inhabited from 300 BCE to 300 CE, was the last stronghold against the invading Romans.

THE DRIVE
It's a 16km drive from Citânia de Briteiros to Braga. The N309 northwest heads through undulating countryside sprinkled with orchards, woods and church-topped villages. Before reaching Braga, allow time to visit Bom Jesus do Monte.

03 BRAGA

Stay the night in Braga and your wake-up call will be the alarm of some three dozen church bells. *Bemvindo* (welcome) to Portugal's most devout city. Highest on your list should be the Romanesque **Sé** (*se-braga.pt*), Portugal's oldest cathedral dating to 1070. Don't miss the intricate west portal, carved with scenes from Reynard the Fox, the filigree Manueline towers and the cloister lined with Gothic chapels. But Braga is more than the sum of its prayers – students and a vibrant cafe scene inject it with youthful spirit. Start or finish your evening in one of the cafes lining the **Praça da República**. Lying around 5km east of central Braga, Bon Jesus do Monte is the goal of legions of penitent pilgrims every year. One of Portugal's most recognisable icons, the sober neoclassical church stands atop a forested hill that affords grand sunset views across the city. But most come for the extraordinary tiered baroque staircase, **Escadaria do Bom Jesus** (Monte do Bom Jesus). The lowest staircase is lined with chapels representing the Stations of the Cross. The area is chocked with tourists on summer weekends – best avoided if you want to experience the place at its peaceful best.

THE DRIVE
On the A11 it's a 23km drive west to Barcelos. A slightly slower alternative is to take the prettier, more relaxed N103 through pinewoods, cultivated fields and low-rise hills.

04 BARCELOS

Sitting on the Rio Cávado and hiding a pretty medieval core, dinky Barcelos is worth more than a cursory glance. This town is famous for its roosters (adorning every souvenir stall), pottery and, above all, its massive **Feira de Barcelos** market, still a largely rural affair, with villagers hawking everything from scrawny chickens to hand-embroidered linen and carved ox yokes.

THE DRIVE
The N103-1 takes you straight west through countryside and small settlements for the 16km drive to Esposende.

05 ESPOSENDE

After immersing yourself in the rural delights of the hinterland, it's time to hit the coast for a restorative blast of Atlantic air. Consistent swells and breezes attract surfers and kitesurfers to Esposende's broad golden beaches flanked by low dunes.

Photo opportunity

Escadaria do Bom Jesus – a real baroque stunner of a staircase.

THE DRIVE
Trace the contours of the coast north on the N13 past fields, little farms and villages on the 28km drive to Viana do Castelo. Or hop on the A28 instead to carve 15 minutes off your journey.

06 VIANA DO CASTELO

The Costa Verde's biggest stunner, Viana do Castelo is a double shot of medieval centre and gorgeous beaches. Narrow lanes lined with Manueline manors and rococo palaces unfurl to **Praça da República**, with its Renaissance fountain and fortress-like town hall. For wondrous views down the coast and up the Lima Valley, hop on the funicular up to the eucalyptus-cloaked **Monte de Santa Luzia** and linger to glimpse the fabulously over-the-top, neo-Byzantine **Templo do Sagrado Coração de Jesus** (*templosantaluzia.org*). A five-minute **ferry** trip across the river brings you to **Praia do Cabedelo**, one of the Minho's best beaches, where powder-soft sands fold into grassy dunes and wind-blown pines.

THE DRIVE
The 30km drive east along the N202 to Ponte de Lima weaves past orchards, fields and a succession of low-key, whitewashed villages.

07 PONTE DE LIMA

The name is a giveaway – Ponte de Lima's showstopper is its 31-arched **Ponte Medieval** (Ponte Romana) loping across the Rio Lima – the finest medieval bridge in all Portugal. Most of it dates from the 14th century, though the segment on the north bank is bona fide Roman. The town itself is mellow and photogenic, with **Ecovia cycling trails** (*ciclovia.pt*) along the river, two crenulated 14th-century towers and a cute old town for a mosey. The town cranks to life at weekends and every other Monday, when a vast market spreads along the river bank.

THE DRIVE
It's a 19km drive east of Ponte de Lima on the quaint and countrified N203 to Ponte da Barca.

PARQUE NACIONAL DA PENEDA-GERES

Spread across four impressive granite massifs in Portugal's northernmost reach, this 703-sq-km park encompasses boulder-strewn peaks, precipitous valleys, and lush forests of oak and fragrant pine. It shelters more than 100 granite villages and hamlets that have changed little over the centuries. Many of the oldest villages are found in the Serra da Peneda and remain in a time warp, with oxen being trundled along cobbled streets by black-clad widows; distinctive *espigueiros* (stone granaries); and shepherds herding livestock up to high pastures for five months each year.

This is a wild landscape and in its remotest parts, a few wolves roam, as do wild boar, badgers and otters. With luck, you may catch a glimpse of roe deer and wild ponies. Hiking trails ranging from 1km to 30km abound in all sections of the park and mountain-bike rental is easy to source. For the lowdown on the park, including marked trail descriptions and an accommodation booking service, visit *adere-pg.pt*.

FOTOKON/SHUTTERSTOCK ©

Templo do Sagrado Coração de Jesus

08 PONTE DA BARCA

Serene Ponte da Barca takes its name from the *barca* (barge) that once ferried pilgrims and others across the Rio Lima. Slow the pace here with a stroll along the willow-shaded riverfront or a bike ride into a wooded valley. **ADERE Peneda-Gerês** (*adere-pg.pt*) is a great source of information on the national park.

THE DRIVE

From Ponte da Barca, the N203 swings northeast, with snap-shot views initially of the Rio Lima, then twists and turns through the verdant, mountainous heart of the Parque National de Peneda-Gerês, affording fabulous views on almost every corner. It's around an hour and a half's drive (60km) to Peneda.

09 PENEDA

There are many bases for striking out into the Parque Nacional da Peneda-Gerês, but few rival Peneda for sheer beauty. This is one of the park's most stunning mountain villages and the serra's namesake. It straddles both sides of a deep ravine and is backed by a domed mountain and gushing waterfall. Come for a quiet slice of village life and terrific hiking opportunities. A 1km trail takes you to a lake high in the hills where wild horses graze.

31

PORTUGAL

Tasting the Dão

BEST FOR FOODIES

Head to Tres Pipos for regional food cooked to a tee and paired with superb Dão wines.

DURATION	DISTANCE	GREAT FOR
2-4 days	151km/ 94 miles	History, wine

BEST TIME TO GO	Spring through autumn for mild weather and seasonal colour.

Santa Comba Dão

The Dão is off-the-beaten track Portugal in a nutshell. Get ready to slow-tour the country's rural heartland, an enticing ensemble of vineyards, pine and eucalyptus woods, family-run wineries and whitewashed villages full of sleepy charisma. Cellar tours, manor-house sleeps, hearty meals with beefy red wines and hikes in the wilds of the country's highest peaks in Serra da Estrela all await. Wind down the window. Hear that? Silence.

Link your trip

26 Atlantic Coast Surf Trip

Swing over to the Atlantic coast for a sun and surf fix. Praia de Pedrogão is 120km southwest from Santa Comba Dão.

32 Highlands & History in the Central Interior

Detour 52km southwest of Santa Comba Dão to Coimbra, the start of a drive with historic cities and evocative fortress towns on every turn.

01 SANTA COMBA DÃO

With its cluster of whitewashed, red-roofed houses tucked among low-rise hills, *miradouros* (lookouts) gazing across the Rio Dão, and a fine, twin-towered baroque church, this market town makes an appealing stop for an hour or so. Santa Comba Dão is the start of the wine region proper and used to be the terminus of the narrow-gauge Dão railway line to and from Viseu. Most Portuguese recognise the name as the birthplace of the notorious dictator and former prime minister António de Oliveira Salazar, who was born and buried in the nearby village of Vimieiro.

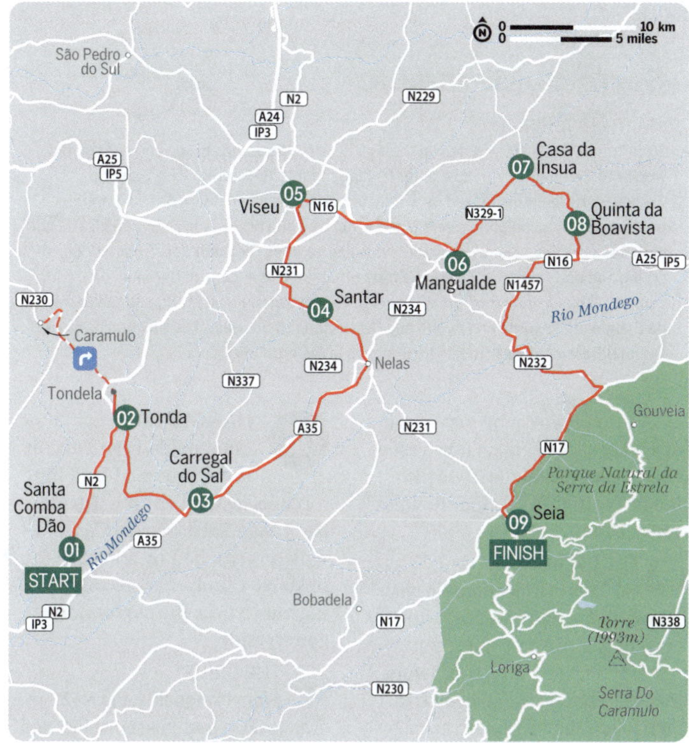

THE DRIVE

From Santa Comba Dão, the N2 blazes 15km north past arable countryside, woodlands of pine and eucalyptus, and small settlements, with Serra do Caramulo rippling northwest in the distance. Before reaching Tondela, exit right following the signs to Tonda, Couço and Mouraz.

02 TONDA

For a hearty meal while on the wine trail, head straight to **Tres Pipos** (*3pipos.pt*) in the small village of Tonda. It's a convivial, family-run affair, dishing up spot-on regional dishes like *cabrito* (roast kid) and *polvo à lagareiro* (octopus cooked with potatoes, garlic and olive oil) in atmospheric dining rooms with old wooden ceilings and thick stone walls. There's a good selection of Dão wines on the list and also a shop where you can stock up on local *vinho* as well as regional honeys, preserves, sausages, oils and black earthenware from nearby Molelos.

THE DRIVE

From Tonda, a minor road threads 14.5km south through pine and eucalyptus woodlands and past tiny orchards and vineyards and unassuming villages like Nagozela, before crossing the Rio Dão. As you approach Carregal do Sal, turn right at the roundabout to reach Quinta de Cabriz.

03 CARREGAL DO SAL

The main attraction in Carregal do Sal is **Quinta de Cabriz** (*globalwines.pt*), the headquarters of Global Wines Portugal, one of the region's major producers. Here you can stock up at the wine boutique, savour regional dishes expertly paired with wines in the restaurant, enjoy a tasting or hook onto a guided tour of the vineyards (no booking required, just turn up). Fine wines produced here include the Cabriz Touriga Nacional, a spicy, dark-fruit number, and Cabriz Encruzado, a crisp, lemony white.

THE DRIVE

The A35, N234 and N231 take you northeast from Quinta de Cabriz to Santar, 26km away. The second half of the route is more attractive, leading past pockets of pine woodland, neat rows of vines and cultivated fields.

04 SANTAR

Santar is a dinky little village and one of the Dão's prettiest, with narrow lanes twisting past baroque villas. The biggest draw, however, is its standout wineries. Top billing goes to the centrally located **Paço dos Cunos de Santar** (*facebook.com/pacodoscunhas*), a 17th-century estate, where you can tour the vineyard before a tasting of its noble wines and olive oils, which go nicely with the seasonal, creative takes on regional cuisine in the contemporary restaurant. Close by is the **Casa de Santar** (*casadesantar.com*), a family-owned winery with attractive grounds and baroque architecture. A guided visit takes you deep into its granite cellars, where robust reds are aged in oak barrels. There is also a gourmet shop where you can pick up some bottles and regional specialities.

THE DRIVE
The N231 swings north from Santar to Viseu, a 16km drive away. It's a relaxed country road, taking you past small vineyards and stands of olive and pine.

05 VISEU

Viseu merits at least half a day of your time, or stay overnight to really absorb the atmosphere of the alley-woven medieval city. Start off the day by paying a visit to the **Catedral de Viseu**, a striking hybrid of architectural styles. Originally built in the 13th century, it now has a 17th-century mannerist facade and a soaring 16th-century columned interior. Particularly impressive is the vaulted Manueline ceiling with ribs carved to resemble knotted strands of rope and the double-tier cloister, an early example of Italian-inspired Renaissance architecture. Nearby, the **Museu Grão Vasco** showcases an important collection of works by local-born Vasco Fernandes, aka Grão Vasco (the Great Vasco; c 1475–1543), one of Portugal's seminal Renaissance artists.

THE DRIVE
Take the meandering N16 east of town through pinewoods, with views of low-rise mountains and past stone-walled vineyards before crossing a bridge over the Rio Dão. Then follow the A25, taking exit 22 onto the N329-1 to Mangualde. It's a 17km drive.

DETOUR:
Serra do Caramulo

START: 02 TONDA

From Tonda, the N230 wiggles up through little hamlets and spruce and eucalyptus woods to Caramulo, a good base for striking out into the surrounding Serra do Caramulo. Here fields flanked by woods of oak, pine and chestnut rise to granite, boulder-speckled heights, where small waterfalls and brooks run swift and clear. The mountains are loveliest when wildflowers like heather, oleander and broom bloom in spring and early summer. The range tops off at the 1076m peak of Caramulinho, worth climbing if it is a clear day for far-reaching views stretching all the way to the Serra da Estrela in the south and Aveiro and the Atlantic to the west. The trail begins close to Hotel Caramulo – ask locals to point you in the right direction.

06 MANGUALDE

Mangualde is an elegant town, crowned by a hilltop neoclassical church, **Igreja de Nossa Senhora do Castelo**, which is reached by a long flight of steps. Climb up here for sweeping views over the surrounding countryside.

THE DRIVE
From Mangualde, the N329-1 swings 12km north past hamlets and hills thickly cloaked in pines and eucalyptus. As you enter Penalva do Castelo, head straight at the second roundabout for Casa da Ínsua.

07 CASA DA ÍNSUA

Just outside the sleepy village of Penalva do Castelo, you can rejuvenate at the sublime **Casa da Ínsua** (*montebelohotels.com*). This 18th-century manor and winery has been lovingly converted into a five-star hotel, complete with manicured landscape gardens, chandelier-lit salons, high-ceilinged rooms brimming with historic charm, a wine-tasting room and a highly regarded restaurant. Staff arrange activities including afternoons in the vineyards and cheese- and preserve-making workshops.

WINES OF THE DAO

The Dão rivals the Douro and Alentejo when it comes to the quality of its wines, some of Portugal's best. The conditions are ideal for wine-growing, with granitic soils, a temperate climate and shelter provided by the Serra da Estrela, Serra do Caramulo and Serra da Nave.

If the region has sidestepped the global spotlight until recently, it is because viticulture here still tends to be small scale, with vineyards still often little bigger than your average backyard, tucked between cultivated fields, orchards and mountains wreathed with pine and eucalyptus woods. These little wineries work hand in hand with large cooperatives.

Most wine lovers rave about the region's smooth reds, made from grapes like the touriga nacional, tinta roriz, jaen and alfrocheiro. These are ruby-hued, velvety and full-bodied, with aromas of spices, black cherry and other dark fruits. The region also produces some very decent whites – keep an eye out, particularly, for those made from the tangy encruzado grape, which are fresh and citrusy, with flavours of apple, lemon and melon.

THE DRIVE
Veer southeast from Casa da Ínsua and head straight at the roundabout onto a minor road that takes you east through undulating countryside. Continue southeast to Quinta da Boavista, roughly 7km away.

QUINTA DA BOAVISTA

A shining example of ecotourism, **Quinta da Boavista** (*quintadaboavista.eu*) in Penalva do Castelo is a winery run with a passion by João Tavares de Pina and his family. The eco-aware farmhouse sits in a secluded spot and offers well-equipped apartments, wine tastings of its full-bodied reds and delicious home-cooked meals. There's also a swimming pool. It's a chilled spot to wind out your road trip of the Dão wine region.

Photo opportunity

The countryside rippling far and wide from the top of Caramulinho.

THE DRIVE
It's a 43km drive south to Seia on the N1457, N232 and N17. The drive takes you through tranquil countryside streaked with olive trees and vines and backed by low-rise, forested hills.

SEIA

Besides sweeping views over the surrounding lowlands, Seia's big draw is its cluster of museums, including the **Centro de Interpretação da Serra da Estrela** (*cise.pt*), providing an excellent introduction to the mountainous region. This is the best place for information on hiking routes, maps and arranging guided hikes. From here you can easily strike out into the **Parque Natural da Serra da Estrela**, the country's largest protected area at 1.11 hectares. It's a wilderness of rugged boulder-strewn meadows and icy lakes, crowned by mainland Portugal's greatest peak, 1993m-high Torre. Crisp air and immense vistas make this a trekking paradise. As surprisingly few people get off the main roads, you'll often feel as though you have the park all to yourself.

TRABANTOS/SHUTTERSTOCK ©

Viseu

32

PORTUGAL

Highlands & History in the Central Interior

BEST FOR FOODIES

Hiking the Serra da Estrela around Manteigas.

DURATION	DISTANCE	GREAT FOR
5-7 days	770km/ 480 miles	History, nature

BEST TIME TO GO	From May to October for best temperatures.

Universidade de Coimbra

History is tangible at every turn in Portugal's interior and this route combines some of the nation's most evocative historic sights, from the venerable university library of Coimbra or Viseu's cathedral, to picture-perfect traditional villages like Piódão or Idanha-a-Velha. Sturdy fortress towns like Almeida and Trancoso shore up the border with Spain, while the Serra da Estrela mountains offer superb vistas and glorious hiking opportunities.

Link your trip

29 Medieval Jewels in the Southern Interior

Head down to Lisbon from Coimbra to explore more of the interior, or connect part-way along in Tomar, 80km south of Coimbra.

31 Tasting the Dão

From Viseu you can access this pleasure-trip around Portugal's silkiest reds.

01 COIMBRA

While Porto and Lisbon take the headlines, the university town of Coimbra, between the two, is one of Portugal's highlights. Its atmospheric historic centre cascades down a hillside above the Rio Mondego: a multicoloured assemblage of buildings covering a millennium of architectural endeavour. The spiritual heart of the old town is the **Universidade de Coimbra** (*uc.pt/turismo*), whose stunning 16th- to 18th-century buildings surround the Patio des Escolas square. The **Biblioteca Joanina** library is the sumptuous highlight. Within a short stroll are two other Coimbra masterpieces:

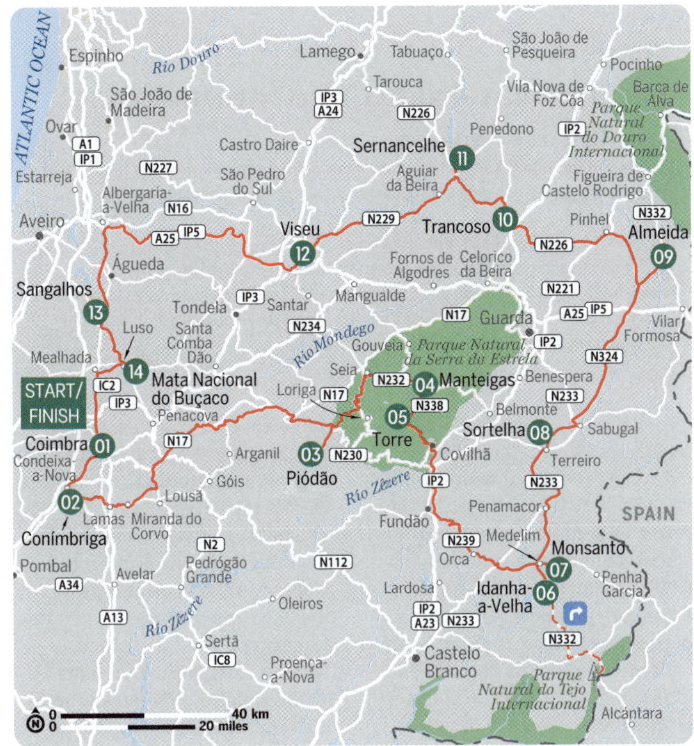

the **Sé Velha** (*sevelha-coimbra.org*) is one of Portugal's finest Romanesque buildings, while the altogether more modern **Museu Nacional de Machado de Castro** (*museumachadocastro.pt*) presents an excellent collection of art as well as taking you down to the city's Roman origins.

THE DRIVE
It's a short drive southeast along the IC3/N1 some 16km to Condeixa-a-Nova, on whose outskirts sit the Roman ruins of Conímbriga.

02 CONÍMBRIGA

Hidden amid humble olive orchards in the rolling country southwest of Coimbra, Conímbriga boasts Portugal's most extensive and best-preserved **Roman ruins** (*conimbriga.pt*), and ranks with similarly lauded sites on the entire Iberian Peninsula. To get your head around the history, begin at the small **museum** near the entrance. Displays present every aspect of Roman life from mosaics to medallions. Then, head out to the **ruins** themselves. A massive defensive wall running right through the site speaks of times of sudden crisis. In contrast, the extraordinary mosaics of the Casa dos Repuxos speak of times of peaceful domesticity.

THE DRIVE
It's two hours in the car to the next stop. The most interesting route is to take the N342 east, turning north onto the N236, then taking the N17 and IC6 northeast. The last stretch on the N230 is a spectacular if occasionally nerve-racking drive, following valleys with breathtaking views, sheer drops and tight curves.

03 PIÓDÃO

Remote Piódão offers a chance to see rural Portugal at its most pristine. This tiny traditional village clings to a terraced valley in a beautiful, surprisingly remote range of vertiginous ridges, deeply cut valleys, rushing rivers and virgin woodland called the Serra de Açor (Goshawk Mountains). Until the 1970s you could only reach Piódão on horseback or by foot, and it still feels as though you've slipped into a time warp. The village is a serene, picturesque composition in schist and slate; note the many doorways with crosses over them, said to offer protection against curses and thunderstorms. Houses descend in terraces to the square, where you'll find the fairy-tale parish church, the **Igreja Nossa Senhora Conceição**, and a low-key touristy scene selling local liqueurs and souvenirs.

THE DRIVE
It's only 66km to the next stop, but with the winding roads, spectacular scenery and intriguing villages en route, it may take you some time. Retrace your steps, then head northeast on the N338. The N231 takes you to Seia; from there the N339 then N232 is one of Portugal's great drives, through typical landscapes of the Serra da Estrela and down a vertiginous descent into Manteigas. At Penhas Douradas, at the top of the hill before the long descent into Manteigas, don't miss the stunning view

from a stub of rock called Fragão do Corvo; just follow the signs.

DETOUR:

Parque Natural do Tejo Internacional

START: 06 IDANHA-A-VELHA

Still one of Portugal's wildest landscapes, this 230-sq-km park shadows the Rio Tejo (Tagus), the border between Portugal and Spain. It shelters some of the country's rarest bird species, including black storks, Bonelli's eagles, royal eagles, Egyptian vultures, black vultures and griffon vultures.

The best-marked hiking trail, the **Rota dos Abutres** (Route of the Vultures), descends from Salvaterra do Extremo (34km southeast of Idanha-a-Velha) into the dramatic canyon of the Rio Erges. It's an 11km circuit that includes a vulture colony viewing point, and great views of a castle over in Spain.

04 MANTEIGAS

In the heart of the Serra da Estrela, Portugal's loftiest and most spectacular highland region, this is the most atmospheric of the mountain towns hereabouts. Cradled at the foot of the beautiful Vale do Zêzere, with high peaks and forest-draped slopes dominating the horizon in all directions, Manteigas enjoys a spectacular natural setting. There are lots of good marked walks in the surrounding area, so you may want to set aside a day to explore the serra landscapes on foot. Walk through the glacial valley above town and you'll still encounter terraced meadows, stone shepherds' huts and tinkling goat-bells, while in Manteigas itself cobblestone streets and older homes still hold their own against the high-rise development that has taken root on the Serra da Estrela's fringes.

THE DRIVE
The drive from Manteigas to Torre (22km, around 35 minutes) is especially breathtaking, first following the N338 along the Vale do Zêzere. After turning right onto the N339 towards Torre, you pass through the Nave de Santo António – a traditional high-country sheep-grazing meadow – before climbing through a surreal moonscape of crags and gorges. Visible near the turn-off for Torre is Cântaro Magro, a notable rock formation, rising 500m straight from the valley below.

05 TORRE

In winter, Torre's road signs are so blasted by freezing winds that horizontal icicles barb their edges. Portugal's highest peak, at 1993m, Torre ('Tower') produces a winter freeze so reliable that it has a small ski resort with mainly beginners' slopes. Outside the snow season (mid-December to mid-April), Portugal's pinnacle is rather depressing, though a park visitors centre with displays about the region's natural and cultural history is worthwhile. Even if you give Torre itself a miss, it's worth the drive here to survey the astoundingly dramatic surroundings.

THE DRIVE
Retrace your steps from Torre and continue straight on along the N339 to eventually descend steeply into Covilhã. Take the IP2/A23 motorway south, then the N18 and N239 roughly eastwards, finally reaching the N332 which takes you the last stretch to Idanha-a-Velha. It's a drive of around 90km.

06 IDANHA-A-VELHA

Extraordinary Idanha-a-Velha is a very traditional small village with a huge history. Nestled in a remote valley of patchwork farms and olive orchards, it was founded as the Roman city of Igaeditânia (Egitania). Roman ramparts still define the town, though it reached its apogee under Visigothic rule: they built a **catedral** and made Idanha their regional capital. It's also believed that their legendary King Wamba was born here. Moors were next on the scene, and the cathedral was turned into a mosque during their tenure. They, in turn, were driven out by the Knights Templar in the 12th century. It's believed that a 15th-century plague virtually wiped out the town's inhabitants. Today a small population of shepherds and farmers live amid the Roman, Visigothic and medieval ruins. Wandering this picturesque village is an enchanting trip back in time.

THE DRIVE
Head north up the N332 again, then turn right at the N239. The turn-off to Monsanto is clearly marked. It's only a 15km drive. Passengers who want to stretch their legs could walk the pretty 7km trail from Idanha to Monsanto.

07 MONSANTO

Like an island in the sky, the stunning village of Monsanto towers high above the surrounding plains. A stroll through its steeply cobbled streets, lined with stone houses that seem to merge with the boulder-strewn landscape, is reason enough to come. But to fully appreciate Monsanto's rugged isolation, climb the shepherds' paths above town to the abandoned and crumbling hilltop **castle**. This formidable stone fortress seems almost to have grown out of the boulder-littered hillside that supports it. It's a beautiful site, windswept and populated by lizards and wildflowers. Immense vistas include Spain to the east and the Barragem da Idanha dam to the southwest. Walkers will also appreciate the network of hiking trails threading through the vast cork-oak-dominated expanses below.

THE DRIVE
Sortelha is about 60km north of Monsanto across a variety of hilly landscapes. Head due north from Monsanto, eventually linking up with the N233. Turn off in the village of Terreiro, following the brown signs for Sortelha.

08 SORTELHA

Perched on a rocky promontory, Sortelha is the oldest of a string of fortresses guarding the frontier in this region. Its fortified 12th-century castle teeters on the brink of a steep cliff, while immense walls encircle a village of great charms. Laid out in Moorish times, it remains a winning combination of stout stone cottages, sloping cobblestone streets and diminutive orchards. 'New' Sortelha lines the Santo Amaro–Sabugal road. The medieval hilltop fortress is a short drive, or a 10-minute walk, up one of two lanes signposted 'castelo'. The entrance to the fortified old village is a grand,

Photo opportunity

The sweeping mountaintop view from Fragão de Covão above Manteigas.

stone Gothic gate. From here, a cobbled lane leads up to the heart of the village, with a *pelourinho* (pillory) in front of the remains of a small castle and the parish church. Higher still is the bell tower – climb it for a view of the entire village. For a more adventurous and scenic climb, tackle the ramparts around the village (beware precarious stairways and big steps).

THE DRIVE
Head east to Sabugal, then turn north, following the N324 north before joining the N340 for the final run northeast to Almeida. It's a drive of around 65km.

09 ALMEIDA

After Portugal regained independence from Spain in the 1640s, the country's border regions were on constant high alert. Almeida's vast, star-shaped fortress is the handsomest of the defensive structures built during this period. The fortified old village is a place of great charm, with enough history and muscular grandeur to set the imagination humming. Most visitors arrive at the fortress via the **Portas de São Francisco**, two long tunnel-gates separated by an enormous dry moat. The long arcaded building just inside is the 18th-century **Quartel das Esquadras**, the former infantry barracks. Not far away, the interesting **Museu Histórico Militar de Almeida** is built into the *casamatas* (casemates or bunkers), a labyrinth of 20 underground rooms used for storage, barracks and shelter for troops in times of siege. Piles of cannonballs fill a central courtyard of the museum, with British and Portuguese cannons strewn about nearby. Make sure you also see the attractive **Picadero d'el Rey**, once the artillery headquarters, and what's left of the castle, blown to smithereens during a French siege in 1810.

THE DRIVE
Retrace your steps down the N340, then head northwest on the N324. At Pinhel, turn westwards onto the N221/N226, all the way to Trancoso, around 60km in total.

10 TRANCOSO

A warren of cobbled lanes squeezed within Dom Dinis' mighty 13th-century walls makes peaceful Trancoso a delightful retreat from the

WALKS FROM MANTEIGAS

The **Trilhos Verdes** (*manteigastrilhosverdes.com*) is an excellent network of marked trails in the Manteigas area. Each route is viewable online and has its own leaflet available at the park information office in town.

The relatively easy ramble (11km one-way) through the magnificent, glacier-scoured **Vale do Zêzere**, one of the park's most beautiful and noteworthy natural features, is a highlight. It's quite exposed in summer.

modern world. The walls run intact for over 1km around the medieval core, which is centred on the main square, Largo Padre Francisco Ferreira. The square, in turn, is anchored by an octagonal *pelourinho* dating from 1510. The Portas d'El Rei (King's Gate), surmounted by the ancient coat of arms, was always the principal entrance, whose guillotine-like door sealed out unwelcome visitors. On a hill in the northeast corner of town is the tranquil **castle**, with its crenellated towers and the distinctively slanted walls of the squat, Moorish Torre de Menagem, which you can climb for views.

THE DRIVE
Head 30km northwest along the N226 to reach the next stop, Sernancelhe.

11 SERNANCELHE

Located 30km northwest of Trancoso, Sernancelhe has a wonderfully preserved centre fashioned out of warm, beige-coloured stone. Sights include a 13th-century church that boasts Portugal's only free-standing Romanesque sculpture, an old Jewish quarter with crosses to mark the homes of the converted and several grand 17th- and 18th-century town houses. The finest manor of all is the **Solar dos Carvalhos** (Praça da República), believed to be the birthplace of the famed 18th-century statesman and strong-armed reformer Marquês de Pombal. Just outside of town are hills that bloom with what are considered to be Portugal's best chestnuts.

THE DRIVE
The N229 leads you 55km southwest through increasingly fertile countryside to Viseu.

12 VISEU

One of central Portugal's most appealing cities, Viseu has a well-preserved historical centre that offers numerous enticements to pedestrians: cobbled streets, meandering alleys, leafy public gardens and a central square – Praça da República, aka the 'Rossio' – graced with bright flowers and fountains. Sweeping vistas over the surrounding plains unfold from the town's highest point, the square fronting the 13th-century granite cathedral (p212w), whose gloomy Renaissance facade conceals a splendid 16th-century interior, including an impressive Manueline ceiling.

THE DRIVE
It's a drive of 90km to the next stop. The quickest way is to take the A25 motorway west, turning south onto the IC2.

13 SANGALHOS

In the village of Sangalhos, in the Bairrada wine-producing region between Aveiro and Coimbra, the extraordinary **Aliança Underground Museum** (*bacalhoa.pt*) is part *adega* (winery), part repository of an eclectic, enormous, and top-quality art and artefact collection. Under the winery, vast vaulted chambers hold sparkling wine, barrels of maturing aguardente, and a series of galleries displaying a huge range of objects. The highlight is at the beginning – a superb collection of African sculpture, ancient ceramics and masks – but you'll also be impressed by the spectacular mineral and fossil collection and the beauty of some of the spaces. Other pieces include *azulejos* (tiles), a rather hideous collection of ceramic and faience animals, and an upstairs gallery devoted to India. The only complaint is that there's no information on individual pieces, and you don't have time to linger over a particular item. Phone ahead to book your visit, which can be conducted in English and includes a glass of sparkling wine.

COIMBRA FADO

If Lisbon represents the heart of Portuguese fado (traditional Portuguese melancholic song), Coimbra is its head. The 19th-century university was male-only, so the town's womenfolk were of great interest to the student body. Coimbra fado developed partly as a way of communicating with these heavily chaperoned females, usually in the form of serenades sung under the bedroom window. For this reason, fado is traditionally sung only by men, who must be students or ex-students.

The Coimbra style ranges from hauntingly beautiful serenades and lullabies to more boisterous students-out-on-the-piss type of songs. The singer is normally accompanied by a 12-string *guitarra* (Portuguese guitar) and perhaps a Spanish (classical) guitar too. Due to the clandestine nature of these bedroom-window concerts, audience appreciation is traditionally indicated by softly coughing rather than clapping.

There are several excellent venues in Coimbra to hear fado, including **À Capella** (*acapella.com.pt*).

THE DRIVE

It's an easy 20km drive down the N235 to the town of Luso and on up the hill to the Buçaco forest.

14 MATA NACIONAL DO BUÇACO

This famous, historic national **forest** (*fmb.pt*) is encircled by high stone walls that for centuries have reinforced a sense of mystery. The aromatic forest is criss-crossed with trails, dotted with crumbling chapels and graced with ponds, fountains and exotic trees. In the middle, like in a fairy tale, stands a royal palace. Now a luxury hotel, it was built in 1907 as a royal summer retreat on the site of a 17th-century Carmelite monastery. This wedding cake of a building is over-the-top in every way: outside, its conglomeration of turrets and spires is surrounded by rose gardens and swirling box hedges in geometric patterns; inside (nonguests are more or less prohibited entry) are neo-Manueline carvings, suits of armour on the grand staircases and *azulejos*. Nearby, **Santa Cruz do Bussaco** (*fmb.pt*) is what remains of a convent where the Duke of Wellington-to-be rested after the Battle of Bussaco in 1810. The atmospheric interior has decaying religious paintings, an unusual passageway right around the chapel, some guns from the battle, and the much-venerated image of *Nossa Senhora do Leite* (Our Lady of Milk), with ex-voto offerings. Outside the forest walls lies the old-fashioned little spa town wof Luso.

THE DRIVE

Heading back to Coimbra, ignore your GPS and make sure to take the lovely foresty N235, which later joins the IP3. It's a picturesque drive.

Santa Cruz do Bussaco

Arriving

Spain's most popular arrival airports by far are Madrid's Barajas airport (15km northeast of central Madrid) and Barcelona's El Prat airport (15km southwest of the centre). Lisbon is the primary point of entry for most travellers visiting Portugal. The airport is about 6km from the city centre.

Car Rental at Airports

All major Spanish and Portuguese airports have car-rental desks in their arrivals halls, and all the international and local companies are represented. It's strongly advised to make your reservation well in advance of your visit, especially during peak periods such as summer or during major festivals or trade fairs. Otherwise you run the risk of waiting in a long queue, paying more for your rental or even not finding a car at all. Airport car-rental desks usually have longer opening hours than in-city offices and – especially in cities such as Madrid, Barcelona and Lisbon – picking up your car at the airport can have the advantage of getting you out on the road and away from complicated inner-city traffic if you're not staying overnight in the city itself. Unlike in some other countries, there's usually no surcharge for picking up your vehicle at the airport.

To the City Centre

	Madrid	Barcelona	Lisbon
TRAIN	29 min, **€2.60**	20-30 min, **€4.20**	No train
BUS	15-35 min, **€5**	30-40 min, **€5.90**	No bus
TAXI	20-30 min, **€30**	30 min, **€30**	20 min **€20**
METRO	40 min **€7.50**	30 min **€4.60**	20 min **€1.50**

OTHER MAJOR ENTRY POINTS

While most travellers arrive at Madrid, Barcelona or Lisbon, other destinations such as Málaga, Alicante, Valencia, Seville, Bilbao and Porto also have busy airports.

VISAS

EU nationals don't need a visa. Non-EU nationals (including UK nationals) can enter Spain or Portugal under the ETIAS visa-waiver system; travellers can then stay visa-free for 90 days within any 180-day period.

WI-FI

Most airports offer free wi-fi; in Spain, look for an Aena network to join. Elsewhere, pretty much everywhere has wi-fi, though getting connected can still be tricky in more remote rural areas.

SIM CARDS

Travellers with EU phones have free roaming. For others, an e-SIM with a data package is a good option; otherwise, local SIM cards are available in Spanish and Portuguese phone shops.

Getting Around

Spain's (and, to a lesser extent, Portugal's) transport systems are excellent. Spain in particular has a super-modern train system, an extensive domestic air network, well-maintained roads, and buses to the country's remotest corners.

DRIVING INFO

Drive on the right.

Speed limits are 30km/h or 50km/h in built-up areas, 90km/h to 100km/h on regular roads and 120km/h on motorways.

.05

Blood alcohol limit is 0.5g/L

Trains

Renfe is the excellent national train system that runs most of the services in Spain, including the high-speed AVE trains that link major destinations. In Portugal there's a decent network between major towns from north to south.

Road Conditions in Spain

Motorways radiate from Madrid to all corners of the country, shadowed by smaller but often more picturesque minor roads, especially in the mountains. Most roads are in good condition. Overtake on the outside only and give way to vehicles that are already on roundabouts.

Buses

There are few places in Spain or Portugal where buses don't go. Numerous companies provide bus links, from local routes between villages to fast intercity connections. Most buses are geared towards locals, so weekend services are often more limited.

Air Travel

Spain has an extensive network of internal flights, operated by Spanish airlines and a handful of low-cost international airlines. Carriers include Air Europa, Iberia (including Iberia Express and Iberia Regional-Air Nostrum), Ryanair, Volotea and Vueling. Portugal's limited domestic routes are expensive.

Spain's Tiny Parking

Spain famously has some of smallest parking spaces in Europe, and just finding a spot (even if you're willing to pay for it) is a headache, particularly in the big cities. So if you're struggling to squeeze your rental wheels into a particularly tight corner in a dimly lit underground car park in the sizzling summer heat, take it slow and don't worry – everyone else has been here too!

CAR RENTAL COSTS

Rental
€35-50 /day

Petrol
Approx €1.70/litre

Train ticket Madrid–Barcelona
From €19

Train ticket Lisbon–Porto
From €23

LEFT: WISELY/SHUTTERSTOCK ©, RIGHT: GEORGE TRUMPETER/SHUTTERSTOCK ©

Accommodation

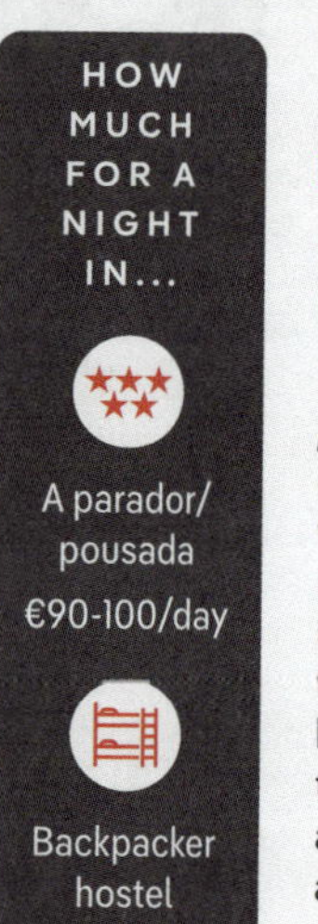

HOW MUCH FOR A NIGHT IN...

A parador/pousada
€90-100/day

Backpacker hostel
€15-20/day

An urban boutique hotel
€100/day

SLEEP IN A SPANISH PARADOR

The state-run Paradores hotel chain has around 100 properties and is one of Spain's most ingenious ideas, with strong sustainability initiatives. Paradores typically inhabit stunning historical buildings, such as monasteries, castles and palaces, and can be surprisingly well priced. Some are legendary addresses, such as the Hostal dos Reis Católicos in Santiago de Compostela and the Parador de Granada (within the Alhambra's grounds).

Sleep Like Portuguese Royalty

Pousadas de Portugal (*pousadas.pt*) is a network of monasteries, convents, forts, castles and palaces transformed into luxury hotels by the Pestana Group, a member of Historic Hotels of Europe. Despite the modern facilities, each hotel respects the history and architectural traits of the former monuments. Prices vary according to location, but rates start at around €100 per night.

Boutique Bliss

Lovers of design should note that Spain and Portugal have a wealth of creative boutique hotels, from Moorish-inspired hideaways to sleekly appointed havens. Most are independent ventures run by charismatic owners keen to share their love for their home. Rental villas (often with private pools) also abound, especially in coastal destinations, and are a great option for families and groups.

Rural Dreams

Rural tourism has become immensely popular, and there are now many charming *casas rurales* to rent. These are usually comfortably renovated village houses or farmhouses with a handful of rooms, which you can usually rent in their entirety. Well-equipped campsites are also dotted across the country, some of them in divinely beautiful settings near rivers, lakes and woodlands.

On a Budget

Not to be confused with hostels, *hostales* are small, simple, comfortable budget hotels, while *pensiones* are fuss-free guesthouses, often family run. Smart modern hostels with dorms and wallet-friendly private rooms are popping up everywhere but particularly in urban destinations; the best have lively social calendars and other extras. Along the Camino de Santiago you'll find rustic *albergues* (guesthouses) for pilgrims.

APARTMENT RENTALS

A wave of private tourist apartments has swept across Spain's most popular areas, particularly the historic centres of major cities. Rental agencies and platforms such as Airbnb have been accused of driving up rents, which then pushes out local residents and independent businesses, inevitably altering the fabric of the neighbourhood. This is particularly the case in (but not only in) Barcelona (p105), where there have been protests against overtourism. Travellers can help by supporting local hotels (ideally a smaller independent property). If you're looking to book an apartment, double-check that it's licensed.

Cars

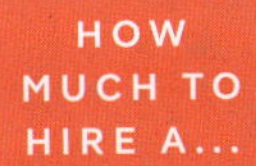

HOW MUCH TO HIRE A...

small car
€35-50/day

EV
€70/day

campervan
€120/day

Car Rental

To rent a car you'll need a licence and to be aged at least 21 in Spain and at least 25 in Portugal. In most cases you'll also need a credit card, as only a few places accept debit cards. Rates and availability very enormously by season. Note that most cars are manual, although this is slowly changing; automatic vehicles are limited and usually cost more. An International Driving Permit (IDP) issued by the automobile association in your home country is rarely (but sometimes) asked for by car-rental agencies if your licence is not in Spanish or Portuguese; get one before leaving home, just in case. If you're here for longer than six months, you'll need a local licence.

EVs

As in much of Europe, the use (and rental) of EVs is growing rapidly, although charging stations don't always keep up with demand, especially during holiday periods. Charging usually costs €8 to €10 per hour. Check online for the latest updates. Travelling in an EV during summer requires careful planning: queues often form at charging stations along major highways, which can make for a long wait. Always 'fill up' before leaving home to minimise delays out on the road. The cost of renting an EV may be slightly higher than that of renting a fuel vehicle, but that too is changing and prices are more often on par.

OTHER GEAR

If you need a child safety seat for your rental vehicle, either bring your own or reserve one well in advance. GPS units, comprehensive insurance, roadside assistance packages and other extras all cost more and may need to be arranged in advance.

Health & Safe Travel

INSURANCE

Though having one isn't mandatory to enter Spain or Portugal, a travel-insurance policy that covers theft, medical issues and travel delays or cancellations is strongly recommended. All EU residents can access state health services in Spain with the free European Health Insurance Card (EHIC), which you must request in your country of residence well before travelling abroad.

Scams & Thefts

Be wary of pickpockets in heavily touristed areas and keep an eye out for distraction techniques (women offering good-luck flowers, people spotting dirt on your shirt, people trying to sidetrack you in motorway rest areas). Never leave anything important lying unattended at the beach, as things can disappear instantly while your back is turned.

Women Travellers

Women travelling in Spain and Portugal report few concerns. That said, women can attract unwanted male attention, especially in small, remote places and if travelling solo. Sticking to common sense and following the same precautions you would at home or anywhere else is best.

Wildfires

Devastating wildfires have become commonplace across both Spain and Portugal, particularly in summer, as global warming has exacerbated and prolonged heatwaves. In 2022 Spain saw more than 40 large wildfires burn almost 3000 sq km of land, and countless towns and villages were evacuated. Keep an eye on the news, and in case of emergency follow instructions from local authorities.

CAR BREAKDOWN

The Real Automóvil Club de España (race.es) and the Automóvel Club de Portugal (acp.pt) are the national automobile clubs. They may come to assist you in case of breakdown, but you should always obtain a local emergency telephone number from your own insurer or car-hire company.

Responsible Travel

Climate Change & Travel

Lonely Planet urges all travellers to engage with their travel carbon footprint, which will mainly come from air travel. While there often isn't an alternative, travellers can look to minimise the number of flights they take, opt for newer aircrafts and use cleaner ground transport, such as trains.

One proposed solution – purchasing carbon offsets – unfortunately does not cancel out the impact of individual flights. While most destinations will depend on air travel for the foreseeable future, for now, pursuing ground-based travel where possible is the best course of action.

The UN Carbon Offset Calculator shows how flying impacts a household's emissions:

The ICAO's carbon emissions calculator allows visitors to analyse the CO2 generated by point-to-point journeys:

---

spain.info

Responsible-tourism ideas from Spain's tourist board.

miteco.gob.es

Spain's national parks.

natural.pt

The best of Portugal's protected areas.

VOLUNTEERING

You don't need to stay for months to lend a helping hand (though pitching in during a longer visit is great, too!). Beach clean-ups are among the drop-in initiatives that travellers can get involved in.

LOCAL & SEASONAL

Wonderful fresh-produce markets where seasonal, locally sourced ingredients are the stars are among the greatest joys of a visit to Spain or Portugal. Pop-up farmers markets also showcase organic bounty sold directly by growers.

SUSTAINABILITY

The Global Sustainability Index (*https://earth.org/global-sustainability*) ranks Spain 12th and Portugal 16th. Both countries have produced a road map to achieve carbon neutrality by 2050, which includes targets to shift to renewable energy.

Nuts & Bolts

GOOD TO KNOW

Time zone
Spain is GMT/UTC + 1 in winter, GMT/UTC + 2 in daylight saving; Portugal is one hour ahead of Spain year-round

Country code
Spain 34, Portugal 351

Emergency number
112

CURRENCY: EURO (€)

Opening Hours

Opening hours vary throughout the year. We provide high-season opening hours; hours will generally decrease in the shoulder and low seasons.

Banks 8.30am–2pm (until 3pm in Portugal) weekdays; some in Spain also 4–7pm Thursday and 9am–1pm Saturday

Restaurants Lunch 1–4pm (Spain), noon–3pm (Portugal); dinner 8.30–11pm or midnight (Spain), 7–10pm (Portugal)

Shops 10am–2pm and 4.30–7.30pm or 5–8pm Monday to Saturday (Spain); 9.30am–noon and 2–7pm Monday to Friday, 10am–1pm Saturday (Portugal)

Electricity

Type C, 220V/50Hz

Type F, 230V/50Hz

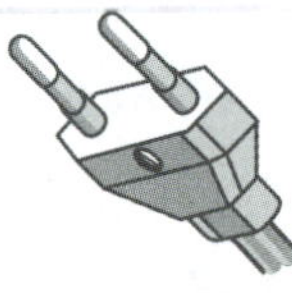

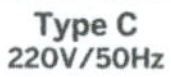

Type C
220V/50Hz

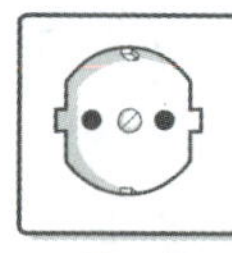

Type F
230V/50Hz

Smoking

Banned in all enclosed public spaces in Spain; allowed in some restaurants and most bars in Portugal.

Tap Water

Tap water is generally safe to drink in Spain and Portugal.

Paying by Card

Most places accept debit- and credit-card payments, although there's sometimes a minimum spend and splitting bills isn't always an option. It's still worth carrying a little cash.

VAT & Refunds in Spain

Most prices in Spain include 21% VAT. Travellers who aren't EU residents can claim a partial refund on purchases made in Spain using the electronic VAT refund procedure (DIVA); this means requesting a form from shops and validating it at airports and ferry ports.

Tipping

Tipping is almost always optional. In restaurants many locals leave small change and others leave up to 5% (considered generous); that said, things are changing slightly and some do tip more. It's rare to tip in bars and cafes, but some people round up for taxis.

HOW MUCH FOR A...

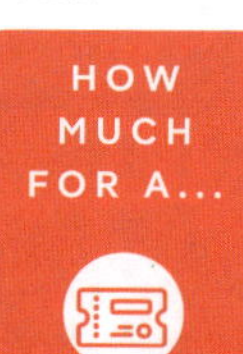

Major-gallery admission
Around €15

Alhambra ticket
€19

Guided walking tour
Around €15

Lisbon (p200)

OFS

Index

C

Drives 000
Map Pages 000, 000

D

E

M

Drives 000
Map Pages 000, 000

Drives 000
Map Pages 000, 000

N

O

Drives 000
Map Pages 000, 000

W

X

Z

THE WRITERS

This is the 3rd edition of Lonely Planet's *Best Road Trips Spain & Portugal* guidebook, updated with new material by Anthony Ham. Writers on previous editions whose work also appears in this book are included below.

Anthony Ham

Anthony is a freelance writer and photographer who specialises in Spain, East and Southern Africa, the Arctic and the Middle East. When he's not writing for Lonely Planet, Anthony writes about and photographs for newspapers and magazines in Australia, the UK and US. In 2001, after years of wandering the world, Anthony finally found his spiritual home when he fell irretrievably in love with Madrid on his first visit to the city. Less than a year later, he arrived there on a one-way ticket, with not a word of Spanish and not knowing a single person in the city. He now divides his time between Spain and Australia.

Contributing writers

Regis St Louis, Gregor Clark, Duncan Garwood, John Noble

SEND US YOUR FEEDBACK

We love to hear from travelers - your comments keep us on our toes and help make our books better. Our well-travelled team reads every word on what you loved or loathed about this book. Although we cannot reply individually to your submissions, we always guarantee that your feedback goes straight to the appropriate writers, in time for the next edition. Each person who sends us information is thanked in the next edition.

Visit **lonelyplanet.com/contact** to submit your updates and suggestions or to ask for help. Our award-winning website also features inspirational travel stories and news.

Note: We may edit, reproduce and incorporate your comments in Lonely Planet products such as guidebooks, websites and digital products, so let us know if you are happy to have your name acknowledged. For a copy of our privacy policy visit **lonelyplanet.com/legal**.

BEHIND THE SCENES

This book was produced by the following:

Commissioning Editor
Sandie Kestell

Production Editor
Graham O'Neill

Book Designer
Eoin T Loughney

Cartographer
Daniela Machová

Assisting Editors
Helen Koehne,
Kate Mathews,
Charlotte Orr

Cover Researcher
Kat Marsh

Thanks to
Ronan Abayawickrema,
Sofie Andersen,
Annemarie McCarthy

Product Development
Amy Lynch, Marc Backwell,
Katerina Pavkova, Fergal Condon,
Ania Lenihan

ACKNOWLEDGMENTS

Cover photograph
Lagos, Portugal; Michael Howard/4Corner Images©